D1216742

The Black Book
of The American Left

The Black Book of the American Left

The Collected Conservative Writings of David Horowitz

Volume IV
Islamo-Fascism and the War Against the Jews

Second Thoughts Books
Los Angeles

©2014 by David Horowitz

All rights reserved. No part of this publication may be reproduced, stored in a retrieval system, or transmitted, in any form or by any means, electronic, mechanical, photocopying, recording, or otherwise, without the prior written permission of Second Thoughts Books, 14148 Magnolia Blvd., Sherman Oaks, California, 91423.

First American edition published in 2013 by Second Thoughts Books.

Manufactured in the United States and printed on acid-free paper. The paper used in this publication meets the minimum requirements of ANSI/NISO Z39.48 1992 (R 1997) *(Permanence of Paper)*.

Book design and production by Catherine Campaigne; copy-edited by David Landau; research provided by Mike Bauer.

FIRST AMERICAN EDITION

LIBRARY OF CONGRESS CATALOGING-IN-PUBLICATION DATA

Horowitz, David, 1939–
    The black book of the American left : the collected conservative writings of David Horowitz / by David Horowitz.
    volumes   cm.
    Includes bibliographical references and index.
    ISBN NEED NEW ISBN # (hardback)
        1. Social movements—United States—History.   2. Radicalism—United States. 3. Anti-Americanism—United States.   4. Horowitz, David, 1939– Political and social views.   I. Title.
    HX86.H788 2013
        335.00973   2013000496

10   9   8   7   6   5   4   3   2   1

Contents

Islamo-Fascism and the War Against the Jews

Like the previous installments of *The Black Book of the American Left*, this volume addresses the role progressives played in undermining the defense of Western civilization against the totalitarian forces determined to destroy it. The present volume focuses on the holy war or *jihad* waged by totalitarian Islamists in their quest for a global empire. It is divided into three sections, the first and third of which contain narratives of campaigns I organized to confront the growing Islamist presence on American college campuses. While these accounts describe a cultural conflict in university communities, they have implications for a parallel culture war in the society at large.

The Achilles' heel of democratic societies, as the Polish philosopher Leszek Kolakowski once observed, is also their moral foundation—the principle of tolerance, which they extend even to those who want to destroy them.[1] The Islamists understand this vulnerability and therefore have exploited it as a central strategy along with the intimidation they conduct through terror. By deploying defamatory expressions like "bigotry" and "Islamophobia," they seek to stigmatize their opponents, namely anyone who attempts to draw attention to the political nature of their movement, its imperialistic ambitions, its support for terrorism, its oppression of women, its hostility to other religions, and its viru-

---

As in previous volumes, the texts have been edited for publication.
[1]Cf. Leszek Kolakowski, "The Self-Poisoning of the Open Society," in *Modernity On Endless Trial*, 1990, pp.162–174

lent hatred of Christians and Jews. By casting themselves as the victims of religious persecution, Islamists have succeeded to a remarkable extent in censoring and marginalizing these critics. The narratives included in this volume illustrate these strategies and their agents in action.

The Islamists' success in the wider society is evidenced in the censorship that even government agencies have imposed on their own utterances, and on the institutional guides they have developed for dealing with national security threats. For example, the *9/11 Commission Report* on the Islamic attacks of September 2001 referred to "Islam" 322 times, used the word "Muslim" 145 times and *"jihad"* (holy war) 126 times. But even though Osama bin Laden called his *jihad* a religious war against "the Jews and Crusaders," the Bush administration described its response to the 9/11 attacks as a "War on Terror" without any reference to Islam. By using the neutered term "terror" to describe the Islamist threat, the administration obscured not only the religious nature of the attacks but the fact that the Islamists did not confine their tactics to military strikes but also pursued their goals through sophisticated political movements designed to infiltrate and subvert non-Muslim societies.[2]

By the end of more than a decade of pressure from domestic Islamists and the political left, the religious nature of the war had become practically invisible, even to American counter-terrorism organizations. In the words of one member of the House subcommittee on crime, terrorism and homeland security, "The current FBI counterterrorism lexicon, [which describes] the language they can use, does not include *'jihad,'* does not include 'Muslim,' does not include 'Islam.' It includes 'violent extremism' many times, but it does not include *'sharia'* [the Islamic law *jihadists* are seeking to impose globally]. It does not even include 'Al-Qaeda,'

---

[2] Robert Spencer, *The Stealth Jihad: How Radical Islam Is Subverting America Without Guns or Bombs,* 2008; Andrew C. McCarthy, *The Grand Jihad: How Islam and the Left Sabotage America,* 2010; cf. David Horowitz and Robert Spencer, "Islamophobia," in this volume

'Hezbollah,' or 'Hamas.' Even the National Intelligence Strategy 2009 does not include references to *'jihad,'*, 'Muslim,' or 'Islam.'"[3]

When the Obama administration took office in 2009, even more changes were instituted to shield not only the public but also the Department of Homeland Security and counter-intelligence agencies from the fact that the war against the West was based on an ideology shared by millions (probably hundreds of millions) of devout Muslims and sponsored by heavily armed Islamic regimes; or from the fact that it was a war at all. Under Obama, even the denatured term "War on Terror" was dropped from official pronouncements and replaced by the meaningless subterfuge, "overseas contingency operations." The Obama administration designated the largest post-9/11 attack on American soil, the 2009 massacre of 13 American soldiers by a *jihadist* screaming *"Allahu Akbar,"* as "workplace violence," denying the 39 soldiers wounded in the attack the Purple Hearts they had earned.[4]

"Islamophobia," the opening chapter of this volume, is an essay co-authored with Robert Spencer, one of the foremost scholars of Islam and a valued colleague. It describes the international campaign to marginalize and ultimately silence critics of the *jihad* through the passage of what would amount to anti-blasphemy laws. Anti-blasphemy laws are the cornerstones of totalitarian states, outlawing speech that challenges their rule. Such laws have already been adopted by several Islamic governments. The agenda of the Islamophobia campaign is to make them universal—a goal reflected in resolutions the Islamic states have been able to push through the UN. Until such time as Islamists are able to establish these laws in the western democracies, the strategy of the *jihadists* is to use the principle of tolerance to justify suppressing criticism of Islam-inspired terror or Islam-mandated oppression by

---

[3]Rep. Louie Gohmert, remarks to the David Horowitz Freedom Center, May 4, 2013; http://frontpagemag.com/2013/frontpagemag-com/congressman-louie-gohmert-the-islamist-enemy-within/
[4]Ibid.

characterizing it as an attack on *all* Muslims, and therefore as "racist" and "bigoted" hate speech.

The first half of this volume contains a running account of the campaign I organized in the fall of 2007 to publicize the term "Islamo-Fascism," and make it part of the national debate. The idea crystallized during an evening event I held on March 2, 2007 at a Conservative Pac Conference (CPAC) attended by 500 college students.[5] One of the attendees, Michael Abdurakhmanov, a student from Pace University had attempted to screen the film *Obsession: Radical Islam's War Against the West* on his campus. Because *Obsession* documented the *jihadist* agendas of Islamist organizations like Hamas and the Muslim Brotherhood, the film became the target of a nationwide campaign led by the Council on American-Islamic Relations (CAIR), a Hamas-linked Muslim Brotherhood front group. The campaign claimed the film was Islamophobic, racist, and an attack on all Muslims, although it was nothing of the kind.[6] Another Brotherhood front, the Muslim Students Association, complained to the Pace administration, prompting the president of the university to issue an order that the film not be shown, a blatant violation of the First Amendment that was reversed months later.[7]

---

[5]Pace Hillel, "Pace University Ignores Anti-Semitism, Threatens Jewish Student Group," *Students for Academic Freedom,* January 8, 2007, http://www.studentsforacademicfreedom.org/news/2355/pace-university-ignores-anti-semitism-threatens-jewish-student-group; Michelle Malkin, "Jewish Student Group Threatened Over 'Obsession' Showing," *MichelleMalkin.com,* January 9, 2007, http://michellemalkin.com/2007/01/09/report-jewish-student-group-threatened-over-obsession-showing/
[6]Michael Abdurakhmanov, "Film Censorship 101," Tuesday, November 28, 2006, *FrontPageMag.com,* http://archive.frontpagemag.com/readArticle.aspx?ARTID=1378
[7]Brendan O'Reilly, "Islam Film Sparks Protests at Local Campuses," *The Hofstra Chronicle,* March 3, 2007, http://www.hofstrachronicle.com/2.1158/islam-film-sparks-protests-at-local-campuses-1.55800; Karen W. Arenson, "Film's View of Islam Stirs Anger on Campuses," *New York Times,* February 26, 2007, http://www.nytimes.com/2007/02/26/movies/26docu.html?pagewanted=all&_r=0

Our speaker for the CPAC evening, former senator Rick Santorum, related how during a White House visit he attempted to persuade President Bush to use the term "Islamo-Fascist" to describe America's global enemy. He said Bush did use it but only one time because of the immediate uproar from Islamist groups like CAIR and the political left, which claimed it was "offensive" to Muslims. Santorum's words prompted me to do something about the suppression of the film and the term. Taking the microphone, I announced that I was declaring April 4 "Islamo-Fascism Awareness Day" and would show *Obsession* simultaneously on 100 college campuses on that date. There had never been such a coordinated conservative event, and, as the words left my lips, I realized that I had stepped out on a very short limb. There was little time to organize such a demonstration, but when the day came we were able to put together showings of the film on 96 college campuses and at four other locations. When it was over, I thought, "If we can do this with a day, we can do it with a week," and began planning to do just that in the fall.

From the attacks of September 2001 until the fall of 2007, the term "Islamo-Fascism" had been all but banned from public discourse—most incomprehensibly in the university community, the center of the nation's intellectual discourse, where presumably every idea exists to be examined. Aside from a handful of conservatives and Christopher Hitchens, a radical chastened by the attacks of 9/11, virtually no one was using this term. Or, more precisely, no one was willing to take the risk of using this term, given the kind of slander that CAIR and its supporters on the left were ready to direct at them. I called our campaign "Islamo-Fascism Awareness Week," which effectively introduced the words and concept to the university public.

The term "Islamo-Fascism" properly identified the religious nature of the *jihadist* threat along with its totalitarian implications—two hitherto-suppressed realities that were vital to understanding the enemy we faced. Beginning October 22, 2007, we held events on over 100 college campuses and were able to organize repeat campaigns, with new themes added, through three semesters. By the fourth semester, the novelty had worn off and we were obliged to come up with a new but related effort, which is described in Part II of this volume.

The most interesting revelations of the Islamo-Fascism campaign were the tacit alliances revealed between the campus Islamists and a broad spectrum of the progressive left. Those on the left who did not actively protest against our events were still not ready to welcome a debate over the appropriateness of the term, or to stand up for our right to express such a view without being subject to vilification; nor were "liberal" faculty members willing to invite us to university platforms to discuss our case. We were universally treated as unwanted intruders in the academic environment. Unlike the Israel-hating "apartheid" weeks organized by the Muslim Students Association and Students for Justice in Palestine, our events received no support from campus administrators or faculty. Instead, the academic community tolerated vicious personal attacks, reckless slanders and even physical threats—all of which violated the "principles of community" and "diversity" it claimed to honor—against the students who organized our events. In any other case, such behavior would have called forth stern admonitions and disciplinary actions from university authorities; but in this case they elicited none. No university or faculty spokesman or organization came to the defense of the students who held the events, or spoke up for their right to express opinions without being subjected to malicious slanders and threats. The campus press also showed itself to be a one-party affair, printing one-sided misrepresentations of what transpired, providing a platform for smears of speakers and student organizers alike, and denying a platform to the targets of this malice when they sought to defend themselves and set the record straight. These attacks were common to every event our students organized, despite the fact that our Islamo-Fascism Awareness Weeks focused on the oppression of women and other minority groups in Islam as their official themes.

The chapter titled "Why Islamo-Fascism," also co-authored with Robert Spencer, is a statement we published to explain our rationale for the use of the term. Unfortunately, given the hysteria of the campaign against us and intimidation of anyone who might speak up in our defense, there was no possibility of stimulating a public discussion of the issue. The conviction that some ideas were too "offensive" to be permitted on a university campus was too prevalent. Despite this, I have no doubt the campaign had a significant impact. While people prudently kept themselves out of the line of fire and did not speak up, privately they could not help being provoked to new thoughts about these issues.

The second half of this volume contains two parts. It is introduced by a summary account of the Middle East conflict, titled, "Why Israel Is the Victim, and the Arabs Are the Indefensible Aggressors in the Middle East." With the facts of this history known, and the genocidal intentions of the Palestinians understood, it is puzzling that any self-respecting liberal or progressive would not be repelled by the Palestinian cause; or, worse, would actually support it. The other chapters in this section were written during the Second Lebanon War, which was caused by Israel's unilateral evacuation of Gaza, its occupation by Hamas and by the ensuing terrorist attacks on Israel by Hamas and its Hezbollah allies. Nothing could demonstrate more clearly that the only peace acceptable to the Palestinians and their supporters is one in which the Jewish state no longer exists.

The next section describes the campaign that followed the conclusion of the Islamo-Fascism Awareness weeks. It was organized to counter the anti-Israel propaganda campaigns conducted by two campus fronts for the Muslim Brotherhood—Students for Justice in Palestine and the Muslim Students Association. The campaigns took the form of "Israeli Apartheid Weeks," accusing Jews of committing genocide against a defenseless people, stealing their land, imprisoning them behind "apartheid walls," and forcing millions of "refugees" to live in squalid camps where they remained homeless and oppressed. These campaigns were designed to demonize the Jewish state and mobilize support for its destruction. Based on blatant lies and promoting ethnic hate, they violated established university codes of behavior that no other campus organization would be able to violate with impunity. Yet they were supported by university funds and university departments, and tolerated by university administrators.

On many campuses there was no public opposition to these anti-Israel events; nor was there official disapproval towards their sponsors on any campus. Moreover, when our students put up an opposition, they were attacked not only by the Muslim Brotherhood groups but by leftists and the liberal organization Hillel, the largest Jewish group on campus. These episodes are described in "Genocidal Acts at U.C. San Diego," and "Jews Who Stand With Their Enemies," but the same themes run throughout the campus narratives in this volume. The stories of these encounters with the Islamist fifth column provide a sobering insight into the education of America's future leaders and thus into political conflicts waiting down the line.

As in previous volumes, the texts have been edited for publication.

PART I

Islamo-Fascism

Islamophobia
(with Robert Spencer)

In George Orwell's futuristic nightmare, *1984*, citizens are targeted by a secret police for "thought-crimes" committed against the totalitarian state. Thought-crimes are simply attitudes and ideas the authorities regard as politically incorrect. Orwell wrote *1984* during the height of the Cold War and its vision reflected an all-too-present reality. The Soviet police state had spread its tentacles over the lives of hundreds of millions of captive people. Tens of millions of them were sent to labor camps and firing squads for ideas that failed to conform to the prescriptions of the totalitarian state. Their offense was to be "anti-Soviet"—to have criticized Communism or the Soviet rulers, or not to have parroted the views and opinions approved by the regime as politically correct.

During the Cold War, the United States led a coalition of democracies opposed to the Communist bloc because America's founders had made the principle of individual liberty the cornerstone of their republic. The very first article of the Bill of Rights restricts the power of the state to control individual speech. This First Amendment freedom guarantees citizens the right to dissent from orthodoxy, to criticize the powerful, and to tell the truth as they see it without fear of reprisal. This freedom is the absolute and indispensable basis of every other freedom that the citizens of

October 4, 2011, http://frontpagemag.com/2011/david-horowitz-and-robert-spencer/american-liberals-and-iranian-mullahs-peddle-fear/

a democracy enjoy, since, without the right to dissent from the opinions of the state, every other freedom can be taken away. Every dissent from the policies and practices of the state would be a thought-crime.

"Islamophobia" is the name that has been given to a modern-day thought-crime. The purpose of inserting the term "phobia" is to suggest that any fear associated with Islam is irrational—whether that fear stems from the fact that Islam's prophet and its current-day imams call on the faithful to kill infidels, or because the attacks of 9/11 were carried out to implement those calls. Worse, it is to suggest that such a response to those attacks reflects a bigotry that itself should be feared. Those with an historical perspective, however, will have a different view, given that Islam's attitude of hostility toward the infidel world has been unchanging since its beginnings.

In the fall of 2005, Muslim riots resulted in the deaths of more than 100 people in Europe and Asia. The riots were incited by imams and triggered by the publication of cartoons in Denmark depicting Islam's prophet Muhammad.[1] The intimidation was so great that when Yale University Press published a scholarly book about the Muhammad cartoons, it refused to print the cartoons themselves in the text, despite the protests of the author.[2]

Responding to these acts of violence, a group of internationally respected writers published a manifesto called "Together Facing the New Totalitarianism."[3] Salman Rushdie, a member of the group, had been the target of a previous attack resulting from a novel he had written that Iran's Ayatollah Khomeini considered "insulting to the prophet." Khomeini issued a *fatwa* calling on all

---

[1] http://en.wikipedia.org/wiki/Timeline_of_the_Jyllands-Posten_Muhammad_cartoons_controversy
[2] Patricia Cohen, "Yale Press Bans Images of Muhammad in New Book," *New York Times*, August 12, 2009; http://www.nytimes.com/2009/08/13/books/13book.html?_r=2&
[3] "Writers' statement on cartoons," *BBC News*, March 1, 2006; http://news.bbc.co.uk/go/pr/fr/-/2/hi/europe/4764730.stm

Muslims to kill Rushdie, who was forced to go into hiding for several years. Every year, the Islamic Republic of Iran renews the sentence. The writers' manifesto said: "After having overcome fascism, Nazism, and Stalinism, the world now faces a new global totalitarian threat: Islamism.... We, writers, journalists, intellectuals, call for resistance to religious totalitarianism and for the promotion of freedom, equal opportunity and secular values for all. We refuse to renounce our critical spirit out of fear of being accused of 'Islamophobia,' a wretched concept that confuses criticism of Islam as a religion and stigmatization of those who believe in it. We defend the universality of the freedom of expression, so that a critical spirit can exist in every continent, towards each and every maltreatment and dogma."[4]

Political Islam

Islam is often defended as a religion no different from Christianity, Hinduism, Judaism and most other faiths. But this overlooks the fact that, unlike other modern faiths, Islam is a political religion. It has had no reformation since its founding in the 7th century, and Muslims recognize no separation between religion and state. In its canonical texts and teachings, Islam regards all other religions (and non-religions) as infidel creeds, and instructs believers to regard themselves at war with those who will not submit to the Muslim deity. Unlike Christians or Jews, Muslim leaders seek to establish a global Islamic political state that would impose Islamic law on individuals everywhere and thus criminalize heretical thoughts.

Political Islam's global ambition is openly stated. The president of the Islamic Republic of Iran, Mahmoud Ahmadinejad, has said: "Have no doubt.... Allah willing, Islam will conquer what? It will conquer all the mountain tops of the world."[5] In 1990, the 56

---

[4] Ibid.
[5] "Iran's New President Glorifies Martyrdom," Middle East Media Research Institute, July 29, 2005; http://www.imra.org.il/story.php3?id=26226

member states of the Organization of the Islamic Conference (OIC) met in Egypt and adopted the "Cairo Declaration on Human Rights in Islam." The Cairo Declaration states that "all human beings form one family whose members are united by their subordination to Allah."[6] These are religious statements, but they are made by *political* authorities. Moreover, they are in complete accord with traditional Islamic theology. In his 1955 book *War and Peace in the Law of Islam*, Majid Khadduri, an internationally renowned scholar of Islamic law, wrote: "The Islamic state, whose principal function was to put God's law into practice, sought to establish Islam as the dominant reigning ideology over the entire world.... The jihad was therefore employed as an instrument for both the universalization of religion and the establishment of an imperial world state."[7] Because the tenets of Islamic belief are not open to question, and because as a religion Islam prescribes moral behavior for every aspect of individual and social life, Islamic law—*sharia*—is by its very nature totalitarian. A religion that recognizes no principle of separation from governmental authority, whose prescriptions dictate what is proper for every aspect of private life, is by definition totalitarian. Where Islam becomes the religion of the state, violations of Islamic doctrine and heretical thoughts are inevitably seen as crimes against the state.

The Organization of Islamic Cooperation (OIC) is composed of the 56 Islamic nations plus the Palestinian Authority.[8] At present, only Saudi Arabia, Iran, Islamic northern Sudan and most of Somalia are states wherein Islamic law is fully implemented. Other Islamic states, such as Pakistan, Egypt and Indonesia, are currently governed by a mixture of Western and Islamic law. Even in such "moderate" majority-Muslim states, however, Christians are

---

[6]"Cairo Declaration on Human Rights in Islam," August 5, 1990; http://www1.umn.edu/humanrts/instree/cairodeclaration.html
[7]Majid Khadduri, *War and Peace in the Law of Islam*, Johns Hopkins University Press, 1955, p. 51
[8]It changed its name in July 2011 from the Organization of the Islamic Conference.

violently persecuted as infidels, and non-Muslims in general are denied basic rights. Even in these states, apostasy is not tolerated. Converts from Islam to other religions are routinely threatened, harassed, jailed and even executed under existing state law. In short, even in "moderate" Muslim states the penalty for deviation from the accepted religious orthodoxy is severe; and in each of these states there are radical Islamic movements pushing for more stringent conformity to Islamic law. Not a single one of the OIC's members—with the arguable exception of Lebanon, which is unique in having a significant Christian population—can be considered a democracy in the Western sense. Even secular Turkey denies equality of rights to Christians in numerous ways. Not a single one of the 56 Islamic states or the Palestinian Authority is tolerant towards gays, women or other minorities, or treats them as equals.

Since the demise of the Soviet Union, the Islamic states of the OIC have comprised the largest voting bloc at the United Nations. Wielding its influence, the OIC has succeeded in having Israel condemned more than 200 times in formal UN resolutions—more often than all the other member states combined. But the same Islamic voting bloc has ensured that the terrorist regimes in Iran, Gaza and the West Bank have not been censured even once. Through the OIC, the Islamic states have also been working for several years to persuade the members of the UN to criminalize "Islamophobia."

Islamophobia and the Muslim Brotherhood

The Muslim Brotherhood is a global organization and the leading force behind totalitarian Islam. It is also the fountainhead of terrorist Islam, in particular of the Islamic terror groups Al-Qaeda and Hamas. The Brotherhood was founded in Egypt in 1928 by Hasan al-Banna, an open admirer and supporter of Adolf Hitler who arranged to have *Mein Kampf* translated into Arabic in the 1930s. His disciple, Haj Amin al-Husseini, the patriarch of Palestinian nationalism, spent the Second World War in Berlin recruiting

Arabs for Hitler's legions. Al-Banna's ambition was to create a global Islamic empire instituting *sharia* as a global law: "It is a duty incumbent on every Muslim to struggle towards the aim of making every people Muslim and the whole world Islamic, so that the banner of Islam can flutter over the earth and the call of the Muezzin can resound in all the corners of the world: God is greatest [*Allahu Akbar*]!"[9] The motto of the Muslim Brotherhood inspires its members to achieve this plan: "Allah is our goal. The Prophet is our leader. The Qur'an is our law. Jihad is our way. Dying in the way of Allah is our highest aspiration."

Al-Banna's movement grew quickly in Egypt, but after a member of the Brotherhood assassinated the Egyptian prime minister on December 28, 1948, the organization was outlawed. Nonetheless, since the days of President Gamel Abdel Nasser (1956–1970), the Brotherhood has been so popular among Egyptians that the Egyptian government has looked the other way as the group terrorized Coptic Christians and others, and enforced Islamic strictures upon the population as a whole. It was only when the Brotherhood showed signs of becoming strong enough to seize state power that the Egyptian government cracked down. In 1966, the Brotherhood's leading theorist, Sayyid Qutb (also an admirer of Hitler), was arrested and executed for calling for the overthrow of the existing regime and its replacement with one that fully implemented Islamic law. But the popularity of the Brotherhood persisted. Nasser's successor, Anwar Sadat, signed a peace agreement with Israel, which led to his assassination by Islamic hardliners. Shortly before his assassination, Sadat had released all the members of the Brotherhood who had been languishing in Egyptian prisons, and had even promised the Brotherhood that Islamic law would be fully implemented in Egypt.

After 9/11, the Brotherhood launched a campaign to sanitize its image and present itself as a moderate organization. Its intention

---

[9]Brynjar Lia, *The Society of the Muslim Brothers in Egypt*, Ithaca Press, 1998, p. 79

was to enter the political process and subvert the secular order. This goal was achieved with the fall of Sadat's successor, Hosni Mubarak, whose removal was demanded by America's president Barack Obama. Immediately following Mubarak's fall, the Brotherhood became the leading political force in Egypt, its influence manifest in the reopening of Egypt's relations with Iran for the first time in 34 years. This entente coincided with Cairo's ending of the arms blockade of Gaza, which had been designed to keep weapons from flowing to the Islamic terrorist group Hamas. Hamas identifies itself as a creation of the Brotherhood in its founding charter: "The Islamic Resistance Movement [Hamas] is one of the wings of the Muslim Brothers in Palestine. The Muslim Brotherhood Movement is a world organization, the largest Islamic Movement in the modern era."[10] Al-Qaeda founders Abdullah Azzam and Osama bin Laden, and top leader Ayman al-Zawahiri, were all members or protégés of the Muslim Brotherhood.[11] The Brotherhood's reach also extended into Shi'ite Iran. Navvab Safavi, founder of the Iranian Islamic group Fadayan-e Islam, was strongly influenced by the Brotherhood. Safavi went on to become a close associate of the Ayatollah Khomeini, who labeled America "the Great Satan" after the name of the large pillar that Muslims stone during their pilgrimage to Mecca—in other words the leader of the anti-totalitarian, anti-*sharia,* infidel world.

The Muslim Brotherhood's designs on the Great Satan are spelled out in an internal document that the FBI seized in the Northern Virginia headquarters of the Holy Land Foundation in 2005. At the time, the Holy Land Foundation was the largest Islamic "charity" in America. It was also a fundraising front for the terrorist organization (and Muslim Brotherhood creation) Hamas. In 2007, the seized document was presented as evidence in

---

[10]"Selected Documents Regarding Palestine," http://www.thejerusalem-fund.org/www.thejerusalemfund.org/carryover/documents/charter.html
[11]"Washington's Schizophrenic Approach Toward the Muslim Brotherhood," *IPT News,* September 28, 2010

the trial of the Holy Land Foundation, which was accused of illegally supporting a terrorist organization. The trial resulted in convictions of the Foundation's leaders. The captured document disclosed at the trial was titled, "An Explanatory Memorandum on the General Strategic Goal for the Group in North America."[12] In it, Muslim Brotherhood members were told: "The general strategic goal of the group in America, which was approved by the Shura Council [upper house of Egypt's parliament] and the Organizational Conference for the year [1987] is Enablement of Islam in North America, meaning: establishing an effective and stable Islamic Movement led by the Muslim Brotherhood, which adopts Muslim causes domestically and globally, and which works to expand the observant Muslim base, aims at directing and unifying Muslims' efforts, presents Islam as a civilizational alternative, and supports the global Islamic state wherever it is."[13] And further: "[Muslims] must understand that their work in America is a kind of grand jihad in eliminating and destroying the Western civilization from within and 'sabotaging' its miserable house by their hands and the hands of the believers so that it is eliminated and Allah's religion is made victorious over all other religions."

To realize the goal of destroying Western civilization and establishing a global Islamic state, the Brotherhood memorandum called for the creation of front organizations that would insinuate themselves into the institutional framework of host societies and of American society in particular. Among the groups the memorandum identified as being part of this network of Brotherhood fronts were the Muslim American Society, the Muslim Students Association, the Islamic Society of North America, the Islamic

---

[12]Mohamed Akram, "An Explanatory Memorandum on the General Strategic Goal for the Group in North America," May 22, 1991, Government Exhibit 003-0085, U.S. vs. HLF, et al. p. 7 (21).

[13]"A Project for an Explanatory Memorandum for the General Strategic Goal for the Group in North America Mentioned in the Long Term Plan"; http://www.discoverthenetworks.org/viewSubCategory.asp?id=1235

Circle of North America, and the Islamic Association for Palestine, the parent group of the Council on American-Islamic Relations (CAIR).[14] Another front group identified in the memorandum—the International Institute for Islamic Thought—invented the term "Islamophobia."[15]

A Global Movement Against Islamophobia

Abdur-Rahman Muhammad is a former member of the International Institute for Islamic Thought. He was present when the word "Islamophobia" was created, but now characterizes the concept of Islamophobia this way: "This loathsome term is nothing more than a thought-terminating cliché conceived in the bowels of Muslim think- tanks for the purpose of beating down critics."[16] So, in its very origins, "Islamophobia" was a term designed as a weapon to advance Islam's totalitarian cause by stigmatizing its critics and effectively silencing them. Although it was invented in the early 1990s, "Islamophobia" did not become the focus of an active Brotherhood campaign until after 9/11. Since then it has become "a matter of extreme priority" for the Organization of Islamic Cooperation; this according to its secretary-general, Ekmeleddin Ihsanoglu.[17] By 2010, the campaign had already achieved notable success. In November of that year, the UN General Assembly voted to condemn what it called the "vilification of

---

[14]Ibid. The document is analyzed in http://www.discoverthenetworks.org/ viewSubCategory.asp?id=1235

[15]Claire Berlinski, "Moderate Muslim Watch: How the Term 'Islamophobia' Got Shoved Down Your Throat," *Ricochet,* November 24, 2010; http://ricochet.com/main-feed/Moderate-Muslim-Watch-How-the-Term-Islamophobia-Got-Shoved-Down-Your-Throat; "The neologism 'Islamophobia' did not simply emerge *ex nihilo.* It was invented, deliberately, by a Muslim Brotherhood front organization, the International Institute for Islamic Thought, which is based in Northern Virginia."

[16]Claire Berlinski, op. cit.

[17]Patrick Goodenough, "New Name, Same Old Focus for Islamic Bloc," *CNSNews.com,* June 30, 2011; http://www.cnsnews.com/news/article/ new-name-same-old-focus-islamic-bloc

religion."[18] Every majority-Muslim state, without exception, supported the resolution. A Reuters report claimed that the resolution's language had been softened before it was finally submitted. The term "defamation" had been changed to "vilification" in order to win more support from Western nations. But the two words are essentially synonyms, and both are dangerously subjective. What actually constitutes "defamation" or "vilification" would presumably be left up to some UN body to determine; in other words, essentially to the Islamic states.

The resolution is a step towards making it criminal to criticize any matter "regarded by followers of any religion or belief as sacred."[19] So defined and made into law, it would be an anti-blasphemy statute. Such statutes are presently on the books in several Islamic states. On the other hand, anti-blasphemy laws are the very reason the American founders created the First Amendment. They themselves were refugees from religious persecution; they wanted to make sure their new republic could not sanctify a particular creed or use it to persecute dissenters. That is what American democracy is essentially about.

To sugarcoat its bitter pill, the UN resolution against "vilification" condemned not only "Islamophobia" but also "Judeophobia and Christianophobia." This was merely a sop to Western sensibilities and bothersome notions of free speech; not something the Muslim framers of the resolution took seriously. Massacres of Christians in Egypt, Iraq, Pakistan and Indonesia, terror attacks against Passover Seders in Israel, and other acts of Muslim hatred did not lead to calls for UN censure from the Islamic bloc. When Andres Serrano's *Piss Christ* became a *cause célèbre*, or a thousand anti-Semitic caricatures appeared in Arab government media (including the "Protocols of the Elders of Zion," which was run as

---

[18]Louis Charbonneau, "Support for U.N. Vote against Defaming Religion Wanes," *Reuters*, November 24, 2010; http://in.reuters.com/article/2010/11/24/idINIndia-53114620101124
[19]Patrick Goodenough, op. cit.

an eleven-part miniseries on Egyptian TV), there were no expressions of outrage from the Islamic bloc nations or the UN, and no formal condemnations. The clear aim of the UN's anti-blasphemy resolution was to proscribe *Islamophobia* in non-Muslim countries, not to curb Muslim hatred against Jews, Christians or other religious believers.

On the contrary, blasphemy laws defined to include the expression of basic Christian and Jewish beliefs are already on the books in many areas of the Islamic world. In Pakistan, a blasphemy law has been used to victimize numerous innocent Christians, sometimes simply for affirming the Christian faith. The punishment is often death. In Saudi Arabia the law allows no non-Muslim religious expression at all, since Muhammad commanded that Jews and Christians be expelled from the Arabian Peninsula, and that there be only one religion there. Thus it is illegal to build a Christian church in Saudi Arabia, or to bring a Bible across its borders; and no Jew or Christian is permitted to set foot in the cities of Mecca and Medina, lest these Muslim holy sites be defiled.

Islamophobia Defined

Just as the Muslim Brotherhood had affinities with the Nazis, so they embraced Marxist indictments of the capitalist West. Their instructors were first their Communist allies and then, in the post-Communist era, "social justice" progressives.[20] Islamic *jihadist* pronouncements regularly incorporate the analyses of these leftists. Among the books recommended in Osama bin Laden's *fatwas* also are Mearsheimer and Walt's conspiratorial treatise, *The Israel Lobby and U.S. Foreign Policy*, and Noam Chomsky's *Hegemony or Survival: America's Quest for Global Dominance.*[21] Indeed, the

---

[20]David Horowitz, *Unholy Alliance: Radical Islam and the American Left*, Regnery, 2004; Andrew McCarthy, *The Grand Jihad: How Islam and the Left Sabotage America*, Encounter, 2010

[21]Noam Chomsky, *Hegemony or Survival: America's Quest for Global Dominance*, Metropolitan, 2003; Chomsky is also an enthusiast of Hezbollah.

anti-Islamophobia movement has been built on foundations created by progressives and so is already well advanced in the West. In 1996, the Runnymede Trust, a progressive group in England, established a "Commission on British Muslims and Islamophobia." Its elaborate definition of Islamophobia has since become a model for Muslim Brotherhood fronts like CAIR and the Muslim Students Association. Under the Runnymede definition, Islamophobia includes any one of these eight components:

1. Islam seen as a single monolithic bloc, static and unresponsive to new realities;
2. Islam seen as separate and other—(a) not having any aims or values in common with other cultures (b) not affected by them, or (c) not influencing them;
3. Islam seen as inferior to the West—barbaric, irrational, primitive, sexist;
4. Islam seen as violent, aggressive, threatening, supportive of terrorism, engaged in 'a clash of civilizations;'
5. Islam seen as a political ideology, used for political or military advantage;
6. Criticisms made by Islam of 'the West' rejected out of hand;
7. Hostility towards Islam used to justify discriminatory practices towards Muslims and exclusion of Muslims from mainstream society; or
8. Anti-Muslim hostility accepted as natural and 'normal'.[22]

Note, at the outset, how contradictory these proscriptions are. The very first Runnymede injunction seeks to ban all references to Islam as a "single monolithic bloc." But then, with one exception, every other Runnymede proscription presents Islam as a single monolithic bloc: "Islam seen as separate ... Islam seen as inferior ... sexist ... Islam seen as violent," "Criticisms made by Islam of

---

[22]"Islamophobia, A Challenge for Us All," The Runnymede Trust, 1997; http://www.runnymedetrust.org/projects/commissionOnBritishMuslims.html

'the West' rejected out of hand ..." These statements presume that Islam is a unitary entity and can, for example, make judgments about the West with a single voice that are rejected out of hand. The definition of Islamophobia is made as though there were no separatist Muslims to be concerned about, no violent Muslims to fear, no doctrines associated with "Islam" that are backward and sexist, and no Muslim criticisms of the West that should be rejected out of hand. There is a reason the Runnymede statement and its imitators take a monolithic view of Islam. It serves their primary goal, which is to conflate criticisms of some Islamic doctrines and opposition to Islamic terrorists with attacks on Muslims as such. As the signers of the Rushdie manifesto put it: "'Islamophobia' [is a] wretched concept that confuses criticism of Islam as a religion and stigmatization of those who believe in it." Thus, critics of Islam's relegation of women to second-class citizenship are labeled anti-Muslim even though they are defending Muslims; and opponents of Islamic terror are called Islamophobes.

Each one of the Runnymede criteria is so vague as to be easily applied to any criticism of Islam. Is Islam sexist?—i.e., do women have diminished rights in Muslim societies and cultures? It is undeniable that they do. But in the Runnymede view, to say so is *Islamophobic.* Is Islam engaged in a clash of civilizations? The leaders of Islamic *jihadist* organizations like the Muslim Brotherhood, Hamas, and Hezbollah, and the rulers of Muslim states like the Sudan and Iran, proclaim that they are in a war of civilizations with the West. But to recognize this fact is *Islamophobia.* Is Islam a political ideology? It is the ideology of political organizations like the Muslim Brotherhood and the Taliban; it is the official view of states like Saudi Arabia and Iran. Islamic apologists all over the world criticize the idea of the separation of religion and state, and compare Islam favorably to Christianity precisely *because* Islam has a political doctrine and Christianity does not. Yet to note this fact is anti-Muslim. There is no mystery as to how the Runnymede principles will be interpreted. They have already been used to condemn every critic of the Islamic oppression of women, of Islamic support for suicide bombings and other acts of terror, and of Islamic intolerance. Such critics are *Islamophobes.*

Outlawing Cartoons and Films

The Organization of Islamic Cooperation campaign against Islamophobia began in earnest at its annual meeting in Senegal in March 2008. At this meeting, the OIC declared its intention to craft a "legal instrument" to fight against the threat to Islam "from political cartoonists and bigots."[23] The reference was to the Danish cartoons that had appeared in 2005, touching off the international protests that included riots, the burning of embassies, and even murders of non-Muslims, including a Catholic nun. In the eyes of those attending the meeting, however, Muslims were the victims. "Muslims are being targeted by a campaign of defamation, denigration, stereotyping, intolerance and discrimination," fumed Ekmeleddin Ihsanoglu, who gave attendees "a voluminous report by the OIC that recorded anti-Islamic speech and actions from around the world. The report concludes that Islam is under attack and that a defense must be mounted."[24] The attacks by Muslims on non-Muslims, and the hundred-plus fatalities the protests caused, went un-noted and un-deplored.

Ihsanoglu even compared the appearance of the Danish cartoons to the 9/11 atrocity, warning that "the Islamic world took the satirical drawings as a different version of the September 11 attacks against them." He then urged the European Union to adopt new laws against Islamophobia.[25] At the Senegal meeting, Ihsanoglu declared: "Islamophobia cannot be dealt with only through cultural activities but [through] a robust political engagement." The political engagement he referred to was a campaign to

---

[23]Rukmini Callimachi, "Defame Islam, Get Sued?," The Associated Press, March 14, 2008; http://usatoday30.usatoday.com/news/world/2008-03-14-1763755799_x.htm

[24]Ibid.

[25]"Offensive Cartoons Like 9/11 of Islamic World," *The Journal of Turkish Weekly*, February 14, 2006

restrict freedom of speech. Abdoulaye Wade, president of Senegal and chairman of the Organization of Islamic Cooperation, explained: "I don't think freedom of expression should mean freedom from blasphemy. There can be no freedom without limits."[26] In a July 2008 briefing on Capitol Hill, Pakistani embassy representative Asma Fatima defended the anti-cartoon outrages as necessary and called for restrictions on speech that insulted Islam: "The ideal of freedom of speech is precious to you, but it's not value-neutral. You don't have to hurt people's sentiments and bring them to the point where they have to react in strange ways."[27]

The new anti-Islamophobia campaign also focused on *Fitna*, a short film by Dutch politician Geert Wilders. The film consisted of passages from the Qur'an exhorting Muslims to violence, then depictions of the violence directly inspired by those passages and imams drawing on those passages. The Organization of Islamic Cooperation condemned *Fitna* in "the strongest terms," claiming that Wilders' film was "a deliberate act of discrimination against Muslims," intended only to "provoke unrest and intolerance."[28] There was no suggestion that the citations from the Qur'an were inaccurate or that the incidents they inspired hadn't taken place. Physical threats against Wilders by Muslims resulted in the Dutch government providing him with a 24-hour security detail, and forced Wilders to live in hiding, separated from his family. But the same government indicted Wilders for having created the film. It was extraordinary enough that a member of the Dutch parliament and leader of the nation's third-largest party would have to live in hiding, but the indictment by the Dutch government was even

---

[26]Ibid.

[27]Julia Duin, "Religious Speech Debated," *The Washington Times*, July 17, 2008; http://www.washingtontimes.com/news/2008/jul/17/religious-speech-debated/

[28]"Muslims Condemn Dutch Lawmaker's Film," *CNN*, March 28, 2008; http://www.cnn.com/2008/WORLD/europe/03/28/islam.film/index.html?_s=PM:WORLD

more outrageous. It charged that Wilders had "intentionally offended a group of people, i.e. Muslims, based on their religion"; had "incited to hatred of people, i.e. Muslims, based on their religion"; and had "incited to discrimination ... against people, i.e. Muslims, based on their religion." It also claimed that he had incited people to hate Muslims because of their race.[29] All this was based on statements Wilders had made about Islam that were entirely true and accurate; the indictment was an attempt to criminalize the airing of unpleasant facts and the expression of politically incorrect opinions.

Instead of defending Wilders's right to his opinions, many Western officials rushed to support the condemnations. Ihsanoglu noted that the anti-free speech campaign had made "convincing progress at all these levels mainly the UN Human Rights Council in Geneva, and the UN General Assembly. The UN General Assembly adopted similar resolutions against the defamation of Islam." He added: "In confronting the Danish cartoons and the Dutch film 'Fitna,' we sent a clear message to the West regarding the red lines that should not be crossed. As we speak, the official West and its public opinion are all now well aware of the sensitivities of these issues. They have also started to look seriously into the question of freedom of expression from the perspective of its inherent responsibility, which should not be overlooked."[30]

Doudou Diène, the UN special *rapporteur* on contemporary forms of "racism, racial discrimination, xenophobia and related intolerance," went further, suggesting that even quoting the Qur'an accurately but in a critical manner was an act of bigotry: "One may note that a number of Islamophobic statements have

---

[29]Robert Spencer, "Geert Wilders Receives Summons: a Sledgehammer Blow to the Freedom of Speech," Jihad Watch, December 4, 2009; http://www.jihadwatch.org/cgi-sys/cgiwrap/broncos/managed-mt/mt-srch.cgi?IncludeBlogs=1&tag=Geert%20Wilders&limit=20

[30]Ekmeleddin Ihsanoglu, "Speech of Secretary General at the Thirty-fifth Session of the Council of Foreign Ministers of the Organisation of the Islamic Conference," June 18, 2008

been falsely claimed to be scientific or scholarly, in order to give intellectual clout to arguments that link Islam to violence and terrorism. Furthermore, the manipulation and selective quoting of sacred texts, in particular the Qur'an, as a means to deceptively argue that these texts show the violent nature of Islam has become current practice."[31]

Perhaps the most disturbing aspect of the international campaign against free speech was the readiness of western politicians of a leftist bent, including government leaders, to support the Muslim assault and to impose restrictions on their own people. This was especially egregious in the Netherlands, the scene of shocking acts of Islam-related violence. The gay politician Pim Fortuyn was murdered in 2002 by a leftist Dutchman, Volkert van der Graaf, who explained that he had done it on behalf of the country's Muslims, to stop their "scapegoating" by Fortuyn. In 2004, an Islamic *jihadist*, Mohammed Bouyeri, murdered filmmaker Theo van Gogh—also gay—in broad daylight on a street in Amsterdam, on grounds that van Gogh had insulted Islam with his film *Submission*, criticizing the Islamic treatment of women.

The trial of Geert Wilders ended in an acquittal in June 2011. On receiving the verdict, he said: "It is my strong conviction that Islam is a threat to Western values, to freedom of speech, to the equality of men and women, of heterosexuals and homosexuals, of believers and unbelievers." These claims are founded in the behavior of the Organization of Islamic Cooperation and the failure of any Muslim authority to defend Wilders; in the clear and elaborate strictures about women and homosexuals in Islamic teachings and Islamic law; and in the persecution of non-believers, especially Christians, in Muslim countries like Egypt, Pakistan, and Indonesia, all of

---

[31]Doudou Diène, "Racism, Racial Discrimination, Xenophobia and Related Forms of Intolerance: Follow-Up To and Implementation of the Durban Declaration and Programme of Action," United Nations Human Rights Council, August 21, 2007; http://unispal.un.org/UNISPAL.NSF/0/E218497A128230AA8525734F0049BA57

which go un-noted and un-lamented in the pronouncements of the 56 Muslim states and the Palestinian Authority that constitute the Organization of Islamic Cooperation.

Nonetheless, Wilders's post-verdict statement is precisely the sort of utterance that led to his indictment. Even as the Dutch court acquitted him, moreover, it affirmed the false and dangerous premises that underpinned the prosecution, including the idea that one could and should face legal action for saying things that others deem offensive. Amsterdam judge Marcel van Oosten explained: "The bench finds that your statements are acceptable within the context of the public debate. The bench finds that although gross and denigrating, it did not give rise to hatred."[32] In other words, the presiding judge would not have hesitated to fine or jail Wilders if he had determined that his words had "given rise to hatred." Thus, the false and dangerous premise of Wilders's indictment is still in place in Dutch law. Upon his acquittal, Wilders said: "Today is a victory for freedom of speech. The Dutch are still allowed to speak critically about Islam, and resistance against Islamization is not a crime."[33] At least for now.

Islamophobia Witch-Hunts

In many European countries, governments already preemptively silence critics of Islam in the name of fighting racial hatred. In June 2002, well before the OIC had begun its Islamophobia campaign in earnest, Muslims in Switzerland targeted the Italian journalist Oriana Fallaci for her post-9/11 book, *The Rage and the Pride.* In it, she had argued that Europe was being colonized by Muslims who refused to assimilate into their host societies and

---

[32]"Victory for Free Speech—Dutch MP," *AAP*, June 23, 2011; http://www.dailytelegraph.com.au/news/breaking-news/victory-for-free-speech-dutch-mp/story-e6freuyi-1226080864102

[33]Pamela Geller, "Geert Wilders Verdict: Not Guilty All Counts! Eureka! 'Today Is a Victory for Freedom of Speech,'" *Atlas Shrugs*, June 23, 2011; http://atlasshrugs2000.typepad.com/atlas_shrugs/2011/06/geert-wilders-verdict-not-guilty-all-counts-eureka.html

remained hostile to their cultures and values. Citing Swiss laws against racism, the Islamic Center of Geneva demanded that Fallaci's book be banned. Hani Ramadan, grandson of Muslim Brotherhood founder Hassan al-Banna, declared that "Fallaci is insulting the Muslim community as a whole with her shameful words." The Islamic Center called on Swiss authorities not only to ban her book but to prosecute those who were distributing it. Swiss officials moved to have Fallaci extradited to face trial but failed in their attempt.[34] Then, in May 2005, the Italian government itself indicted Fallaci for her book, which it said "defames Islam."[35] The campaign to silence Fallaci spread to France, where a group calling itself the Movement Against Racism and for Friendship Between Peoples (MRAP) also filed racism charges, arguing that "Freedom of expression is and will remain a fundamental right … but when this great writer resorts to outrageous stigmatization of Islam, the limits of what is tolerable are breached."[36] In the end, Fallaci escaped prosecution only because she fled Europe and took refuge in America, where the Bill of Rights still prevailed. Shortly before she died of cancer in 2006, she predicted that, when the case came to trial, she would be found guilty.[37]

The guardians of tolerable speech had better luck against Sixties screen siren Brigitte Bardot, who was convicted five times in her native France for "inciting racial hatred," in every case for remarks considered denigrating to Muslims. In June 2008, a court fined the 73-year-old Bardot €15,000 (around $23,000) as punishment for writing that the Islamic community in France was

---

[34]"Swiss Muslims File Suit Over 'Racist' Fallaci Book," IslamOnline, June 20, 2002; http://www.milligazette.com/Archives/01072002/0107200263.htm

[35]Christopher Orlet, "Oriana in Exile," *American Spectator,* July 18, 2005; http://spectator.org/archives/2005/07/18/oriana-in-exile

[36]"Swiss Muslims File Suit Over 'Racist' Fallaci Book," IslamOnline, June 20, 2002; http://www.milligazette.com/Archives/01072002/0107200263.htm; http://www.islam-online.net/english/News/2002–06/20/article29.shtml

[37]Tunku Varadarajan, "Prophet of Decline," *The Wall Street Journal,* June 23, 2005; http://online.wsj.com/article/SB111948571453267105.html

"destroying our country and imposing its acts."[38] The court apparently didn't consider the possibility that imposing Islamic law was precisely what many Muslims in France had in mind. Although they had not moved, like their coreligionists in Britain, to establish separate *sharia* courts, they enforced many *sharia* provisions in the suburbs of major French cities, most of which are inhabited by Muslim majorities.

These prosecutions were ongoing. Wilders noted shortly after his acquittal that "Danish journalist Lars Hedegaard, Austrian human-rights activist Elisabeth Sabaditsch-Wolff and others ... have recently been convicted for criticizing Islam."[39] In October 2009, journalist Jonathan Turley noted that Ireland had passed a blasphemy law, and that "in Holland, Dutch prosecutors arrested cartoonist Gregorius Nekschot for insulting Christians and Muslims with cartoons, including one that caricatured a Christian fundamentalist and a Muslim fundamentalist as zombies who want to marry and attend gay rallies." Christian fundamentalists, of course, were not the ones complaining. Turley added that "the 'blasphemy' cases include the prosecution of writers for calling Muhammad a 'pedophile' because of his marriage to 6-year-old Aisha (which was consummated when she was 9). A legislator in Austria, a publisher in India and a city councilman in Finland have been prosecuted for repeating this view of the historical record."[40]

Such prosecutions have already come to North America as well. On February 14, 2006 a Canadian magazine, the *Western Standard*, became one of the few publications in the Western world to reprint the Danish Muhammad cartoons. The Islamic

---

[38]"Bardot Fined Over Racial Hatred," *BBC News*, June 3, 2008; http://news.bbc.co.uk/2/hi/entertainment/7434193.stm

[39]Geert Wilders, "In Defense of 'Hurtful' Speech," *The Wall Street Journal*, June 24, 2011; http://online.wsj.com/article/SB10001424052702304569504576403682863549032.html

[40]Jonathan Turley, "Just Say No To Blasphemy: U.S. Supports Egypt in Limiting Anti-Religious Speech," *jonathanturley.org*, October 19, 2009; http://jonathanturley.org/2009/10/19/just-say-no-to-blasphemy-u-s-supports-eygpt-in-limiting-anti-religious-speech/

Supreme Council of Canada and the Edmonton Muslim Council complained that the *Standard*'s publisher, Ezra Levant, was "Islamophobic," sparking an investigation of Levant by the Alberta Human Rights and Citizenship Commission. During his interrogation by a commission investigator, Levant delivered a ringing defense of freedom of speech. Many voices were raised in protest against the prosecution, even including some on the left, such as that of Megan McArdle, a senior editor of *The Atlantic*.[41] Facing a groundswell of support for Levant, the Islamic Supreme Council withdrew its complaint.[42] But an even higher profile case was brought against *Maclean's* magazine in Canada for running an excerpt from *America Alone*, a book by the popular columnist Mark Steyn.

Charging that Steyn's "flagrantly Islamophobic" writing subjected Canadian Muslims to "hatred and contempt," the Canadian Islamic Congress filed complaints against *Maclean's* with three separate human-rights commissions.[43] One of the Canadian Islamic Congress's complaints was about Steyn's comment that, in Europe, "the number of Muslims is expanding like mosquitoes."[44] *New Republic* writer Jim Henley labeled Steyn a "racist" because of this phrase.[45] One small problem with these attacks was that

[41]Megan McArdle, "Restoring My Libertarian Street Cred," *The Atlantic*, January 16, 2008; http://www.theatlantic.com/business/archive/2008/01/restoring-my-libertarian-street-cred/2564/

[42]Syed Soharwardy, "Why I'm Withdrawing My Human Rights Complaint against Ezra Levant," *Toronto Globe and Mail*, February 15, 2008; http://www.freerepublic.com/focus/f-news/1970789/posts

[43]"Neocon Book Offends Canada Muslims," *IslamOnline*, January 1, 2008; https://www.onislam.net/english/news/americas/431811

[44]"Clueless Would-be Censors Attack Mark Steyn Again," *Western Standard Shotgun Blog*, February 29, 2008; http://westernstandard.blogs.com/shotgun/2008/02/clueless-would.html; Mark Steyn, "The Future Belongs to Islam," *Maclean's*, October 20, 2006; http://www.macleans.ca/culture/books/article.jsp?content=20061023_134898_134898

[45]Jim Henley, "Sympathy for the Devil," *Unqualified Offerings*, December 8, 2007; http://www.highclearing.com/index.php/archives/2007/12/08/7517

the mosquito remark had been a quote from Mullah Krekar, a Muslim *jihadist* who continues to reside in Norway despite long-standing efforts to deport him. Moreover, Krekar's prediction of Islam's demographic conquest of Europe is hardly original. As far back as 1974, Algerian leader Houari Boumédienne had declared at the United Nations: "One day, millions of men will leave the Southern Hemisphere to go to the Northern Hemisphere. And they will not go there as friends. Because they will go there to conquer it. And they will conquer it with their sons. The wombs of our women will give us victory."[46]

In fact, this is a commonly expressed aspiration of Islamic supremacists. It wasn't Steyn who said that "Islam will return to Europe as a conqueror and victor," or that "The conquest this time will not be by the sword but by preaching and ideology." These are the sentiments expressed by the Muslim Brotherhood's spiritual leader Sheikh Yusuf Al-Qaradawi, who is inexplicably misperceived as a "moderate" in the West.[47] Qaradawi is also on record saying that the Holocaust was God's punishment of the Jews and that, "Allah willing, the next time it will be by the believers."[48] Nor was it Steyn who said that Muslims "will control the land of the Vatican; we will control Rome and introduce Islam in it." This was said by a Saudi sheikh, Muhammad bin Abd Al-Rahman Al-Arifi, imam of the mosque of the King Fahd Security College.[49] In

[46]Lorenzo Vidino, "Forceful Reason," *National Review,* May 4, 2004; http://old.nationalreview.com/comment/vidino200405040834.asp

[47]"Leading Sunni Sheikh Yousef al-Qaradawi and Other Sheikhs Herald the Coming Conquest of Rome," *Middle East Media Research Institute*—Special Dispatch Series No. 447, December 6, 2002; http://www.memri.org/report/en/0/0/0/0/0/0/774.htm

[48]Oren Kessler, "Analysis: Yusuf al-Qaradawi—a 'Man for All Seasons,'" *Jerusalem Post,* February 20, 2011; http://www.jpost.com/Middle-East/Analysis-Yusuf-al-Qaradawi-a-man-for-all-seasons

[49]Steven Stalinsky, "The Next Pope and Islamic Prophecy," *FrontPageMag.com,* April 14, 2005; http://archive.frontpagemag.com/readArticle.aspx?ARTID=8931

the end, Steyn's offense was identical to Wilders's—to quote the statements of Muslims themselves revealing agendas that many Westerners would find worrisome. The actions of the Canadian Islamic Congress show the lengths to which Western-based Muslim advocacy groups will go to carry water for the Organization of Islamic Cooperation in its campaign to silence public discussion of *jihadists'* self-stated goals in their holy war against the West. The Canadian Islamic Congress doesn't file complaints against the *jihadists* who actually advocate an Islamic conquest of Europe; it just goes after western critics of these agendas. In other words, it is "Islamophobia" to reveal the unpleasant reality of the Islaminspired war against the West.

Islamophobia and National Security

Stigmatizing critics of the Islamic jihad as "Islamophobes" not only threatens free speech; it cuts large holes in our security defenses against a terrorist attack. In April 2009, Barack Obama appointed Arif Alikhan, the deputy mayor of Los Angeles, as Assistant Secretary for Policy Development at the Department of Homeland Security. While serving as Los Angeles' deputy mayor, Alikhan (who once called the *jihad* terror group Hezbollah a "liberation movement") blocked a Los Angeles Police Department project to assemble data about the ethnic makeup of mosques in the Los Angeles area. This was not an attempt to conduct surveillance of the mosques or monitor them in any way. LAPD Deputy Chief Michael P. Downing explained that it was actually an outreach program: "We want to know where the Pakistanis, Iranians and Chechens are so we can reach out to those communities."[50] But Alikhan and other Muslim leaders claimed that the project manifested racism and "Islamophobia," and the LAPD ultimately discarded all plans to study the mosques and gain invaluable

---

[50]"Los Angeles Police Plan to Map Muslims," Associated Press, November 9, 2007; http://www.huffingtonpost.com/huff-wires/20071109/lapd-muslims/

contacts in the Muslim community that might prevent terrorist attacks. Alikhan's reward for this disservice was to be appointed by President Obama to a key role at Homeland Security, the department charged with managing the defenses of the entire country. In December 2010, the Los Angeles City Council passed a resolution condemning "Islamophobia."[51]

The effect of this multifaceted societal onslaught has been a weakening of necessary defenses. On November 5, 2009, Army psychiatrist Nidal Malik Hasan gave a neighbor a copy of the Qur'an and told her, "I'm going to do good work for God."[52] Later that day, he entered a center at Fort Hood in Texas where soldiers receive medical examinations before deployment overseas. Shouting *"Allahu Akbar!"* Hasan pulled out a handgun and began firing.[53] Before he was finished, he had murdered thirteen unarmed American soldiers and wounded 32. Yet long before this massacre, Hasan had displayed unmistakable signs of sympathies for *jihadist* terror. He routinely harassed his colleagues with harangues about Islam, and proclaimed that he was "Muslim first and American second."[54] His business card read "SOA," a well-known acronym among *jihadists* for "Soldier of Allah."[55]

---

[51]Jo R. Hicks and David A. Lehrer, "Hyperbole Rules in Muslim Debate," *Los Angeles Daily News*, December 26, 2010; http://www.dailynews.com/opinions/ci_16943041

[52]Nick Allen, "Fort Hood Gunman Had Told US Military Colleagues that Infidels Should Have Their Throats Cut," *The Telegraph*, November 8, 2009; http://www.telegraph.co.uk/news/worldnews/northamerica/usa/6526030/Fort-Hood-gunman-had-told-US-military-colleagues-that-infidels-should-have-their-throats-cut.html

[53]James C. McKinley, Jr. and James Dao, "Fort Hood Gunman Gave Signals Before His Rampage," *New York Times*, November 8, 2009; http://www.nytimes.com/2009/11/09/us/09reconstruct.html?pagewanted=all&_r=0

[54]Nick Allen, *The Telegraph*, op. cit.

[55]"Inside the Apartment of Nidal Malik Hasan," *Time, Magazine*, n.d.; http://www.time.com/time/photogallery/0,29307,1938378_1988330,00.html

Hasan gave a PowerPoint presentation to his colleagues in which he proposed to show "what the Qur'an inculcates in the minds of Muslims and the potential implications this may have for the U.S. military." He argued that Muslims must not fight against other Muslims (as is mandated by Qur'an 4:92), and that the Qur'an also mandates both defensive and offensive jihad against unbelievers, in order to impose upon those unbelievers the hegemony of Islamic law. He quoted the Qur'anic verse calling for war against the "People of the Book" (that is, mainly Jews and Christians) until they "pay the tax in acknowledgment of [Islamic] superiority and they are in a state of subjection" (9:29). According to reports of his talk, Hasan seems then to have told the assembled (and no doubt stunned) physicians that Muslims had a religious obligation to make war against and subjugate non-Muslims as inferiors under their rule. An official who spoke to some of those who attended the lecture said: "Hasan apparently gave a long lecture on the Qur'an and talked about how if you don't believe, you are condemned to hell. Your head is cut off. You're set on fire. Burning oil is poured down your throat."[56] According to the Associated Press, "he gave a class presentation questioning whether the U.S.-led War on Terror was actually a war on Islam. And students said he suggested that *sharia,* or Islamic law, trumped the Constitution and he attempted to justify suicide bombings."[57] Above all, he warned that Muslim soldiers should not be sent to fight for the U.S. in Muslim countries. As evidence of what could happen if they were forced to do so, Hasan invoked the earlier *jihad* murders by another Muslim serviceman, Sgt. Hasan Akbar, of his commanding officers in Kuwait.

But those in his audience did nothing to report him. It was fear of being accused of "Islamophobia" that prevented Hasan's Army

---

[56]Tom Gjelten, Daniel Zwerdling and Steve Inskeep, "Officials Begin Putting Shooting Pieces Together," *National Public Radio,* November 6, 2009; http://www.npr.org/templates/story/story.php?storyId=120162816
[57]Ibid.

superiors from acting upon the warning signs of his commitment to *jihad*. According to the Associated Press, "a Defense Department review of the shooting rampage at Fort Hood, Texas, has found the doctors overseeing Major Nidal Hasan's medical training repeatedly voiced concerns over his strident views on Islam and his inappropriate behavior, yet they continued to give him positive performance evaluations that kept him moving through the ranks."[58] In other words, he rose through the Army ranks even as he justified suicide bombing and spouted hatred for America while wearing its uniform. He was even promoted from captain to major *after* the notorious lecture at the school of medicine. While his colleagues and superiors noted his statements, and were worried about them, "no one in Hasan's chain of command appears to have challenged his eligibility to hold a secret security clearance even though they could have because the statements raised doubt about his loyalty to the United States."[59]

What was the reason for the silence in the face of all these warnings? If Nidal Hasan had been removed from his position or merely reprimanded in the months or years before he massacred thirteen people at Fort Hood, it isn't hard to imagine what might have happened. Groups like the Council on American-Islamic Relations (CAIR) and the Muslim Public Affairs Council (MPAC) would have been quick to charge the Army with *Islamophobia*. The mainstream media would have embarked on a full-bore witch-hunt about the alleged persecution of Muslims in the military, interviewing the teary-eyed mothers of Muslim soldiers killed in the line of duty while fighting for the U.S. in Iraq or Afghanistan. Army Generals would have had to answer questions about alleged discrimination against Muslims in the military on the Sunday morning talk shows. And ultimately, the President of the United States would order a special effort to make Muslims in the military feel welcome.

---

[58]"In Hasan Case, Superiors Ignored Own Worries," Associated Press, January 11, 2010; http://www.nbcnews.com/id/34802972/ns/us_news/t/hasan-case-superiors-ignored-own-worries/
[59]Ibid.

Those who might have complained about Hasan understood that they could have faced public abuse from organizations like CAIR and MPAC as Islamophobes and possibly even disciplinary action from their superiors. Chris Matthews, Jon Stewart and Bill Maher would have subjected them to nationally broadcast ridicule. All Army personnel would have been ordered into sensitivity training, perhaps run by CAIR itself. It isn't hard at all to imagine such a scenario, because it has played out in real life more than once. For years now, CAIR, MPAC and other Brotherhood front groups have done all they can to demonize everyone who speaks honestly about the threat of *jihad* and Islamic supremacism. For CAIR and MPAC, the Fort Hood massacre was in a very real sense a mission accomplished: "Islamophobia" was duly avoided. The U.S. Government's official report on the Fort Hood massacre doesn't mention Islam or *jihad* or terrorism even once. Homeland Security Secretary Janet Napolitano declared: "This was an individual who does not represent the Muslim faith."[60] The U.S. Army Chief of Staff, George Casey, went further: "Our diversity, not only in our Army, but in our country, is a strength. And as horrific as this tragedy was, if our diversity becomes a casualty, I think that's worse."[61] So recognizing signs of Muslim hostility (which, of course, is Islamophobia) is worse than mass murder. That is the judgment of the U.S. Army Chief of Staff.

CAIR's Islamophobia Campaign

The Muslim Brotherhood front group CAIR is the leader of the anti-Islamophobia campaign in the United States. CAIR presents itself as a mainstream civil-rights organization for Muslims,

---

[60]Daniel Bardsley, "Fort Hood Killer 'Does Not Represent Muslims': American Security Chief," *The National*, November 9, 2009; http://www.thenational.ae/news/uae-news/fort-hood-killer-does-not-represent-muslims-american-security-chief

[61]"General Casey: Diversity Shouldn't Be Casualty of Fort Hood," *Reuters*, November 8, 2009; http://blogs.reuters.com/talesfromthetrail/2009/11/08/general-casey-diversity-shouldnt-be-casualty-of-fort-hood/

"similar to a Muslim NAACP," in the words of CAIR spokesman Ibrahim Hooper.[62] The group says its mission is "to enhance understanding of Islam, encourage dialogue, protect civil liberties, empower American Muslims, and build coalitions that promote justice and mutual understanding."[63]

Like so many pronouncements from Brotherhood fronts, this is just a smokescreen for CAIR's real agendas. On June 4, 2007, the Justice Department named CAIR an unindicted co-conspirator in the Holy Land Foundation case, in which the Foundation was accused and then convicted of funding the terrorist organization Hamas, a Brotherhood offshoot. Federal prosecutors identified CAIR as an organization created out of "the U.S. Muslim Brotherhood's Palestine Committee and/or its organizations." To set itself up in business, CAIR had received half a million dollars from the Holy Land Foundation, which made it party to a criminal conspiracy on behalf of Hamas.[64] When confronted with this fact by terrorism analyst Steven Emerson in 2003, CAIR cofounder and executive director Nihad Awad declared: "This is an outright lie. Our organization did not receive any seed money from the Holy Land Foundation. CAIR raises its own funds and we challenge Mr. Emerson to provide even a shred of evidence to support his ridiculous claim." Emerson then produced the canceled check.[65]

CAIR was created in 1994 as a spinoff of a Hamas front group, the Islamic Association for Palestine. Founded in 1981 by Hamas

---

[62]Daniel Pipes and Sharon Chadha, "CAIR: Islamists Fooling the Establishment," *Middle East Quarterly*, Vol. XIII, No. 2, Spring 2006, http://www.meforum.org/916/cair-islamists-fooling-the-establishment

[63]"Our Vision, Mission, and Core Principles," Council on American-Islamic Relations; http://www.cair.com/about-us/vision-mission-core-principles.html

[64]Josh Gerstein, "Islamic Groups Named in Hamas Funding Case," *The New York Sun*, June 4, 2007; http://www.nysun.com/national/islamic-groups-named-in-hamas-funding-case/55778/

[65]"HLF's Financial Support of CAIR Garners New Scrutiny," The Investigative Project on Terrorism, October 12, 2007; http://www.investigativeproject.org/513/hlfs-financial-support-of-cair-garners-new-scrutiny

operative Mousa Abu Marzook, the IAP was shut down in 2005 by the U.S. government for funding terrorism. In 1994, at Barry University in Florida, Nihad Awad conceded, "I'm in support of [the] Hamas movement more than the PLO."[66] In 1998, CAIR cofounder and longtime Board chairman Omar Ahmad told a Muslim audience: "Islam isn't in America to be equal to any other faith, but to become dominant. The Qur'an should be the highest authority in America, and Islam the only accepted religion on earth."[67] Since 9/11, CAIR executives have learned to be more careful with their public statements, and today Ahmad denies uttering the quote. But the journalist who reported it stands by the accuracy of her story.[68]

In 2007, six Muslim clerics sued US Airways after being removed from a flight for behavior that could only be described as mimicking that of airline terrorists. The lawyer for the "Flying Imams," as they became known, was Omar T. Mohammedi, who has served as president of CAIR's New York chapter.[69] The imams also attempted to sue the anonymous passengers who reported them, but House Republicans pushed through a measure protecting whistleblowers in such circumstances.[70] If the imams' suit had been successful, it would have essentially placed Muslims beyond

---

[66]Daniel Pipes and Sharon Chadha, "CAIR: Islamists Fooling the Establishment," *Middle East Quarterly*, Vol. XIII, No. 2, Spring 2006; http://www.meforum.org/916/cair-islamists-fooling-the-establishment

[67]Art Moore, "Did CAIR Founder Say Islam to Rule America?" *WorldNet-Daily*, December 11, 2006; http://www.wnd.com/2006/12/39229/

[68]Ibid.

[69]Liza Porteus, "US Airways Passengers Who Reported 'Suspicious' Imam Activity May Be Sued," *FoxNews*, March 19, 2007; http://www.foxnews.com/story/0,2933,259263,00.html; Omar Mohammedi was identified as the President of CAIR-NY in the Speaker Biographies published at the National Association of Muslim Lawyers conference, "Advancing Justice & Empowering the Community," March 31–April 2, 2006.

[70]Major Garrett, "Congress to Protect Citizens Who Report 'Flying Imams'-Type Suspicions," *FoxNews*, July 25, 2007; http://www.foxnews.com/story/0,2933,290678,00.html

the pale of security-related scrutiny; anyone who reported suspicious behavior by a Muslim in an airport or airplane would have risked being sued as an "Islamophobe."

Six years earlier, CAIR had already gone on the offensive in a campaign that made clear its real aim: to suppress any association between Islam and the terrorists who act in its name. In 2001, Tom Clancy's novel about Islamic terrorists, *The Sum of All Fears*, was being made into a movie. CAIR launched a successful campaign to pressure the filmmakers into changing the terrorists of the script into some other kind of villain. Despite the fact that the film was targeted for a post-9/11 audience, the filmmakers bowed to CAIR's pressure and recast the villains as neo-Nazis. Film director Phil Alden Robinson wrote abjectly to CAIR, "I hope you will be reassured that I have no intention of promoting negative images of Muslims or Arabs, and I wish you the best in your continuing efforts to combat them."[71]

In June 2011, CAIR published a report on Islamophobia in America. It was called *Same Hate, New Target: Islamophobia and its Impact in the United States.* The title reflected a main theme of the anti-Islamophobia campaign, which is to portray the effort to silence critics of Islamic *jihad* as following in the footsteps of the civil-rights struggles of the past. As OIC Secretary General Ihsanoglu explained, "Islamophobia represents a contemporary manifestation of racism and the phenomenon must be addressed in that context."[72] The CAIR report was published with an introduction by Niwad Awad, who thanked Dr. Hatem Bazian for his input. Bazian, an instructor at UC Berkeley, is a ubiquitous speaker for terrorist support groups like the Palestine Solidarity Movement. He gained notoriety in 2004 when he called for "an

---

[71]Reihan Salam, "The Sum of All PC: Hollywood's Reverse Racial Profiling," *Slate*, May 28, 2002; http://www.slate.com/articles/arts/culture-box/2002/05/the_sum_of_all_pc.html

[72]Patrick Goodenough, "New Name, Same Old Focus for Islamic Bloc," *CNSNews.com*, June 30, 2011; http://cnsnews.com/news/article/new-name-same-old-focus-islamic-bloc

intifada in this country" in a speech at Berkeley; he is a co-founder of the Hamas-supporting campus organization, Students for Justice in Palestine.[73]

The CAIR report is careful to begin with a gesture of fairness, suggesting that not every critic of Islam is an Islamophobe ("it is not appropriate to label all, or even the majority of those, who question Islam and Muslims as Islamophobes"), but then fails to provide a single example of what those legitimate questions might be or to identify a single individual whose criticisms of Islam might be so regarded. It then defines Islamophobia as "closed-minded prejudice against or hatred of Islam and Muslims," and lists the eight sweeping principles of the Runnymede document as tests of closed-mindedness.[74] Not surprisingly, CAIR has repeatedly and consistently used the vagueness of those principles to characterize as "prejudice" and "hatred" any resistance to the global *jihad*, including virtually all of the anti-terror legal measures and policy procedures adopted by the United States government, beginning with the Patriot Act. In its report, CAIR displays its own open-mindedness by demonizing as "Islamophobic" every public figure who has worked effectively against Islamic terrorism and supremacism.

In a section titled "The Worst"—meaning the worst Islamophobes—CAIR's report smears Daniel Pipes ("the grandfather of Islamophobia in America"), Robert Spencer ("intellectualized

---

[73]Cinnamon Stillwell, "UC Berkeley's Hatem Bazian: Academic or Activist?," *Campus Watch*, May 10, 2007; http://www.campus-watch.org/article/id/9732; Daniel Greenfield, *Muslim Hate Groups on Campus*, Kindle ebook: http://www.amazon.com/Muslim-Hate-Groups-Campus-ebook/dp/B006W050N4/ref=sr_1_1?ie=UTF8&qid=1370643626&sr=8-1&keywords=muslim+hate+groups+on+campus

[74]Same Hate, New Target: Islamophobia and its Impact in the United States, January 2009–December 2010, Council on American-Islamic Relations, June 2011; pp. 11–12; http://pa.cair.com/files/CAIR%20Islamophobia%20Report%20-%20Same%20Hate,%20New%20Target.pdf

Islamophobia"), Steven Emerson ("anti-Muslim propaganda mouth-piece"), former Deputy Assistant Secretary of Defense Frank Gaffney ("loony-tunes bigotry"), Brigitte Gabriel ("makes no attempt to hide her efforts to de-humanize Muslims), Newt Gingrich ("a consumer of the Islamophobic narrative"), and Pamela Geller ("an anti-Islam activist").[75]

Robert Spencer is a co-author of the present essay. The CAIR report claims that "Spencer offers an intellectualized Islamophobia through 'selectively ignoring' Islamic texts and principles that do not fit his view of Islam as the enemy," i.e., as purveyor of violent *jihadist* doctrines.[76] As in so many instances of CAIR's claims, this is simply a fabrication. In his books *Onward Muslim Soldiers* and *The Complete Infidel's Guide to the Koran*, Spencer discusses the peaceful and tolerant verses of the Qur'an in detail. But he also explains how mainstream Muslim exegetes regard the peaceful verses, which are confined to the earlier sections of the Qur'an, as being superseded by the later violent ones. Instead of responding to these observations and possibly challenging them, CAIR prefers to demonize the messenger and warn others not to consider his analysis and its implications.

CAIR's principal charge against Spencer is that he "operates the blog *Jihad Watch*, which is notorious for its depiction of Islam as an inherently violent faith that is a threat to world peace."[77] The irony, of course, is that so many Muslims behave on a daily basis as if Islam *were* an inherently violent faith. If they were to stop acting on this belief, *Jihad Watch* would have nothing to report and would cease to exist. But it is characteristic of CAIR's Islamophobia campaign to pretend that "Islamophobes"—not the *jihadists*—are the problem. CAIR also condemns Spencer for participating in a 2006 conference honoring the murdered Pim Fortuyn. CAIR doesn't mention, of course, why Fortuyn was murdered, for to

---

[75]Ibid. pp. 16–18
[76]Ibid. p. 16
[77]Ibid.

do so would have revealed that the real targets of violence in the Netherlands are non-Muslim critics of Islam, not Muslims. A comment on CAIR's report by its legislative director, Corey Saylor. reveals its bottom line, which is to silence critics of Islamic supremacism and global *jihad* by pretending that their critiques are directed against all Muslims: "This report shows that Americans who embrace pluralism must act together to prevent Islamophobia from being accepted in mainstream society." In other words, in the name of tolerance, Americans are being asked to suppress the criticism of Islamic *jihadism* that CAIR finds objectionable.[78] To speak out against Islamic jihad and Islamic supremacism, in this Orwellian perspective, is to discriminate against Muslims.

Worse, it is to collude with anti-Muslim terrorists. As of July 2011, there had been more than 17,000 terrorist attacks by Islamic *jihadists* since the September 11 attacks, with an even greater number of victims.[79] During the same period, there had been no terrorist attacks against Muslims—at least not by non-Muslims. But on July 22, 2011 a violent attack against alleged supporters of the "Islamization" of Norway took place in Oslo.[80] The attack was committed by a deranged individual, Anders Behring Breivik, who blew up a government building in Oslo, killing eight, and who then proceeded to the youth camp of the reigning Norwegian political party on the island of Utoya, where he killed 68 others.[81] Two days later, *The New York Times* ran a front-page story purporting

---

[78] *Islamophobia, A Challenge for Us All*, The Runnymede Trust, 1997; http://www.runnymedetrust.org/projects/commissionOnBritishMuslims.html

[79] "About the List of Terrorist Attacks," *TheReligionofPeace.com*; http://www.thereligionofpeace.com/Pages/TheList.htm

[80] Elisa Mala and J. David Goodman, "At Least 80 Dead in Norway Shooting," *The New York Times*, July 22, 2011; http://www.nytimes.com/2011/07/23/world/europe/23oslo.html?pagewanted=all

[81] "Death Toll Declines after Confusion," *Views and News from Norway*, July 26, 2011; http://www.newsinenglish.no/2011/07/26/death-toll-declines-after-early-confusion/

to link Robert Spencer and other anti-*jihad* writers to the killings. The evidence? A 1,500-page manifesto, written by the killer, which contained clippings of articles with references to Spencer's writings on Islam and Islamic *jihad*. The majority of the references actually appeared in a single article in which Spencer was quoted alongside Condoleezza Rice and Tony Blair.[82] Other Spencer references were contained in an article by a third party, in which Spencer was cited on the history of Islam. Not a single Spencer quote called for violence against Muslims or their supporters. Indeed, not a single one of the Oslo killer's victims was a Muslim.[83] Yet, without any other evidence, the *Times* article claimed that these scattered references to Spencer's scholarly descriptions of Islam "deeply influenced" a mass murderer. The *Times* article was headlined: "Killings in Norway Spotlight anti-Muslim Thought in the U.S." In other words, according to *The Times*, Robert Spencer had committed a thought-crime.[84]

No doubt, *The Times* would have been outraged if anyone had suggested that Al Gore was responsible for the terrorist attacks committed by the Unabomber because Gore's writing on the environment was cited in *his* manifesto; or that Noam Chomsky was complicit in Osama bin Laden's crimes because the late terrorist had recommended a Chomsky book in one of his *fatwas*. The difference is that, while Gore's and Chomsky's views mirrored *The Times'* own attitudes, Spencer had already been identified as an Islamophobe, and was thereby worthy of burning.

The Islamophobia Campaign on American Campuses

Following its grand strategy of "destroying the Western civilization from within," the Muslim Brotherhood created the Muslim

---

[82]Daniel Greenfield, "In Defense of Robert Spencer," *FrontPageMag.com*, July 26, 2011; http://frontpagemag.com/2011/07/26/in-defense-of-robert-spencer/

[83]Ibid.

[84]Scott Shane, "Killings in Norway Spotlight Anti-Muslim Thought in U.S.," *The New York Times*, July 24, 2011; http://www.nytimes.com/2011/07/25/us/25debate.html?_r=2&hp

Students Association as the first in its network of organizations designed to carry out the mission. Universities are receiving money from the Organization of Islamic Cooperation to promote the anti-Islamophobia campaign. For example, the OIC funneled $325,000 through CAIR to Georgetown University to finance anti-Islamophobia efforts. But the activists directly involved in those efforts on college campuses are groups like the Muslim Students Association and its aggressive ally, Students for Justice in Palestine. These are sponsors of the "Israeli Apartheid Weeks" designed to demonize the state of Israel and accuse Jews of stealing Muslim land.

In the spring of 2011, student legislators at three University of California campuses—Davis, Santa Barbara and Los Angeles—passed identical resolutions against Islamophobia. The text of each of the resolutions was lifted almost verbatim from the Runnymede document, and was sponsored by the Muslim Students Association and supported by a coalition of leftwing student groups. The UCLA resolution was passed on May 24. Two weeks earlier, David Horowitz had delivered an hour-long lecture at the university, sponsored by Bruin Republicans. The speech was videotaped and Frontpagemagazine.com posted the video and an unedited transcript of the speech on its website. The "Resolution Against Islamophobia" was sponsored by the Muslim Students Association and passed the student government council at UCLA by a 10–0 vote. The resolution declared, "UCLA is a UC Campus Against Islamophobia." Among the "Whereas" clauses justifying its necessity, the resolution cited as "Islamophobic" the speech Horowitz had given opposing Israeli Apartheid Week. The UCLA resolution, in its opening clause, described "Islamophobia" in these words taken almost verbatim from the Runnymede proclamation: "Whereas, Islamophobia is defined as ideologies, beliefs, and actions that perpetuate inaccurate and xenophobic views toward the culture and practice of Islam and the personification of its followers, such as being seen as monolithic, seen as a separate and 'other' culture that does not share common values, seen as inferior to the West, seen as violent, aggressive, and supportive of terrorism, seen as sexist and oppressive of women, seen as a political ideology used for political advantage, anti Muslim hostility, and exclusionary or discriminatory practices against Muslims from mainstream society .."

In other words, the UCLA student government has declared itself against any statement to the effect that Islamic law discriminates against women and gays; that Islamic texts denigrate "infidels" and encourage violence against them; that Islamic imams support terrorism; or that Islamic political parties regard Islam as a political ideology. By this resolution, UCLA students are instructed not to assert that the ruling Islamic party in Gaza, Hamas, is actually political—to take one example. Nor may they link the Islamic teachings codified by a warrior named Muhammad, urging his followers to slay infidels and cut off their heads, to Islamic terrorists who invoke those beliefs when slaying infidels by cutting off their heads. Absurd and dangerous as was this effort to outlaw speech, not a single elected student government leader voted against this resolution. Not one.

This is how the UCLA resolution characterized the Horowitz speech: "Whereas, on Wednesday May 11th controversial speaker David Horowitz made false allegations on campus against the Muslim Students Association and the Afrikan Student Union, and further instilled hate against Muslims by stating that, 'Islam is a sick, sick culture ...'" No evidence was provided—nor does any exist—that Horowitz made any allegations against the Afrikan Student Union, let alone false ones.[85] The resolution did provide a

---

[85]Leaders of the Afrikan Student Union protested a statement Horowitz had made ten years earlier. The statement in its entirety is: "If not for the dedication of Americans of all ethnicities and colors to a society based on the principle that all men are created equal, blacks in America would not enjoy the highest standard of living of blacks anywhere in the world, and indeed one of the highest standards of living of any people in the world. They would not enjoy the greatest freedoms and the most thoroughly protected individual rights anywhere."

citation for the alleged Horowitz statement that Islam is a sick culture, via an audio version of the speech Horowitz had given on May 11. Both a video and unedited transcript of the speech were published on Frontpagemag.com, had any of the student legislators thought to consult it. In the speech, Horowitz discussed the practice of suicide bombing, which had become the weapon of choice for the second Palestinian *Intifada*. He observed that American leftists who support the Palestinians excuse the practice by arguing that the Palestinians are "desperate" and have "no choice" but to use this weapon. Then he criticized these justifications: "People have been oppressed for thousands of years, horribly oppressed. Enslaved. Massacred. And yet, in thousands of years of recorded history, there has never before, *never* been a people that has strapped bombs onto its own children, told them to go ahead and blow up other children. And if you do, you're going to go to heaven. And if you're lucky enough to be male, you're going to get 72 virgins. That is sick. That's a sick death cult...."[86]

It is obvious, from this excerpt of the unedited transcript of Horowitz's speech, that the adjective "sick" refers to the practice of suicide bombing and its rationale, which views suicide bombers as martyrs who will enter paradise. The reference is specifically to the *Palestinian* culture of death, obviously framed by the Hamas version of Islam. In other words, what the Muslim Students Association and the resolution were actually saying was that Hamas's death- cult version of Islam *is* Islam. Horowitz didn't say this; the Muslim Students Association and the UCLA student legislators in effect did. These students aspire to be political leaders. They are students at one of the top dozen schools in America, and there didn't seem to be an adult around to teach them what a democracy is or what a totalitarian concept like "Islamophobia" portends. And that should be troubling to all Americans.

---

[86]David Horowitz, "Confronting the Anti-Israel *Jihad* on Campus," *FrontPageMag.com*, May 24, 2011; http://frontpagemag.com/2011/05/24/confronting-the-anti-israel-jihad-on-campus/

Unholy Alliances

The Muslim Brotherhood's grand-strategy memorandum contains a section emphasizing the crucial importance of gaining "a mastery of the art of coalitions" in order to achieve the *jihadists'* goal—conquest of the non-Muslim world. The coalitions mentioned in the Brotherhood document are coalitions of Muslim organizations. But perhaps the chief asset possessed by the *jihadists* is a coalition of non-Muslims—European and American progressives—who support the anti-Islamophobia campaign. This coalition has a venerable antecedent in the support that progressives provided to Soviet totalitarians during the Cold War.

In 2008, the leftwing watchdog organization "Fairness and Accuracy in Reporting" (FAIR) published a lengthy report called *Smearcasting: How Islamophobes Spread Bigotry, Fear, and Misinformation.* The FAIR report focused on a list of "Islamophobia's Dirty Dozen," which began with FoxNews anchors Bill O'Reilly, Sean Hannity and Glenn Beck, and went on to include the two authors of this essay, investigative reporter Steven Emerson, scholar Daniel Pipes, authors Michelle Malkin and Mark Steyn, and others.[87] The FAIR "study" was entirely made up of quotes lifted out of context or misreported in the first place, then presented as self-evident examples of anti-Muslim bigotry. Thus an observation made by David Horowitz, who is described as "the Islamophobia movement's premier promoter," is presented as a claim by Horowitz that "between 150 million and 750 million Muslims support a holy war." What Horowitz actually said is that public opinion surveys in the Muslim world after 9/11, including one conducted by Al Jazeera, reported that between 10 and 50 percent of Muslims considered Osama bin Laden a hero.

In December 2010, *The Huffington Post* ran a lengthy diatribe by Max Blumenthal called "The Great Islamophobic Crusade,"

---

[87]Steve Rendall and Isabel Macdonald, "The Dirty Dozen," *Fairness & Accuracy In Reporting,* October 21, 2008; http://fair.org/article/the-dirty-dozen/

which began with the claim that "Nine years after 9/11, hysteria about Muslims in American life has gripped the country." According to Blumenthal, "this spasm of anti-Muslim bigotry ... [is] the fruit of an organized, long-term campaign by a tight confederation of right-wing activists and operatives who first focused on Islamophobia soon after the September 11th attacks, but only attained critical mass during the Obama era."[88] It did so, according to Blumenthal, because of conservative resentment over Obama's election and because "representatives of the Israel lobby and the Jewish-American establishment launched a campaign against pro-Palestinian campus activism that would prove a seedbed for everything to come." According to Blumenthal, "[Islamophobia] reflects an aggressively pro-Israel sensibility, with its key figures venerating the Jewish state as a Middle Eastern Fort Apache on the front lines of the Global War on Terror...."[89] Not surprisingly, Blumenthal's list of conspirators mirrored the "Worst" list of the CAIR report and included several of the "Dirty Dozen" from the FAIR document. Among those Blumenthal identified as members of the cabal were Robert Spencer, Pamela Geller, Newt Gingrich, David Horowitz and the Dutch politician Geert Wilders. Like every attack on Islamophobia, Blumenthal's screed did not devote a single sentence to examining the analyses or answering the arguments laid out in a library shelf of books written by the targets of his defamation.

Six months later, the Southern Poverty Law Center published an "Intelligence Report" called "Anti-Muslim Bigotry." In a previous report, the SPLC tarred establishment conservative organizations like the American Enterprise Institute, to which former Secretary of State Condoleezza Rice belonged, as "racist." The new report summarized the Blumenthal article and featured one of

---

[88]Max Blumenthal, "The Great Islamophobic Crusade," *The Huffington Post*, December 20, 2010; http://www.huffingtonpost.com/max-blumenthal/the-great-islamophobic-cr_b_799277.html
[89]Ibid., p. 2

its own: "The Anti-Muslim Inner Circle" by Robert Steinback.[90] Steinback lists ten members of this inner circle (including Robert Spencer, David Horowitz and Brigitte Gabriel) who have never been in a room together and in most cases never met or corresponded. It is a "circle" which exists only as a means of defaming its alleged members.

In September 2010, the Hamas-associated CAIR joined the pack, publishing a "Guide to Challenging Islamophobia."[91] One month later, the Center for American Progress, a Democratic Party brain-trust, put on a panel with essentially the same title: "Challenging Islamophobia."[92] The panel included an Episcopal priest and Wajahat Ali, author of a blog that, among other complaints, bemoaned the "persecution" of the American Taliban John Walker Lindh, and referred to him as "an innocent victim of America's 'War on Terror.'"[93] A third panelist was Haris Tarin, Washington office director of the Muslim Public Affairs Council, a Muslim Brotherhood front that has previously declared, "Israelis are the worst terrorists in the world," and described Hezbollah as "a liberation organization."[94]

---

[90]Robert Steinback, "Jihad Against Islam," *Southern Poverty Law Center*, Summer 2011, Issue No. 142; http://www.splcenter.org/get-informed/intelligence-report/browse-all-issues/2011/summer/jihad-against-islam; Robert Steinback; "Anti-Muslim Inner Circle," *Southern Poverty Law Center*, Summer 2011, Issue No. 142; http://www.splcenter.org/get-informed/intelligence-report/browse-all-issues/2011/summer/ the-anti-muslim-inner-circle; For a response to the fabrications in the SPLC report, see Robert Spencer, "SPLC Fronts for the Jihad, Smears Freedom Fighters," *Jihad Watch*, June 22, 2011; http://www.jihadwatch.org/2011/06/splc-fronts-for-the-jihad-smears-freedom-fighters.html

[91]"Guide to Challenging Islamophobia," *Council on American-Islamic Relations*, July 13, 2012; http://cair.com/press-center/press-releases/3551–guide-to-challenging-islamophobia.html

[92]"Challenging Islamophobia," *Center for American Progress*, October 4, 2010; http://www.americanprogress.org/events/2010/10/04/17005/challenging-islamophobia/

[93]Wajahat Ali, "America's 'Detainee 001 —The Persecution of John Walker Lindh," *GoatMilk Blog*, July 11, 2011; http://goatmilkblog.com/2011/07/11/americas-detainee-001—the-persecution-of-john-walker-lindh/

[94]http://www.discoverthenetworks.org/printgroupProfile.asp?grpid=6177

Manufacturing Hate Crimes

A major feature of the anti-Islamophobia campaign is the misrepresentation of the status of Muslims in America. Thus, according to the OIC's Ihsanoglu, "Muslims are being targeted by a campaign of defamation, denigration, stereotyping, intolerance and discrimination."[95] According to CAIR's 2011 Islamophobia report: "In 2009 and 2010, Muslims continued to face barriers to their full and equal participation in American society."[96] Again, according to Max Blumenthal, "hysteria about Muslims in American life has gripped the country." Neither the barriers nor the hysteria, however, prevented President Obama from appointing Arif Alikhan, a Muslim with a record of opposing anti-terror efforts, as Assistant Secretary for Policy Development at the Department of Homeland Security. Nor did they prevent the president from appointing Kareem Shora to the Homeland Security Advisory Council. As executive director of the American-Arab Anti-Discrimination Committee, Shora has consistently joined CAIR and other Islamic supremacist groups in lobbying against anti-terror initiatives. Nor did they prevent the president from appointing Rashad Hussain as special envoy to the OIC. Hussain had distinguished himself by decrying the alleged "persecution" of convicted terrorist and Palestinian Islamic Jihad leader Sami al-Arian. Nor did barriers to Muslims and anti-Muslim hysteria prevent President Obama from making Dalia Mogahed a presidential advisor on Muslim affairs. In October 2009, Mogahed declared on British television that most Muslim women worldwide associate Islamic law with "gender justice."

---

[95]Rukmini Callimachi, "Defame Islam, Get Sued?," Associated Press, March 14, 2008; http://usatoday30.usatoday.com/news/world/2008-03-14-1763755799_x.htm

[96]"Same Hate, New Target: Islamophobia and its Impact in the United States, January 2009–December 2010," Council on American-Islamic Relations and the University of California, Berkeley—Center for Race & Gender, June 2011, p. 29; http://pa.cair.com/files/CAIR%20Islamophobia%20Report%20-%20Same%20Hate,%20New%20Target.pdf

Obama even included Ingrid Mattson, president of the Islamic Society of North America, as one of the clerics chosen to pray at the National Cathedral on his Inauguration Day. The Islamic Society of North America is a Muslim Brotherhood front. Obama also sent his senior advisor, Valerie Jarrett, to be the keynote speaker at ISNA's national convention in 2009. Huma Abedin, deputy chief of staff to Secretary of State Hillary Clinton, comes from a prominent Muslim Brotherhood family, and worked for 12 years in a Brotherhood-associated institute before joining Hillary Clinton's staff. These examples do not begin to exhaust the Brotherhood's penetration of the highest levels of the political establishment.[97] Such instances aside, the idea that anti-Muslim prejudice is an urgent problem which needs to be aggressively addressed is greatly exaggerated. According to the 2009 FBI report on "hate crimes," Jews, not Muslims, made up three-fourths of victims of what are classified as religiously motivated hate crimes—not a few of which were committed by Muslims against Jews. By contrast, hate crimes against Muslims made up only 8 per cent of crimes thus classified, or a total of 132 in a nation of 300 million people.[98]

To support its case that rampant Islamophobia is a problem, the leading Muslim civil-rights organization, CAIR, has not hesitated to fabricate anti-Muslim hate crimes. In 2005, Daniel Pipes and Sharon Chadha published an article identifying six incidents falsely described as hate crimes in CAIR's 2004 report. These included "the July 9, 2004 case of apparent arson at a Muslim-owned grocery store in Everett, Washington," in which "investigators quickly determined that Mirza Akram, the store's operator, staged the arson to avoid meeting his scheduled payments and to collect on an insurance policy. Although Akram's antics had

---

[97]Frank Gaffney, *The Muslim Brotherhood in the Obama Administration*, David Horowitz Freedom Center, 2012
[98]"Blacks, Jews Most Likely Victim of US Hate Crimes: FBI," *Agence France-Presse*, November 22, 2010; http://www.google.com/hosted-news/afp/article/ALeqM5gGFEGzxiZ_ZyoPZ_Ty6TyzhUYVWQ?docId=CNG.abc73085fe90435beeac2a10705c6628.3e1

already been exposed as a fraud, CAIR continues to list his case as an anti-Muslim hate crime. In another incident, a Muslim-owned market was burned down in Texas in August 2004. Although the Muslim owner was arrested the following month for having set the fire himself, CAIR included the case in its report.[99]

If the people at CAIR sincerely wanted to diminish the concerns that reasonable Americans may have about the Islamic *jihad* and the extent of its support in the Muslim community, they could do so effectively by condemning the jihad instead of attacking its opponents. They could direct their indignation towards those Muslims and Muslim organizations that commit violent acts in the name of Islam. They could repudiate the statements their own leaders have made, expressing their desire to see the Constitution replaced by Islamic law. They could state clearly and unequivocally that American and Israeli civilians are innocent victims of Islamic terrorists. They could condemn their sister organization Hamas for targeting them and for urging the "obliteration of Israel." They could promote the teaching in mosques and madrassas that Muslims must coexist peacefully as *equals* with infidels on a permanent basis. And they could oppose blasphemy laws, such as the anti-Islamophobia resolutions they are promoting, which are a direct assault on the American Bill of Rights.

Conclusion

In 2009, the Obama administration broke ranks with other Western nations and joined Egypt in supporting a resolution in the UN's Human Rights Council to recognize exceptions to free speech for "any negative racial and religious stereotyping."[100]

---

[99]Daniel Pipes and Sharon Chadha, "CAIR's Hate Crimes Nonsense," *FrontPageMag.com*, May 18, 2005; http://archive.frontpagemag.com/Readarticle.aspx?ArtId=8559

[100]Jonathan Turley, "Just Say No To Blasphemy: U.S. Supports Egypt in Limiting Anti-Religious Speech," *jonathanturley.org*, October 19, 2009; http://jonathanturley.org/2009/10/19/just-say-no-to-blasphemy-u-s-supports-eygpt-in-limiting-anti-religious-speech/

Egypt has long prosecuted journalists and others for insulting Islam. One Egyptian journal was even banned for publishing a poem that compared Allah to a villager who feeds ducks and milks cows. In praising the resolution, the Egyptian ambassador to the UN observed that "freedom of expression has been sometimes misused" and that an understanding of the "true nature of this right" would require government restrictions. Instead of dissenting from this attack on free speech, the U.S. ambassador praised "this joint project with Egypt" as an attempt to achieve "tolerance and the dignity of all human beings."[101] This troublesome attitude was reaffirmed by Secretary of State Hillary Clinton in July 2011, when she commented on attempts by the Organization of Islamic Cooperation to criminalize Islamophobia. Secretary Clinton spoke of "the false divide that pits religious sensitivities against freedom of expression."[102] But from the point of view of the Islamic states, this is not about religious sensitivities. It is about religious *obligations*, and in that view the only way to end the divide is to restrict freedom of expression.

In a column drawing attention to this resolution, "Just Say No to Blasphemy Laws," George Washington University law professor Jonathan Turley wrote: "Thinly disguised blasphemy laws are often defended as necessary to protect the ideals of tolerance and pluralism. They ignore the fact that the laws achieve tolerance through the ultimate act of intolerance: criminalizing the ability of some individuals to denounce sacred or sensitive values. We do not need free speech to protect popular thoughts or popular people. It is designed to protect those who challenge the majority and its institutions." Turley concluded: "Criticism of religion is the very measure of the guarantee of free speech—the literal sacred institution of society."[103]

---

[101]Ibid.

[102]Daniel Greenfield, "The Cartoonphobia War Goes On," *Front-PageMag.com*, July 22, 2011; http://frontpagemag.com/2011/07/22/the-cartoonphobia-war-goes-on/

[103]Ibid.

The rise of secular messianic movements like communism, socialism and progressivism has paralleled the decline of organized religion. Not coincidentally, their worldviews bear a striking resemblance to the creeds they have replaced. It is not surprising, therefore, that the chief sponsors of blasphemy laws and the attitudes associated with them have been the movements associated with the political left. It is no accident that the movement to outlaw Islamophobia should be deeply indebted to the secular left and its campaign to stigmatize its opponents by indiscriminately applying repugnant terms to them like "racist." Therefore, the left has sponsored the creation of "hate crime" laws as precursors of the desired blasphemy laws. "Hate crimes" are by their very nature crimes against thought. A crime of violence is a crime whatever the motivation. Making it a "hate crime" merely criminalizes the alleged motive. The very term "Islamophobe" has roots in leftist political jargon, as a variation on the term "homophobe." "Homophobe" is itself a coinage akin to "racist" and "sexist," which the left has detached from any meaning other than disagreement with its own agendas, and has then deployed to stigmatize and silence its critics. "Islamophobe" is but the latest of these verbal weapons.

The demagogue Huey Long once said that if totalitarianism came to the United States, it would come calling itself anti-totalitarianism—or tolerance. Islamophobia is the perfect totalitarian doctrine and perfect Orwellian concept, as it is the first step in outlawing freedom of speech, and therefore freedom itself, in the name of religious tolerance.

2

Islamo-Fascism Awareness Week

Next month, student groups across the nation will hold Islamo-Fascism Awareness Week on their campuses.[1] These protests will feature a series of events designed to bring a message to academic communities that challenges most of what students are taught about the so-called War on Terror, both in the classroom and on the quad. The week's events will include speeches about Islamo-Fascism by prominent figures including former Senator Rick Santorum (Penn State, Temple and UPenn), Ann Coulter (Tulane and USC), Robert Spencer (Brown, Dartmouth, and DePaul), Daniel Pipes (Northeastern and UPenn), David Horowitz (Columbia, Emory, Ohio State, Michigan and Wisconsin), Michael Ledeen (Maryland), Nonie Darwish (UCLA and Berkeley), Wafa Sultan (Stanford) and radio talk show hosts Mark Levin (Princeton), Melanie Morgan (San Francisco State), Michael Medved (University of Washington), Martha Zoeller (Georgia Tech), Alan Nathan (George Mason), Mark Larson (to be named) and many others.

A major theme of Islamo-Fascism Awareness Week will be the oppression of women in Islam. The photo accompanying this article, showing a teenage girl buried before being stoned to death for alleged sexual offenses, will serve as the poster for the protest

---

The week started on October 22, 2007.

[1] "A Student's Guide to Hosting Islamo-Fascism Awareness Week," *Terrorism Awareness Project*, October 2007; http://www.terrorismawareness. org/islamo-fascism/49/a-students-guide-to-hosting-islamo-fascism-awareness-week/

week. The stoning took place in Iran.[2] The plight of Muslim women will be featured at "teach-in" panels and also at sit-ins in Women's Studies departments, designed to protest the absence of courses that focus on Islamic gynophobia. The silence of Women's Studies departments in the face of this oppression is a national outrage. College students are offered the opportunity to study the "oppression" of women in Boston and Beverly Hills in hundreds of Women's Studies courses across America. But there is not a single course that addresses the real oppression of women in Teheran and Riyadh. In Saudi Arabia, to take one horrendous example, Saudi police recently shot to death schoolgirls who were fleeing a burning building without their veils. Better that they should be dead than seen. A pamphlet on the subject of women's oppression in Islam, written by Robert Spencer and Phyllis Chesler, will be distributed on campuses (and posted on Frontpage next week) along with a petition protesting the campus blackout of this issue.[3]

Many of our campus protests will show the uncut version of the ABC miniseries *The Path to 9/11*, which has been suppressed by ABC under pressure from the Clintons in order to help Hillary's presidential run. This is the most spectacular episode of political censorship in recent memory. It is also relatively unreported, although the *Los Angeles Times* carried an informative story.[4] *The Path to 9/11* was a film that cost $40 million to make and was seen by 28 million viewers, yet ABC has refused to release the DVD. Other films being shown during the week are *Obsession*,

---

[2] We were not aware at the time that the photo was not of an actual stoning but a still from a film that had been made about a stoning in Iran. This error became a point of attack against our protests, leading MSNBC's Keith Olbermann to name me "Worst Person" of the week, in his ongoing segment attacking conservatives. See Chapter 4, below, "The Worst Person in the World."

[3] "Islamo-Fascism Petition," *Terrorism Awareness Project,* October 2007; http://www.terrorismawareness.org/petitions/63/islamo-fascism-petition/

[4] Martin Miller, "Is Clinton's Candidacy Blocking 'Path to 9/11'?," *Los Angeles Times,* September 5, 2007; http://www.latimes.com/entertainment/la-et-path5sep05,1,2480129.story?ctrack=2&cset=true

Suicide Killers, Islam: What the West Needs to Know, and *Islam v. Islamists.* The purpose of Islamo-Fascism Awareness Week is as simple as it is critical: to confront two Big Lies of the political left—that George Bush created the War on Terror, and that global warming is a greater danger to Americans than the global *jihad* and Islamic supremacism. Nothing could be more politically incorrect than to point out these unpleasant facts. But nothing could be more important for American students to hear.

In the face of the greatest danger Americans have ever confronted, the academic left has mobilized to create sympathy for the enemy and to fight anyone who rallies Americans to defend themselves. Already, CAIR and the Muslim Students Association—which are fronts for the Muslim Brotherhood and Hamas—are planning to hold counter-demonstrations during our Islamo-Fascism Awareness Week, entitled "Peace Not Prejudice." Since the Islamic radicals whom these organizations represent and defend are among the most prejudiced people on earth, and since their own sponsoring organizations, Hamas and the Muslim Brotherhood, have declared a global war against the West, this can only be regarded as high-order satire. The Muslim Students Association is welcome to sign our petition denouncing Islamo-Fascism and defending the dignity of all individuals, infidels included.

Islamo-Fascism Awareness Week is a protest against the censorship in America whose chief enforcer is the progressive left. Anyone who links Islamic radicalism to the terrorist campaigns that are being waged against America, Europe and Israel, and against non-radical Muslims in places such as Darfur, is automatically labeled an "Islamophobe." It is the means by which the enemy seeks to paralyze the defenses of its intended victims. The progressive left is the enabler and abettor of the terrorist *jihad.* It has forged an unholy alliance with the most reactionary forces in the world today. The institutional base of the left is the university system, from whose classrooms it is conducting a behind-the-lines psychological warfare campaign against its own countrymen and the democratic, secular and tolerant society they have created. It is time for Americans to rally in their own defense and answer the corrosive lies and libels whose goal is to sap their will to fight. Islamo-Fascism Awareness Week is the beginning of that answer and the first line of that defense.

3

Why "Islamo-Fascism"?
(with Robert Spencer)

When President Bush used the term "Islamo-Fascism" to describe the *jihadists* who have attacked us, many complained that it reflected a prejudice against Muslims. The Council on American-Islamic Relations, a self-designated civil rights organization with ties to the Muslim Brotherhood and Hamas, protested that the term "feeds the perception that the War on Terror is actually a war on Islam." In fact, the opposite is the truth. As the Algerian sociologist Marieme Helie Lucas explains, the term "Islamo-Fascism" was "initially coined by Algerian people struggling for democracy, against armed fundamentalist forces decimating people in our country, then later operating in Europe, where a number of us had taken refuge."[1] In other words, the term "Islamo-Fascism" originates with moderate Muslims under attack from Muslim radicals, who murdered more than 150,000 Muslims they regarded as infidels in Algeria in the 1990s.

Helie Lucas is the founder of the group Women Living Under Muslim Laws, which resists the oppression of women by these fanatics. The term Islamo-Fascism, as she explains, refers to "political forces working under the cover of religion in order to

October 2007, http://www.terrorismawareness.org/news/76/why-islamo-fascism/

[1] Marieme Helie-Lucas, "Those Who Lived Under 'Islamo-fascism'," *Butterflies & Wheels*, October 24, 2007; http://www.butterfliesandwheels.org/2007/those-who-lived-under-islamo-fascism/

gain political power and to impose a theocracy ('The Law'—singular—of God, unchangeable, ahistorical, interpreted by self appointed old men) over democracy (i.e. the laws—plural—voted by the people and changeable by the will of the people)." The term "Islamo-Fascism" does not propose a generalized "war on Islam" but a defensive war against radicals who have murdered hundreds of thousands of moderate Muslims, Jews, Christians, gays, women and infidels since the first radical Islamic state was formed in Iran in 1979, and the modern global *jihad* was launched in earnest.

Moderate Muslims who observe the precepts of Islam as a religion but reject its political ambitions are happy to live in pluralistic societies that separate religion from the state. Moderate Muslims are willing to live with non-Muslims as equals. It is these Muslims who are the victims of the Islamo-Fascists and the natural allies of the West, which is also the target of the *jihad*. The *jihadists* who wage this war are exponents of political—rather than religious—Islam. They are indeed fascists, sharing crucial ideological convictions with secular fascist movements.

The founder of the Muslim Brotherhood, Hassan al-Banna, was an open admirer of Adolf Hitler, as was the principal theorist of the modern *jihad*, Sayyid Qutb. During World War II, Hajj Amin al-Husseini, the Grand Mufti of Jerusalem, cousin of Yasser Arafat and spiritual godfather of Palestinian nationalism, was openly pro-Nazi. In May 1941, he issued a *fatwa* calling upon the Germans to bomb Tel Aviv. In November 1941, he traveled to Berlin and met with Hitler. Then he went to the Balkans, where he spearheaded the creation of Muslim units of the Waffen SS. The Islamic *jihad* launched by the Muslim Brotherhood, and carried on by its offshoots Al-Qaeda and Hamas, is a totalitarian movement seeking the control of every aspect of human life through the powers of the state. The *jihadists* want to bring all social and family life under the sway of Islamic law through the creation of a global Islamic empire with a caliphate in Baghdad. Like the Nazis before them, they believe in the inherent superiority of one group of human beings over all the rest, whom they regard as "infidels" and "unbelievers." These infidels, according to the passages of the Qur'an that they invoke, are the "vilest of creatures" (Qur'an 98:6).

The term "Islamo-Fascism" describes the agendas of the *jihadists* accurately. It supports moderate Muslims who are seeking to defend themselves and distinguish their religious beliefs from the totalitarian faith of the *jihad*. No one who wants to see moderate Muslims succeed in their efforts to resist the oppressive doctrines of the Islamo-Fascists should oppose the use of this term. Islamo-Fascism Awareness Week is an effort to educate the public about the enemy we face and, in the process, to give moderate Muslims support in their struggle.

4

The Worst Person in the World

L ast Friday, on his MSNBC television show "Countdown," Keith Olbermann named me "The Worst Person in the World." "The Worst Person" is a regular feature of "Countdown," which pretends to be humorous but is a good barometer of the nastiness that animates its progressive host and his fans. The same program featured an attack on a previous "worst person," Fox anchor Bill O'Reilly, whom Olbermann called "unhinged" and slandered as a "racist" despite the absence of any evidence that would justify such a claim. What act of mine, you might wonder, qualified me for such a distinction? Had I provided, as Columbia University did, a prestigious platform for the president of Iran, the Persian Hitler whose agents are presently killing American troops in the Middle East and who has openly called for the obliteration of the Jewish state? Had I perhaps produced a full-page ad in *The New York Times*, declaring the leader of our troops in Iraq a traitor, as the progressives at MoveOn.org did? Did I then perhaps come up with the pun "Less Petraeus, more Betray Us" as a not-so-clever way to tarnish an American war hero? No, as a matter of fact, Keith Olbermann did that.

What I did to deserve this distinction was organize a nationwide campus effort called "Islamo-Fascism Awareness Week," which will be held on over 100 campuses on October 22–26. This is shaping up to be the largest conservative student protest ever in

October 1, 2007, http://archive.frontpagemag.com/Printable.aspx?ArtId= 28301

the United States, and it has the anti-American left in a frenzy. Its purpose is to alert the academic world to the dangers America faces from Islamic terrorists such as Mahmoud Ahmadinejad, whom the president of Columbia University called a "petty tyrant" when in fact he is a global menace. An even more damning sin of mine, it seems, was to make a theme of the week's events "the oppression of women in Islam." To dramatize the barbaric treatment of women in some Islamic countries, I selected a photograph which I had been led to believe was of an actual stoning in Iran.[1] In fact, it was a still photograph from a 32–minute Dutch film called *The Stone*, which is based on an actual stoning and was made to dramatize the barbaric treatment of women in Islamic countries such as Iran.[2] The film was made by Mahnaz Tamizi about an Iranian man who has an affair with a married woman. When they are found out, the man is jailed, while—in accord with the doctrinal niceties of Islamic law—the woman is stoned to death.

The subject and brief duration of the film indicate that its purpose was to spread a message about the oppression of women in Islam—precisely the purpose of our Islamo-Fascism Awareness Week. In other words, the photo we used was perfectly appropriate for a week of events designed to make Americans aware of the terrible oppression of women under the Islamic law that Islamo-Fascists seek to impose everywhere, and that already exists in Iran. According to Amnesty International, for example, despite Iran's agreement to end the practice in 2002, two women were stoned to death in May 2006 and another seven were sentenced to death by stoning in the same year.[3] So what is the problem? Since it was

---

[1] *Windows On Iran*, Fatemeh Keshavarz; http://windowsoniran.files. wordpress.com/2008/09/slide0019.jpg
[2] *The Stone* (1994), *New York Times*; http://movies.nytimes.com/movie/ 435835/The-Stone/overview
[3] Alison Langley, "Death Penalty: Seven Women Face Stoning in Iran," *Inter Press Service*, September 29, 2006; http://www.ipsnews.net/2006/ 09/death-penalty-seven-women-face-stoning-in-iran/

just a matter of misunderstanding that the picture represented an actual stoning, it is a minor issue. But that hasn't prevented it from becoming the focal point of a leftist campaign whose target is the Islamo-Fascism Awareness Week itself. As Olbermann put it: "Keep plugging away, Mr. Horowitz. Let's go on spending billions to stoke up religious hatred and send our kids to die on the battlefield." Ah, so we're the ones, rather than the Islamic terrorists, who are stoking up hatreds. Perhaps inspired by Olbermann, history professor Ralph Luker, who blogs on the History News Network, commented: "Beginning October 22, David Horowitz and Frontpage Rag [sic] will bring 'Hate Your Neighbor Week' to a campus near you"[4]—which is true if your neighbor happens to be bin Laden, or his right hand Zawahiri, or Ahmadinejad.

In other words, according to progressives like Olbermann and Luker, there are no Islamo-Fascists who stone women as instructed by Islamic law; or perhaps it's just that we should not notice them. Or the institution of such laws is not an agenda of the Islamic *jihad* against us. Or, as George Soros and other Democrats maintain, there is no *jihad* or holy war against us that we ourselves did not instigate. George Bush created the terrorists by responding to their attacks and declarations of war on *America.* Anyone who denies this, or has the temerity to observe that the attacks were unprovoked and were the work of Islamic fanatics who regard murder as martyrdom and a path to heaven, is stoking religious hatred. This is the sum and substance of what is a classic left-wing campaign against Islamo-Fascism Awareness Week.

Every leftist campaign eventually becomes a witch-hunt to demonize its opponents, and this one is no different. "Using Racism to Sell War: The West v. Islam?" is not the title of Keith Olbermann's next "Countdown" segment (though it might be). It is the title of a meeting on the Columbia University campus to

---

[4]Ralph Luker, "20th Century Notes," *History News Network,* September 28, 2007; http://www.hnn.us/blogs/entries/43207.html

organize a protest against Islamo-Fascism Awareness Week.[5] The meeting is being put together by the International Socialist Organization which has conducted violent attacks on conservative campus speakers in the past. The announcement for this little planning session on the Columbia/Barnard website is precious: "In the summer of 2006 Bush declared that 'Islamic Fascism' is the biggest threat facing the U.S. today. In October this year, David Horowitz will tour campuses with his 'Islamo-Fascism Awareness Week.' From the hysteria surrounding Ahmadinejad's NYC visit to a spike in horrific hate crimes, the vilification of Arabs and Muslims is on the rise. Islamophobia provides a justification for the U.S.' ongoing wars and must be opposed at every chance. Come be a part of a discussion about the roots of this racist 'clash of civilizations' theory and what we can do to challenge it."

Leon Trotsky once described the world Communist parties and their progressive allies as "frontier guards for the Soviet Union." Through half a century of the Cold War, Communists and progressives made America the bad guy and complained about America's "cold warriors" being too harsh on totalitarians. They presented Communism as the voice of the oppressed and lent America's enemies "critical support" as the counter-weight to American "imperialism," the great oppressor. Today, Keith Olbermann and leftwing activists are performing the same service for the Islamic totalitarians. They are attempting to defame a week of awareness that's designed to educate America's students about the enemies they face in the global War on Terror. Instead of making Americans aware of the threat from Islamic terrorism, they are telling Americans to wonder about "Why they hate us"—as though there were some answer other than the fact that they are religious fanatics who regard America as "the Great Satan" and hate us for who we are.

---

[5]Barnard-Columbia International Socialist Organization, "Using Racism to Sell War: The West vs Islam?" September 28, 2007; http://barnard-columbiaiso.wordpress.com/2007/09/28/using-racism-to-sell-war-the-west-versus-islam/

The scurrilous slander campaign that has been launched against Islamo-Fascism Awareness Week casts an illuminating spotlight on the war at home. The left in America has taken its stand. Just as progressives ran interference for the Soviet empire during the Cold War, today they are running interference for the Islamo-Fascists. They ran interference for Saddam Hussein before the war in Iraq, and if successful would have prevented the overthrow of one of the world's most monstrous tyrannies. Now they are running interference for the terrorists who are fighting our troops and attempting to force an American retreat, just as they did in Vietnam. If successful, they will have provided the Islamo-Fascists in the Middle East with oil-rich Iraq as their new military and political base. And they have run interference at home for those whose agendas include the oppression of women and gays, Christians and Jews, and any infidel who stands in their path. This is why the brave young students who are organizing Islamo-Fascism Awareness Week on campuses across the country deserve everyone's support.

5

Pre-Emptive Strike

Several weeks ago, when we first started billing Islamo-Fascism Awareness Week as the largest demonstration ever by conservative college students, some were skeptical of the claim. But as the week of October 22 approaches—it is now seven days away—it is evident the event we are putting together has more than justified our vision.

We will have events at over 100 schools, and there will be major speeches at more than 30 by figures such as former Senator Rick Santorum, Ann Coulter, Daniel Pipes and Robert Spencer. At more than twenty, students will show an uncut version of *The Path to 9/11*, the ABC mini-series the Clintons censored. At another dozen there will be an unheard-of event: sit-ins at Women's Studies Departments to protest their silence in the face of the oppression of women in Islam. Most importantly, the protest week is getting major coverage in the press. The campus papers of many schools are publishing multiple articles discussing "Islamo-Fascism"—even if only to decry the term. Making the nature of the threat we face a public issue was the goal of our protest to begin with. Moreover, the buzz is becoming louder every day.

As we foresaw when we adopted the name "Islamo-Fascism Awareness Week," the Left has reacted with a campaign to shut us down. But it has in the process guaranteed our success. The goal of

October 15, 2007, http://archive.frontpagemag.com/Printable.aspx?ArtId=28485

the left is to suppress the term Islamo-Fascism because, for the left, America is the enemy. Since the left is at war with America, it cannot afford to have the evils of Islamo-Fascism discussed. So the Internet is abuzz with denunciations of Islamo-Fascism Awareness Week and with the left's plans to disrupt it. The American-Arab Anti-Discrimination Committee has written intimidating letters to the presidents of all the universities where we have planned events, trying to pressure them to cancel our events preemptively. Hardcore organizations like the Socialist Workers Party and the Revolutionary Communist Party have promised violent disruptions. Accordingly, we have assigned bodyguards to our main speakers and alerted campus security wherever we are planning to go.

The lesson is clear: the left will defend the "free speech" rights of the Iranian dictator Ahmadinejad, a murderer of American troops in Iraq, but will go all out to try to suppress a discussion of Islamo-Fascism itself. Even the mainstream media seem to be getting the picture. Last week at George Washington University, one of the campuses where I will personally be speaking, leftists papered the campus with a flyer headlined, "Hate Muslims? So Do We." The flyer was presented as a publication of the Freedom Center and the GWU students organizing the event. Purportedly in our voice, it said: "Your typical Muslim has: laser eyes, venom at the mouth [and a] peg-leg for smuggling children and heroin." Despite the obvious hoax, the campus left reacted with sanctimonious outrage and was backed by the university president, who condemned those behind the flyer in the harshest terms, hinting they would be expelled when caught. The story was picked up by *The Washington Post* and other media. By Wednesday, however, the authors, who had previously hidden in cowardly anonymity, admitted they had published the forgery to discredit us. When the president of GW realized the perpetrators were leftists, he did not expel or otherwise discipline them. He backed off entirely, letting the culprits crow and leaving the conservative students who had been defamed without a campus defender.

We immediately took out an ad in the school paper, denouncing the fraud and pointing out that Tawana Brawley and those who had persecuted the Duke lacrosse players used the same kind of Big Lie to justify their destructive actions. We pointed out that the flyer itself was a hate crime by current standards. Ironically, the Muslim Students Association was also appalled by its contents.

Islamo-Fascism Awareness Week will be a major national story when it unfolds on October 22–26. With enemies like this, who needs friends?

6

Columbia Protests

Why is an idea so frightening to some members of the Columbia University community that they need to organize a campaign to suppress it before it is even aired? Why have some Columbians taken it upon themselves to conduct a hate campaign against students who want to discuss issues that affect us all? Why, on the other hand, were many of these same groups determined to welcome to Columbia a dictator who is providing weapons to kill American men and women in Iraq, who has called for the extermination of the Jewish state, and who presides over a regime that has murdered 4,000 gays and hanged women from cranes for alleged sexual improprieties? If the welcome mat was out for Ahmadinejad, why do these people want to deny a platform to Columbia students who are concerned about the threat from Islamo-Fascists? Is Islamo-Fascism a threat? If the left disagrees, this is exactly the kind of question that will be discussed during the week of Oct. 22–26 at Columbia,[1] unless the activists obstruct it the way they did Jim Gilchrist's attempt to discuss the border issue at Columbia last year. The fascist threat is real, and not just in Iraq or Iran.

October 16, 2007, http://archive.frontpagemag.com/Printable.aspx?ArtId=28507 (This first appeared as a column in the *Columbia Daily Spectator*.)
[1] "A Student's Guide to Hosting Islamo-Fascism Awareness Week," *Terrorism Awareness Project*, October 2007: http://www.terrorismawareness. org/islamo-fascism-awareness-week/49/a-students-guide-to-hosting-islamo-fascism-awareness-week/

Writing in a recent issue of the *Columbia Daily Spectator*, Zahra Khimji, a Columbia sophomore, complained that Islam should not be part of the discussion, while suggesting that the Islamo-Fascists constitute "an incredibly minute minority" of her religion. Would that this were so. Some polls estimate that 10 percent of Muslims support Osama bin Laden and Al-Qaeda. An Al Jazeera poll put the number at 50 percent. In other words, somewhere between 150 million and 750 million Muslims support a holy war against Christians, Jews, and other Muslims who don't happen to be true believers in the Quran as interpreted by Al-Qaeda. This is not an "incredibly minute" cohort. I am sorry that Khimji feels discomfort as a result of the fear that terrorists have struck in the hearts of sensible people. But this complaint should be directed at the holy warriors themselves, not at their current and potential victims.

The very term "Islamo-Fascism" was coined by moderate Muslims who were being slaughtered in Algeria during the 1990s. A group now calling itself "Al-Qaeda in the Islamic Maghreb" killed between 150,000 and 200,000 "unclean" Muslims during that decade. In holding Islamo-Fascism Awareness Week, students at Columbia will be standing up for the survivors and for all Muslims under the threat of fanatical terrorist organizations such as Al-Qaeda, Hezbollah, and Hamas. Is it possible to talk about these terrorist armies without reference to Islam? Hardly. They see themselves as engaged in a holy war that promises them tickets to paradise if they blow up Jewish children, Christian children, or atheist children for that matter. Their community of Islam—which includes the Palestinian Authority—anoints the killers as martyrs and saints for the murders they commit.

Is it possible to talk about these religious fanatics without reference to fascism? Consider the facts. The founding organization of their holy war is the Muslim Brotherhood, which is also the creator of Al-Qaeda and Hamas. The founder of the Muslim Brotherhood, Hassan al-Banna, was an admirer of Hitler, as was Haj Amin al-Husseini, the Grand Mufti of Jerusalem and the father of

Palestinian nationalism. The Ba'ath Party which rules Syria, and ruled Iraq until the overthrow of Saddam, is modeled on Mussolini's Fascist party. It is no accident that Hezbollah's warriors and Iran's Republican Guard goose-step like Hitler's storm troopers; it is an homage. They believe in their superiority and deny basic human dignities to those whom they regard as "infidels." Their goal is to establish a theocratic totalitarian state that will control every aspect of an individual's existence in accordance with the regime's interpretation of Islamic law. This is a fascist agenda and creed. Reasonable people may disagree. Our purpose in holding Islamo-Fascism Awareness Week is not to suppress disagreement or close the argument. That is the agenda of our opponents. Our goal is to initiate a discussion. We are not going to be intimidated by our intolerant opponents; we will not be dissuaded from opening a discussion of matters that are vital to us all.

7

Vocabulary of War

The left is up in arms over the effort to hold an Islamo-Fascism Awareness Week on one hundred American college campuses. The goal of the awareness week is to alert Americans to the threat from Islamo-Fascism and to focus attention on the violent oppression of Muslim women under theocracies in Iran, Saudi Arabia, the Sudan and other Islamic states. It has been attacked as "Islamophobic" and "racist" by the Muslim Students Association, the Revolutionary Communist Party, the American-Arab Anti-Discrimination Committee and FoxNews Channel's Alan Colmes. Is this not puzzling? Why would the left—which claims to be anti-fascist, anti-sexist and *progressive*—oppose Islamo-Fascism Awareness Week rather than support it? Why isn't the left outraged by the genital mutilation of women in countries such as Nigeria, Somalia and Yemen, or the sanctioning of wife-beating under Islamic law in Pakistan and other Islamic states? Across America, Women's Studies programs will teach students about the oppression of women in Peoria and Ann Arbor but not in Teheran or Riyadh. Why not? Why isn't the left appalled by the *jihad*—the holy war that has been declared against the West, and by the sanctifying of murderers as holy "martyrs" when Muslim terrorists kill innocent Americans, Christians and Jews? Perhaps it is because the left is engaged in its own holy war against

October 19, 2007, http://archive.frontpagemag.com/Printable.aspx?ArtId=28551

the same targets: the Great Satan, America, and the Little Satan, Israel.

As the left's response to our campus events shows, it is not only indifferent to the issues of Islamic terror and oppression but is ready to declare war on anyone who wants to raise them. We are all familiar with the way the left wages its political wars. If you disagree with its positions on racial issues—if you believe, for example, that government-enforced racial preferences are misguided and unconstitutional—the left will denounce you as a "racist." In our culture, this is the moral equivalent of a bullet in the heart. If the president of Harvard cites scientific data showing that men and women have different aptitudes for mathematics, the left will denounce him as "sexist," a cultural bullet in the head. If a person believes that children should not be instructed about sex in public schools at the kindergarten level, the left will denounce her as a "homophobe"—another mortal blow. And if students wish to discuss the holy war that Muslim fascists have declared against the West, the left will denounce them as *Islamophobes* and bigots.

To drive home the point that critics of Islamo-Fascism are bigots, the American-Arab Anti-Discrimination Committee will send threatening letters to 100 university presidents across the country, urging them to deny a platform to students who are practicing "hate speech," as they did in regard to Islamo-Fascism Awareness Week, and liberal TV anchors will defend the witch-hunt. Here is a statement made by FoxNews anchor Alan Colmes when I appeared on his show: "The words, the phrase 'Islamo-Fascism' is hate speech. It equates an entire religion with fascism. That's what people object to. It conflates the two, and it's wrong." In other words, students can't even hold a discussion about "Islamo-Fascism" because the idea itself is hateful, and therefore *forbidden.*

Islamo-Fascism Awareness Week is explicitly designed to raise public awareness about the oppression of *Muslim* women by Islamic radicals who abuse them. How can that be equating all Muslims with oppressors? The term "Islamo-Fascism" was coined by moderate Muslims in Algeria who were being slaughtered in the tens of thousands by Islamic radicals bent on *jihad*. How does using a term invented by Muslims to describe their oppressors equate all Muslims with the fascists? Does the term "Italian Fascism" equate all Italians with fascism? Or does it merely identify those Italians who were followers of Mussolini? Is the term "Italian Fascism" hate speech? What about the term "white racism?" By Colmes's logic, such a term equates an entire race—including Colmes—with racism, and is therefore hate speech. Obviously, the attacks on Islamo-Fascism Awareness Week by Colmes and others, including the Revolutionary Communist Party and the Muslim Students Association, are based on reasoning that is absurd. Their only logic is emotional, and the character of that emotion is hate—hate towards those who want to raise awareness of the threats we face from radical Islam. This hatred has only one purpose, which is to defame those who oppose the *jihad* and marginalize their discourse.

8

Opening Day:
University of Wisconsin

I've been told that the cold weather blew in just today, so I planned this event to warm things up. Actually, it wasn't my plan to warm things up. The heat has been provided by a national hate campaign that the political left has organized to intimidate and discredit the students holding this event in order to prevent the discussion they hoped to initiate from taking place. Some of that hate crowd is present tonight. Yes, I can hear you. You attack this event by alleging that it is put on by racists and bigots and Islamophobes. I'm going to disappoint you, if you listen. This evening is not about prejudice against Muslims. On the contrary, this evening is on behalf of all those Muslims who are oppressed by Islamo-Fascism, which you already would know if you had read what we have said.

If you want to understand what this week is about, here is a poster we designed for our events. It is a photograph of an execution on a soccer field in Afghanistan. The figure with the AK–47 pointed at the woman's head is a Taliban soldier. This poor woman, whose femininity and even identity have been hidden by a *burqa*, is about to have her head blown off at point-blank range. She has been accused of sexual improprieties that violate Islamic law. As you may or may not know, in countries where Islamic law or *sharia* is imposed by the state, women cannot be witnesses. So

---

This speech was part of the Islamo-Fascism Awareness Week program at the University of Wisconsin, Madison; October 31, 2007, http://archive.frontpagemag.com/Printable.aspx?ArtId=28660

no women could testify in her behalf. Islamic law forbids it. This poor woman had no defense. The person who took the video from which this still is taken asked the Taliban soldiers why they were executing this woman on the soccer field. It happens that the United States, in its never-ending generosity, gave Afghanistan that soccer field. The soldier replied, "If the United States will give us a place for executions, we will play soccer on the soccer field." These are the religious barbarians we face.

Every person in this photo is a Muslim. The executioner is a Muslim and the victim is a Muslim. There are 130 million girls in Islamic countries who have had their genitals sliced off at puberty, without anesthetic, because sexual pleasure in a woman is held to be evil in some perverted interpretation of Islamic law. The clitorectomies are performed to save these girls from evil. This evening's event and the events of this week are to protest that barbaric treatment of young Muslim women. There are 4,000 homosexuals who have been executed in Iran. This evening is to protest that as well. There are 52 countries in the world where there have been honor killings of Muslim women. If a Muslim woman is raped, her family is shamed. To remove the stain of that shame, one of her relatives, a brother, an uncle, or a parent, murders her. This is a week to bring awareness about that barbaric practice by Islamo-Fascists and to try to stop it.

One of our concerns in this regard is the failure of the Women's Studies Movement in our universities to educate students about these atrocities. There are probably 600 Women's Studies programs on American campuses focusing on the unequal treatment of women in American society. We have been unable to locate a single class that focuses on the oppression of women under Islamic law.

As you probably know, women under Islamic law receive half the inheritance a man does. In some countries where *sharia* is enforced, women can't even get an education. In Saudi Arabia, there is currently a campaign for women's liberation, which is attempting to secure for women the right to drive an automobile.

To drive an automobile! Why aren't Women's Studies departments up in arms about all this? You can probably go to a Women's Studies class at this university and learn about the oppression of women in the faculty lounge, but you can't learn about the oppression of women in Tehran or Riyadh or Kuala Lumpur.

For the information of our opponents here tonight, this week is already a tremendous success, because no matter how hostile you are to what you imagine to be our views—which have been grossly distorted in the attacks this week—you yourselves are already now discussing the issues we set out to raise: "Why is it that American feminists are not up in arms about the savage abuses of women by Islamo-Fascists, about those 130 million young girls who have their genitals sliced off every year?" We have already done a service to Muslim women all over the world, just by raising this issue. I know that there are people here who feel that the Muslim community is under threat in the United States. But think of the Muslim community in Algeria, where between 150,000 and 200,000 moderate Muslims were slaughtered in the 1990s by an organization calling itself Al-Qaeda of the Islamic Maghreb. Think about the Muslims in the Sudan who are being slaughtered by a Taliban-like regime, simply because they don't subscribe to the regime's version of Islam. This is a serious problem in the Islamic world, which lacks the separation of church and state. In these countries, if radical clerics get control of the state, they will use the power of the state to enforce their reading of the Qur'an.

In Iran, just last week, the modesty police issued a new edict forbidding couples to hold hands in public. A totalitarian state is a state that controls every aspect of a person's life. Religions in general, and Islam in particular, are concerned with numerous aspects of a person's life. Religion is about morality, about the family, and about social relations. So when interpretations of religious law are enforced by the state, it spells the end of individual freedom. It means that priests in power are going to set the rules for what you can and cannot do. The end result of that process is this poor woman in the photo, whose life is about to be terminated for allegedly violating a government edict about her sex life. I don't think there is anybody in this room who would support that. I hope there isn't.

That's really what we intended to do with this week, to make people aware of this problem. I have called it "Islamo-Fascism." That is not a term designed to say that all Muslims or a majority of Muslims are fascists. In fact, a majority of Muslims are either victims of Islamo-Fascists or threatened by them. A FoxNews channel anchor, along with other misguided individuals, thinks that the term "Islamo-Fascism" is *hate speech.* In a democracy, at least in our democracy as it has been degraded by so-called liberals today, the way you ban ideas is by calling them "hate speech." But the claim that the term Islamo-Fascism implicates all Muslims makes no logical sense. We use the term "Italian Fascism" without assuming that all Italians are fascists. Hitler did not even win a majority of the vote in Germany, yet we use the phrase "German Fascism" without implying that all people of German descent are fascists. People will throw around the term "white racism" pretty casually. Everyone in this room has either used the phrase "white racism" or read it without objection. Did you intend to call every white person a racist when you used that term? That would make all white liberals racists. Yet that is precisely what the opponents of Islamo-Fascism Awareness Week are claiming when they object to it.

The attacks on this awareness week are quite stupid, when you think about it. If I intended to come on a college platform to say hateful things about all Muslims and did so, I would be hooted off the stage. No campus organization would invite me to say such things; and if I did say them I would never be invited by any campus organization again. Since no one on a college campus is prepared to hear hate speech, why bother to protest it in advance? It's self-discrediting. Yet we live in such Orwellian times that no one laughs when the left and their liberal sympathizers make these preposterous claims about their opponents. On the one hand, the hate campaign against us is a very stupid campaign, and on the other it is malicious. And it is inarguably effective and sinister. When you are called a racist from one end of the country to the other, when you are identified as somebody who is preaching hate against a religious or ethnic or racial group, someone is going to believe those charges. The effect, in other words, is to put a target on your back. Which is why there is so much security present tonight.

America was attacked on 9/11. It was attacked by religious fanatics carrying the Qur'an and screaming *"Allahu Akbar"* as they flew planes....

[At this point, 9/11 conspiracy theorist Kevin Barrett, previously an adjunct lecturer at Wisconsin, seized a floor microphone intended for the question period and began a rant calling for an investigation of 9/11. The audience, half of which was leftist, was not amused. Collectively they began a Wisconsin football chant— "Asshole, asshole"—the sheer volume of which blew the speaker out of the room.]

I want to thank everyone here, including my detractors, for restoring order. This just shows how easy it is to destroy—even if it was only momentarily—the fabric of a conversation. I will open these microphones for questions afterwards, hopefully not rants but actual questions. I find that, when I am in a conversation with somebody I strongly disagree with, I often learn—even if I'm not persuaded by their arguments—that there are people on the other side of these debates who are sincere in their beliefs and who are committed to their country and its democracy. I hope that some of my opponents here, if we can manage to keep this at a civilized level, will also come away with that kind of impression and will think about these issues in a new way. That is the whole idea of having this conversation.

The term Islamo-Fascism is, in my view, a useful and justifiable term because of the merger of religion and state in the totalitarian ideology we are facing. It is also historically based. What we are facing is a global religious movement that is a movement within Islam. It is not to be confused with Islam itself. The Islamo-

Fascists want you to confuse them with the Muslim community as a whole. They want to hide behind the Muslim community. And they are inflicting great damage on the Muslim community by doing so. When Ahmadinejad speaks or when Zawahiri speaks, they do so in the name of the Muslim *ummah*. But they do not actually speak for the Muslim *ummah*. And that distinction has to be made by us as well. What we are facing is a radical force within Islam that originated in Egypt in the 1920s with the Muslim Brotherhood. Hassan al-Banna was the founder of this movement, which aims to seize control of states and impose Islamic law on their populations. The Muslim Brotherhood attempted to assassinate the Egyptian dictator Gamal Abdel Nasser. It assassinated Anwar Sadat, and it would probably like to assassinate the present ruler of Egypt, Hosni Mubarak—all of them Muslims.

Hassan al-Banna was an admirer of Adolf Hitler. Osama bin Laden drew his vision of Islam from teachers who were members of the Muslim Brotherhood. Hamas was created by the Muslim Brotherhood. The Grand Mufti of Jerusalem and godfather of Palestinian nationalism, Haj Amin al-Husseini, was a protégé of the Brotherhood and also an admirer of Hitler. He went to Berlin during the Second World War to meet with Hitler and to recruit Arabs to the Nazi cause. He had his own plans for a death camp in the Middle East to get rid of the Jews in Palestine. The Baathist parties in Syria and Iraq were modeled on the European fascist parties. I could go on and on, but the reality is that there is a historical relationship between Islamic radicals and European fascists, and one of the links in this chain is Jew-hatred. Historically, within the Islamic Empire, Christians and Jews were second-class citizens. They had to identify themselves with insignias and pay an extra tax, and were called *dhimmis*. When Jews settled in the Islamic world, on the other hand, even this inferior status was better than what they experienced in the Christian world. They fled from Christendom because during the Middle Ages, as you know, they were expelled from entire countries and burned at the stake by the Catholic Church if they didn't convert to Christianity.

The virulent Jew-hatred which is now endemic in the Arab Muslim world stems directly from the Arabs' association with the Nazis during the 1930s and 1940s, when Germany attempted to bring the whole Arab world into its orbit.[1] By Jew-hatred I mean the publication of forgeries like the "Protocols of the Elders of Zion." I mean teaching little children to want to kill Jews from an early age.

The goal of the crusade we are calling Islamo-Fascism is the restoration of the caliphate and its establishment in Baghdad. I'm merely describing here the plan that was laid out by Al-Qaeda's second in command, Ayman al-Zawahiri, in one of his *fatwas*. The idea is to create a global totalitarian Islamic empire. These Islamic radicals despise nation-states. They want a universal Islamic *ummah* under their ruthless thumb.

It is claimed by many that the reasons for the Muslim attacks are America's policies towards Israel or the war in Iraq, or President Bush. "Bush created the War on Terror" has become a mantra in some powerful circles of the Democratic Party around George Soros. But there is no basis in fact for these claims. The first leader of the modern Islamo-Fascist movement and the leader of the first Islamo-Fascist state was the Ayatollah Khomeini. It was Khomeini who declared America the Great Satan, and in 1979 led crowds a million strong in chants of "Death to America." It was Jimmy Carter—not George W. Bush—who was president when he did that. Jimmy Carter was a supporter of the Ayatollah and an enemy of the Shah whom he overthrew. Carter pulled the rug out from under the Shah, accusing him of human rights violations; Carter persuaded the Shah to release Khomeini's cohorts from prison and allow Khomeini to return to Iran. In doing so, Carter made the Islamic Revolution possible.

When people say that the United States and its policies are responsible for 9/11, they're forgetting this history. In the past twenty-five years, far from being an imperialist oppressor of

---

[1]Cf. Jeffrey Herf, *Nazi Propaganda for the Arab World*, 2010

Muslims, as the Islamo-Fascists and the American left would have you believe, the United States saved the lives of millions of Muslims. When the Soviet Union invaded Afghanistan in 1979, its armies conducted a scorched-earth policy killing everything in their way. A million Muslims were slaughtered in Afghanistan until the United States came to their aid, providing them with stinger missiles, which helped the mujaheddin to defeat the Soviet empire. The United States went to war in Kosovo for Albanian Muslims and saved them from extermination. The United States sent the Army Rangers into Mogadishu to feed starving Muslims in Somalia, and those Rangers were attacked for doing so by an Al-Qaeda warlord.

Al-Qaeda and the Islamo-Fascist movement have killed more Muslims than all the members of Bush's "coalition of the willing" and all of Israel's soldiers put together. So it is completely absurd to hold Americans responsible for the hatred that is directed against us. The hatred against America is hatred for the fact that America is free and supports Muslims who don't want to submit to the Islamo-Fascists' will.

In the face of these enemies, leftists are deluded. Whom do you think they are going to kill when they get their states and the powers that go with them? I recommend to you all a book called *Reading Lolita in Tehran*. The author, Azar Nafisi, is a university professor of English literature. Its title refers to the fact that she returned to Iran after the Khomeini Revolution in 1979, and taught *The Great Gatsby* and other American novels to her Iranian students at the University of Teheran. The story she tells should be a warning to every leftist in this audience. Nafisi had attended school in the United States at the University of Oklahoma, where she belonged to a group of Marxist radicals. When the Khomeini Revolution took place, they all went back to Iran, believing that Khomeini was a progressive and didn't really mean it when he said he wanted to create an Islamic state and drag Iran back into the 7th century. The American left embraced Khomeini and his revolution. Richard Falk, who is a spokesman of the present movement against the war in Iraq, called Khomeini a liberator. Andrew Young, who was Jimmy Carter's ambassador to the United Nations, called Khomeini a saint.[2] Encouraged by these endorsements, the Iranian Marxists at the University of Oklahoma, who probably belonged to the anti-war action network of the time, went back to Teheran to join the revolution. And one by one, as Nafisi describes in her book, they were executed by the revolutionary state. *Because* they were Marxists. *Because* they were progressives. *Because* they did not toe the Islamo-Fascist line. That is what the "War on Terror" is about.

In the first three years of his revolutionary rule, Khomeini killed twenty-five *times* as many Iranians—Muslims—as the despised Shah had killed in the 34 years of his. Khomeini opposed the Shah because the Shah was actually a progressive reformer who allowed women to be educated in Iran for the first time in their history; and allowed them, if they so chose, to remove the veil. The Shah was a dictator, but he was a progressive dictator. And that's why Khomeini and Islamic fundamentalists hated him, and overthrew him. This is a warning to you progressives in the audience. This is my gift to you, if you will take it. The Islamo-Fascists whom you support will devour you in the end.

Before I finish, I want to say something about the Iraq War. Watching the left mobilize to oppose the war, I was reminded of the Iranian Revolution of 1979, when the constant complaint of the left was that the United States was supporting dictators like the Shah. So it was quite illuminating what happened when George W. Bush set out to overthrow one of those dictators—one of the true monsters of the 20th century, who had murdered 300,000 of his subjects. Whom do you think he murdered? He

---

[2]Eli Lake, "U.N. Official Calls for Study Of Neocons' Role in 9/11," *The New York Sun*, April 10, 2008; http://www.nysun.com/news/foreign/un-official-calls-study-neocons-role-911; Michael D. Evans, "Father of the Iranian Revolution," *The Jerusalem Post*, June 20, 2007; http://www.jpost.com/LandedPages/PrintArticle.aspx?id=65542

murdered Muslims. He dropped poison gas on the Kurds. He put Muslims into plastic shredders. His two sons went on a rape rampage, molesting and killing Muslim girls. Then Bush came along and overthrew him. And yet, the left hates Bush for that! I watched all of my former comrades go into the streets to try to save Saddam Hussein, a fascist dictator and mass murderer. Now, what is *that* about? It's about the left's hatred for America, which is greater than its hatred for oppressors like Saddam Hussein. The reason the left has entered a *de facto* alliance with the Islamo-Fascists is that the left believes what the Islamo-Fascists believe. They believe that the United States is the Great Satan and Israel is the Little Satan. Leftists see it as their progressive duty to make the United States lose the War on Terror so the Khomeinis of the Middle East can liberate the Muslim world. The left has been on the wrong side of these battles for freedom for almost 100 years.

I think the war in Iraq has been mismanaged, and so has the war at home. The president has failed to explain the war to the American people. But these mistakes don't negate the fact that the overthrow of Saddam Hussein was a good deed. Moreover, the United States cannot afford to lose this war. If we lose the war in Iraq, if we do what Nancy Pelosi and Cindy Sheehan want us to do, which is to pull out in the middle of the war, what will happen in Iraq is exactly what happened in Vietnam when we did the same thing. After we left Vietnam to the mercy of the communists, two-and-a-half million people were slaughtered. Not only will Muqtada al-Sadr and the Republican Guard slaughter every Muslim in Iraq who wanted freedom, who went to vote, who supported the coalition led by America. Iraq will wind up in the hands of Ahmadinejad and Iran, and they will go after the other Arab regimes in the region whose Islamic ways are not pure enough. The result will be a regional war, and because Russia and China will support Iran, it might be a global war as well.

The reason for our intervention in Iraq in the first place was to prevent such a war. Saddam had conducted two wars of aggression, one against Iran and the other against Kuwait. After the Gulf War, we imposed a truce on him. We should have overthrown him, but didn't. Instead we imposed arms-control agreements on Saddam in the form of UN resolutions 687, 688 and 689, which were followed by 14 other UN resolutions, all about arms control and all equally disregarded. The same thing happened after the First World War. The Allied Powers had imposed arms- control agreements on Germany, and Hitler had done exactly what Saddam Hussein did. He systematically defied the agreements and rebuilt his war machine. Instead of stopping him when he was weak but defiant, the western powers, particularly France and Britain, appeased him. If those powers had taken on Hitler in 1937, they would easily have crushed him. But by the time Hitler was strong enough militarily to go to war, it took the sacrifice of 70 million lives to defeat him. The antiwar crowd and appeasers of the Thirties have that on their heads. George W. Bush was right to take down Saddam Hussein when he defied international law. Now we need to win the war in Iraq and defeat the Islamo-Fascists in order to avoid another world war, which will be even more costly than the last.

9

What We Did Last Week

The week of October 22–26 witnessed the most extensive campus demonstrations ever organized by students not associated with the political left. One hundred fourteen college and university campuses participated in "Islamo-Fascism Awareness Week," whose objective was to highlight the threat from the Islamic *jihad* and the oppression of Muslim women. At the beginning of the awareness week, there were 6,000 website references to the protest. By its end, there were more than 644,000. There was coverage—often multiple news reports and opinion columns—by student papers on all the campuses where events took place and many more besides. In short, hundreds of thousands of members of the academic community were exposed to the message of the protests and the arguments over the issues they raised.

The events were reported in the national media by the AP, the *Los Angeles Times*, *The New York Times*, *The Seattle Times*, *The Washington Times* and *The Washington Post*, and abroad by the *International Herald Tribune*, the Iran News Agency, Pakistan's *Daily Star* and IslamOnline. There were syndicated op-ed columns by Maureen Dowd and Ann Coulter; there were multiple columns on heavily-trafficked blogs and webzines such as *Slate*, *The Huffington Post*, DailyKos.com, LittleGreenFootballs.com, *The Atlantic*, *National Review Online*, *The Nation*, and Townhall.com.

October 29, 2007, http://archive.frontpagemag.com/Printable.aspx?ArtId=28662

National Public Radio and talk show hosts Sean Hannity, Michael Medved, Michael Reagan, Martha Zoeller, Alan Nathan and many others carried reports of the events. The O'Reilly Factor, John Gibson's Big Story, the Neil Cavuto Show, Hannity & Colmes, Fox Live and the Glenn Beck Show brought Islamo-Fascism Awareness Week into the homes of millions.

In response to Islamo-Fascism Awareness Week, anti-American leftists and organizations supporting the Islamic *jihad* organized a national campaign of vitriol and hate. This campaign revealed the lengths to which the anti-American left will go to prevent Americans from discussing the nature of the war that has been declared on them. It was characterized by a political McCarthyism whose levels of character assassination and slander had not been seen since the early days of the Cold War. Speakers for the events and students organizing them were attacked as religious bigots and anti-Muslim "racists" and "fascists." Leftwing activists at George Washington University posted a flyer falsely attributed to members of the Young America's Foundation who organized and sponsored the campus event. The flyer was headlined "Who Hates Muslims? We Do." The bogus flyer was designed to impute a hate crime to the student organizers who were in fact defending Muslims. These verbal attacks were accompanied by physical threats, although violence was mercifully avoided by campus police and the private security guards who accompanied the speakers to campus. However, several ejections and arrests were necessary to maintain order. It was only at Emory University that intellectual thugs were successful in closing down a speech, as it happens one that I was scheduled to give. This elicited an apology from Emory president James Wagner to the College Republicans who sponsored the event.

The attacks on Islamo-Fascism Awareness Week exposed the broad scope of the alliance between radical Islam and American leftists who regard it as their political task to run interference for America's *jihadist* enemies. The attacks were spearheaded by the misnamed American-Arab Anti-Discrimination Committee whose founder, former Senator James Abourezk, is an open supporter of Hezbollah.[1] Under the Orwellian banner of defending tolerance, Abourezk's group sent letters to the presidents of all the colleges scheduled to host the events, urging them to shut them down. Abourezk's committee was joined in its censorship attempt by offshoots of the Muslim Brotherhood and Hamas, including the Muslim Public Affairs Council, the Muslim American Society, the Council on American-Islamic Relations and the Muslim Students Association, all of whom set out to stigmatize the students organizing the events as "racists" and "bigots" and haters of Muslims.

While the attackers pretended to speak on behalf of victims of ethnic prejudice, they in fact represented that wing of Islam which is persecuting Muslims and conducting a war against infidels. Leaders of the Muslim Students Association, who attended our events, got up during the question periods after the speeches to raise objections. The vice president of the Muslim Students Association at Columbia protested my use of the word "*jihad*," which she said meant spiritual "struggle" rather than "holy war." In fact, I hadn't used the word "*jihad*" in my speech. It was just one of the talking-points her organization had given her in advance of the event. I asked whether she would denounce the terrorist group Hamas, which the Muslim Brotherhood had created along with her organization. I asked her several times and she repeatedly evaded the question, in effect refusing to answer it.

Supporting the Islamists' efforts to discredit our concerns was an array of leftist websites and organizations that included the Revolutionary Communist Party, its front "World Can't Wait," another front "The Columbia Coalition Against the Iraq War," the International Socialist Alliance, the Orwellian-named "National Project to Defend Dissent and Critical Thinking in Academia," *The Nation* magazine, *The Huffington Post*, Alternet.com, IndyMedia.org, the

---

[1] "Former U.S. Senator James Abourezk to Hizbullah TV," *The Middle East Media Research Institute*, August 30, 2007; http://www.memritv. org/clip/en/1551.htm

ACLU, "College Democrats and Campus Progress," a campus organization created by the Center for American Progress, which is headed by former Clinton chief of staff John Podesta and functions as a brain-trust for the Democratic Party. Progressive bloggers like Joshua Micah Marshall and Matthew Yglesias piled on. Cliopatria blogger Ralph Luker described our events as "Hate Your Neighbor Week."

The commotion caused by the witch-hunters succeeded in intimidating several student groups, who declined to sponsor the events. Some were prepared to give the counter-protesters the benefit of the doubt and meet their expressed concerns by holding the events under a different banner, calling them "Terrorism Awareness," and leaving out the announced link to Islamo-Fascism. This was fine with us, because our purpose was to foster a discussion, not to impose a conclusion. The students who attempted to meet the detractors halfway were quickly disabused of their illusions, however, as they were attacked along with the rest of us, and in similarly abusive terms. The campaign against Islamo-Fascism Awareness Week had nothing to do with style and everything to do with substance. The purpose of the character assassination and slander was to discredit all opposition to the left's politically correct positions, and to suppress any discussion of the movement spawned by the Muslim Brotherhood, which is the ideological force behind all the terrorist attacks.

Our campus speakers showed admirable courage in their willingness to endure the slander and attacks they knew that challenging the left would entail. But it was our students who braved the fiercest attacks from members of their campus communities. I can't say enough how proud I am of the students I met this week on the campuses I visited, and the many others who worked with us to make this week a success. Without their willingness to stand up and be counted, there would have been no Islamo-Fascism Awareness Week. I have an idea as to why they did. I have been speaking on college campuses for twenty years and I have never seen conservative students so ready to engage in conflicts that would invite such vicious attacks, alienate their professors and cause them to lose friends as a result of the intimidations of the campus left. They have become willing to do this now because of the example set by their brothers and sisters on the frontlines in Iraq.

When the counter-protesters closed down my speech at Emory University, I was put in mind of the first appearance I had made at Emory. It was in 2002, during the controversy over reparations. I had been invited by a student named Michael Motivator, who was chair of the College Republicans. Michael was a bookish, intellectual type, a political science major. Our meeting left me concerned that he would not be aggressive enough to handle the attacks that were already coming his way, not only from students and professors but from "Student Life" deans who were the instigators of the protests against my visit. A few years later, I received an email from Michael which he had sent to a list of his friends, informing us that he was in his second week at Marine boot camp and asking if we would write him to keep his spirits up so that he could get through the ordeals for which his previous life had not prepared him. Our students see members of their generation ready to put their lives on the line to defend their freedoms. They understand that the war is being waged at home as well. And they are not going to let their brothers and sisters in uniform shoulder the burden alone.

Campus Slanders

The biggest news item during Islamo-Fascism Awareness Week was the disruption of my speech at Emory University by leftists who, it so happens, weren't actually students. They were members of the Coalition United for Peace and Justice, one of the leading "antiwar" groups in the movement (described as "moderate" by *The New York Times*) that set out to save the Saddam regime in Iraq from being overthrown by American forces. Shutting down peaceful campus lectures is in fact a fascist tactic, but in a country as committed to the principles of fairness and free speech as this one it is not yet the most threatening. That distinction must be reserved for the massive witch-hunt and smear campaign which was directed at our events—the pursuit of alleged "racists," "bigots" and "Islamophobes," the designation of those who oppose Islamic terrorism as "anti-Muslim." The one effective way to shut down speech in America is to call it "hate speech" and to suggest that employing it constitutes a "hate crime." Fox News Channel host Alan Colmes, generally a reasonable leftist, spoke for the radicals when he told terrorist expert Steven Emerson that "the term Islamo-Fascism is hate speech." Because such attacks were the essence of the campaign against our events, it is worth dissecting an example. It appeared in the form

November 2, 2007, http://archive.frontpagemag.com/ReadArticle.aspx?
  ArtId=28702

of an article in the UC Irvine student paper *New University*, under the headline "Horowitz Disguises Racism as 'Awareness.'"[1]

UC Irvine is a campus at which the Muslim Students Union two years ago held an "Israeli Awareness Week" where speakers denounced the occupation of Palestine and alleged Jewish control of American politics and policy. Some years before that, a Muslim Students Union speaker on the same campus had explained that Jews were possessed by a "psychosis" that caused them to be "unable to coexist equally and brotherly with other human beings." The speaker, Muhammad al-Asi, imam of the Islamic Center in Washington DC, had gone on to say: "You can take a Jew out of the ghetto, but you can't take the ghetto out of the Jew."[2] The *New University* attack was written by a third- year international studies major named Nathan Tumazi. It began: "Last week marked the beginning of a social and political wave of hatred and racist xenophobia emanating from the violent rhetoric of conservative students, politicians and academics everywhere. The perpetrator responsible for what was called 'Islamo-Fascism Awareness Week' is David Horowitz." Tumazi then proceeded not to describe actual events or speeches associated with Islamo-Fascism Awareness Week, but to make *ad hominem* attacks on myself and other speakers such as Ann Coulter. These attacks, not original, were drawn from the falsehoods the collective left has manufactured out of past statements attributed to its targets. I will deal with those that are specific to me because I am familiar with them, and because they amply illustrate the methods used by Tumazi and others. Those people do not want to join an argument but to end one.

---

[1] Nathan Tumazi, "Horowitz Disguises Racism as 'Awareness'," *New University*, October 29, 2007; http://www.newuniversity.org/2007/10/opinion/horowitz_disguises_racism_as45/

[2] "Muslim Students Association Dossier," *The Investigative Project on Terrorism*, October 2007, p. 34; http://www.investigativeproject.org/documents/misc/31.pdf; cf. Mohammad al-Asi, Speech, UC-Irvine, February 21, 2001; http://www.investigativeproject.org/239/muhammad-al-asi-ghetto-jews

A sample of my writing that appeared on every campus I visited during Islamo-Fascism Awareness Week was an article from *Salon* magazine. The citation was selected to prove that I was an anti-black racist; implausible on its face, since *Salon* is a left-wing magazine that would not publish an anti-black racist tract. I was a regular columnist for *Salon* at the time I wrote it, and the left-wing editors of the magazine raised no objections to content. The article was called "Guns Don't Kill Black People, Other Black People Do."[3] It was about an NAACP plan to sue gun manufacturers and hold them responsible for the fact that homicides were the number-one cause of death among young black males. I pointed out the obvious: that many communities, including many poor communities, have gun-owners who do not kill each other with such regularity; that the real causes of this violence were children without fathers, rampant drug epidemics, uncontrolled street gangs, too few police and other social factors, rather than white gun manufacturers. I urged the NAACP to focus on the real causes of these tragic homicide rates among young black males, rather than grandstand the issue by playing the race card and blaming it all on capitalism and whites.

In his article, Tumazi only quoted the title of the piece and presented it thus: "[Horowitz's] Aug. 16, 1999 column for *Salon.com* entitled 'Guns Don't Kill Black People, Other Blacks Do,' is only a sample of his call to arms for all conservatives, angry or not, to return American universities to their religious and white supremacist origins." Instead of someone concerned about the failure of NAACP leaders to pursue a policy that would help inner-city black youths, I was portrayed as someone who wants to make universities religious and white supremacist—and this from a third-year international studies major at an elite university.

A second ubiquitous quote inserted into my dossier by the campus left is the claim that I said blacks "benefited from

---

[3]See Volume VI in this series, *Progressive Racism.*

slavery." Here is Tumazi's version: "Horowitz was again called out for his xenophobia and blatant discriminatory rhetoric for a January 26, 2005 posting on the History News Network website about 'Why I Am Not Celebrating' the 90th birthday of esteemed African-American historian John Hope Franklin.... In the article, Horowitz launched into an attack on Franklin and then proceeded to claim that 'free blacks and the free descendants of blacks ... benefited from slavery.' Horowitz's anger and bitterness against blacks is only outdone by his relentless hatred of Muslims, anyone who doesn't have a penis, non-heterosexuals and the working and poor classes."

Now for the facts: prior to the article Tumazi quotes, John Hope Franklin had written a vicious attack on me because of my campaign against reparations to be paid, 137 years after the fact, to blacks who had never been slaves, and to be paid by all Americans who were not black. As I pointed out in the course of that campaign, this was a plan to force Americans whose ancestors had fought against slavery, and Americans whose ancestors had immigrated to America after slavery and played no part in the slave system, to pay a "debt" to blacks born long after slavery had been abolished, some of whom were multi-millionaires or even billionaires, like Jesse Jackson and Oprah Winfrey. I opposed reparations on grounds that they were divisive and racist, since the payments were to be made merely on the basis of skin-color. I also said the reparations campaign was destructive to the interests of the black community itself.

All these points were made in an ad I ran in campus papers, to which John Hope Franklin responded. According to Franklin, anyone who opposed this plan was "pro-slavery"—that was the term he actually used to describe me. What was particularly appalling was Franklin's distortion of the historical record, since he himself was a much-praised historian. To justify reparations against whites, even those whose ancestors had fought against slavery, or those whose ancestors had arrived in America after slavery was abolished, Franklin concocted several false claims. Among them was the statement that during slavery "all blacks had no rights that they could claim as their own." As I pointed out in my response to his attack, even the African slaves from the slave ship *Amistad*, who were not American citizens, had rights that were recognized by the United States Supreme Court which, even with a slaveholding majority presiding, voted to free them.

The widely-repeated quote attributed to me about the alleged benefits of slavery was also willfully misrepresented by Franklin. In my original article from which the ad was taken, I had said supporters of reparations were claiming (without evidence) that all of America's wealth was based on slavery, a "fact" they adduced to justify the payment of reparations from whites alive today to blacks alive today. *If that were correct,* I had said, then everyone alive today, blacks as well as whites, would have been the beneficiaries of slavery. (I myself never claimed that slavery was the source of all American wealth, nor do I believe it.) In his attack on me, John Hope Franklin changed the terms of the argument in order to refute it. He wrote that "all whites and no *slaves* benefited from American slavery," as though I had said that slaves benefited from slavery (emphasis added). My response to this, as it appeared verbatim on the History News Network site, was as follows: "Neither I, nor the ad ever claimed that any slaves benefited from slavery. The first question my ad raised was that if all whites benefited economically from slavery (and a responsible historian would certainly want to keep an open mind on this question) could one also maintain that free blacks did not? More importantly, the question was: if all whites alive today were beneficiaries of the wealth that slavery produced, how could one say that blacks alive today were not?"[4] This quote, in the hands of Tumazi, became: "free blacks and the free descendants of blacks ... benefited from slavery."

---

[4]David Horowitz, "Why I Am Not Celebrating John Hope Franklin's Birthday," *History News Network*, January 25, 2005; http://hnn.us/roundup/entries/9856.html; John Hope Franklin, "Horowitz's Diatribe Contains Historical Inaccuracies," *History News Network*, January 25, 2005; http://hnn.us/roundup/entries/9856.html

Like many other leftists whom our speakers and students encountered last week, Nathan Tumazi is a hater who has no regard for the facts. But he is more than that. He wants to put his hatred into action and to silence those with whom he disagrees: "For those of us still committed to defending peace, truth, justice and equality there is much uniting to be done. We need to come together and demand that the racist hate of last week's campaign be forced off our campus." This is the face of the new campus fascism, and it is ugly.

11

The Problem for Our Country

I guess it's noteworthy when George Soros singles you out for attack.[1] On the other hand, when you have been targeted by as many leftists as I have, one more billionaire doesn't make much difference. These assaults have been inspired by my efforts to organize an "Islamo-Fascism Awareness Week," whose goal was to identify America's enemies as more than just "terrorists," and specifically to link them to a powerful radical movement within Islam that has declared war on the West. One salutary aspect of the awareness week is to have exposed the breadth of the coalition that now functions as a frontier guard for our enemies. Members of this coalition are apparently determined to run interference for America's enemies because, in their view, a greater danger to America is posed by conservatives such as George Bush and apparently myself.

According to Soros, Bush has made up the War on Terror and thereby created the terrorist threat. In a notable article titled "A Self-Defeating War," Soros wrote: "A misleading figure of speech applied literally has unleashed a real war fought on several fronts—Iraq, Gaza, Lebanon, Afghanistan, Somalia—a war that has killed thousands of innocent civilians and enraged millions around the world.... We can escape it only if we Americans repudiate the War on Terror as a false metaphor."[2] As a principal funder

---

November 23, 2007, http://archive.frontpagemag.com/ReadArticle.aspx? ArtId=28890

[1]George Soros, "From Karl Popper to Karl Rove," *The Korea Times*, November 11, 2007; http://www.koreatimes.co.kr/www/news/opinon/2007/11/137_13501.html

of the Democratic Party, Soros is probably the inspiration for Nancy Pelosi's claim that the terrorists are only in Iraq because we are there and will leave when we do. Soros is certainly behind John Edwards's suggestion that the War on Terror is a "political bumper sticker," and that the way to fight the terrorists is to treat them as individual criminals rather than members of a fanatical religious movement with tens of millions of adherents.[3]

Even as leftists project onto America responsibility for the war against us, so they seek to blame conservatives for the scorched-earth politics they have adopted at home. Thus Soros describes me as a political manipulator who is unwilling to argue issues with my opponents, and instead focuses on destroying them: "Another technique [of conservatives] is transference: accusing opponents of having motives or using methods that characterize the accuser himself. For example, David Horowitz, who accuses me of being 'the Lenin of the anti-American conspiracy,' is a former Trotskyite for whom opponents are never adversaries to be debated, but rather enemies to be crushed."[4] For the record, I was never a Trot-skyite, nor have I ever accused Soros of being the Lenin of a "conspiracy."[5] More to the point, Soros's claim that I never debate my

---

[2]George Soros, "A Self-Defeating War," *The Wall Street Journal*, August 15, 2006, http://online.wsj.com/article/SB115560280788735731.html? mod=opinion_main_commentaries;
http://www.commondreams.org/views06/0815-35.htm

[3]David Horowitz and Richard Poe, "The Cult of Soros," *FrontPageMag.com*, August 25, 2006; http://archive.frontpagemag.com/ readArticle.aspx?ARTID=2916

[4]Soros, op. cit.

[5]The word "conspiracy" is nowhere to be found without quotation marks in the text I wrote with Richard Poe about Soros's activities. It does appear in *The Shadow Party* on three occasions in references to two authors—*New York Times* reporter Matt Bai and Byron York—both of whom had written about "the Vast Leftwing Conspiracy." We did refer to Soros as the "Lenin" of the Shadow Party, adding this proviso: "if one is careful with the analogy." David Horowitz and Richard Poe, *The Shadow Party*, 2006, Nelson Current, p. 1; Matt Bai, "Wiring the Vast Left Wing Conspiracy," *New York Times Sunday Magazine*, July 25, 2004; http://www.nytimes.com/2004/07/25/magazine/25DEMOCRATS.html; Byron York, *The Vast Left-wing Conspiracy*, Crown Forum, 2005

adversaries on the issues is refuted by my writings and actions in the twenty-five years I have been a conservative. Few public figures have answered the arguments of their critics more copiously than I have. I have written hundreds of thousands of words of specific argument, which can be found in my online article archives at Frontpagemag.com titled "Replies to (Leftwing) Critics" and "Debates With (and About) the Left," as well as in published works such as *Radical Son, The Politics of Bad Faith, Left Illusions, Hating Whitey, Uncivil Wars, Indoctrination U,* and *Unholy Alliance.* Contrary to Soros, my entire intellectual work can be seen as an extended argument with the left, not as an attempt to dismiss it with labels.

The basis for Soros's claim that enemies are to be crushed rather than debated is a passage in my work which has been frequently misrepresented by leftists and is actually a description of how the left itself deals with political opponents. A recent reference to this passage by one of my critics, Michael Bérubé, illustrates the point. "Here's Horowitz in his 2000 book *The Art of Political War and Other Radical Pursuits:* "You cannot cripple an opponent by outwitting him in a political debate. You can only do so by following Lenin's injunction: 'In political conflicts, the goal is not to refute your opponent's argument, but to wipe him from the face of the earth.'"[6] People who have actually read *The Art of Political War,* which was written as advice to Republicans, will recognize this as a description of how I believe *Democrats* (and leftists like Bérubé) fight their political wars. It was not my recommendation to conservatives and Republicans. Moreover, I said this in so many words, and in the very next sentence, which Bérubé deliberately omitted: "Well, we needn't go as far as Lenin. After all, we're not Bolsheviks. But destroying an opponent's effectiveness *is* a

---

[6]Stephen H. Aby, *The Academic Bill of Rights Debate: A Handbook,* Praeger, 2007

fairly common Democratic practice. Personal smears accomplish this. And Democrats are very good at it."[7]

My thirty-year effort to engage an argument with the left has not been reciprocated. Except on occasions when I have invited leftists into the pages of Frontpage or onto my public platforms for the specific purpose of debate, few on the left have considered it necessary (or advisable) to engage my work except to ridicule and slander me, as a way of warning others not to take seriously the issues I raise—in short, to "crush" me (as Soros puts it) and remove me from the discussion. In a typical encounter, when I was debating the dean of the faculty at Reed University, he opened his remarks by describing me thus: "So, I hypothesize, engaging in political warfare, doing and saying whatever it takes to win, this is what Mr. Horowitz does for a living. It's his job, it's his way of life. And, of course, if this is true, then clearly what it means is that it's simply impossible to take anything he says or does seriously, including anything he says today."[8] The dean was extrapolating from the same misrepresented Lenin quote used by Soros and Bérubé, and apologized afterwards in the face of protests from his very liberal student body.[9]

In discussing my book *The Professors*, Bérubé recommended the crush-them-and-dismiss-them strategy to other leftists. "My job is to contest [Horowitz's] legitimacy," he wrote. To implement such a strategy, progressives should resort to "mockery and dismissal."[10] Cary Nelson, president of the American Association of University Professors, was more direct. In a review that appeared in *Academe* he advised: "Please ignore this book. Don't buy it.

---

[7] Quoted from the original pamphlet; see also, David Horowitz, *The Art of Political War and Other Radical Pursuits*, Spence, 2000, p. 24.
[8] My debate with the dean is recounted in David Horowitz, *Indoctrination U: The Left's War Against Academic Freedom*, Encounter, 2007.
[9] The entire episode is described in David Horowitz, *Indoctrination U: The Left's War Against Academic Freedom*, Encounter, 2007.
[10] Michael Bérubé, "Discipline and Puzzle," Crooked Timber, March 29, 2007; http://crookedtimber.org/2007/03/29/discipline-and-puzzle/

Don't read it. Try not to mention it in idle conversation."[11] I am not the only conservative to be treated this way in "liberal" venues.

Bérubé's strategy of mockery and dismissal might be an effective tool for crushing an opponent in academic circles, but in the political arena rougher methods are the order of the day. These will also be familiar to most conservatives, but here is a sample of some recent attacks directed at me, taken from the Google index: "Fat-assed," "faux-intellectual," "a quintessential slobbering lackey," "neo-con," "insane," "Trotskyist turned neo-con scumbag," "Stalinist," "Maoist," "former communist," "brimming with self-hate," "hyperventilating about commies," "traitor," "anti-education fanatic," "witch-hunter," "far-right fanatic," "far-right wacko," "Ahmadinejad's double," "little Fuehrer," "right-wing nut," "Grand Wizard," "anti-Muslim," "religious bigot," "arch-racist," "Zionist neo-conservative," "racist Zionist Jew," "extremist racist Zionist Jew," "a Nazi mind with a Zionist face," "a notorious icon of Zionist Islamophobia," "a blatant Judeo-fascist crusader of Zionism and social regressivism," "Zionist poof."

Some of these sobriquets have appeared on widely trafficked "liberal" sites such as *The Huffington Post*. Others can be found on Islamist websites and venues of the radical left. Here is how I am described in a broadside by the Revolutionary Communist Party, which appeared on Indymedia.org: "[Horowitz] is a vitriolic defender of everything from the extermination of the Native Americans and the enslavement of Black people, to the savage and criminal wars against Iraq and Afghanistan and the torture of those whom this regime deems to be terrorists. He has set up a website that clamors for the arrest and imprisonment of revolutionaries, radicals, dissenters and liberals and reports every slander, rumor, lie and innuendo that comes his way.... In short, Horowitz defends every crime that this system has ever

---

[11]Cary Nelson, "Ignore This Book," (review of *The Professors* by David Horowitz), *Academe*, November-December 2006, pp. 81–84

committed and is now preparing to justify even more, and to intimidate and silence any who would question or resist this."[12] In my speech during Islamo-Fascism Awareness Week at Columbia University, I observed that malicious, fabricated slanders like this were the equivalent of targets painted on one's back.

In fact, such attacks are entirely representative of the wall of hate that greeted students on a hundred campuses who invited speakers to address the issue of Islamo-Fascism in the last week of October. Yet, when I described this as a hate campaign, *Time* magazine blogger Andrew Sullivan was inspired to add another epithet to my list, as he accused me of "turning [the event] into polarizing McCarthyism."[13] Nor did any "liberals"—in the media or on university faculties—step forward to defend the students or the speakers, whose only crime was attempting to start a discussion about an issue that affects us all. When liberals did come forward, it was to attack us and run interference for the left. As political sophisticates, they naturally gravitated to Bérubé's strategy of "mockery and dismissal" rather than the slash-and-burn tactics of the radical street. But their intentions were unmistakable all the same.

A case in point was the appearance of two videos on Talking-PointsMemo.com. They were created and narrated by its editor, Joshua Micah Marshall, who is a contributor to publications such as *Salon, The New Yorker* and *The Atlantic.* The fairly elaborate videos were designed with the clear intent of denigrating our efforts, thus lending tacit support to our campus enemies. The first, about my appearance at Columbia, was billed as "the search for the true meaning of Islamo-Fascism Awareness Week."[14] This turned out to claim that the awareness week had been concocted

---

[12]Giovanni, "Resist David Horowitz's 'Islamo-Fascism Awareness Week'," September 29, 2007; http://www.indybay.org/newsitems/2007/09/29/18450453.php

[13]David Horowitz, "The Problem for Our Country," *FrontPageMag.com,* November 23, 2007; http://archive.frontpagemag.com/readArticle.aspx?ARTID=28890

[14]http://talkingpointsmemo.com/

as a fund-raising stunt built around the abusive notion that there might be any threat to the participants. This "bogeyman" (the term actually used in the film) was alleged to be a pretext for bilking donors out of funds that would buy the security. The allegation was spelled out in a series of interviews with Max Blumenthal, whom Marshall failed to identify as a leftist partisan of Hamas with a personal axe to grind and an obsessive interest in my comings and goings. Blumenthal's father was a White House official who targeted female critics of Bill Clinton. The son has made a small career out of stalking me at events and then fabricating preposterous fictions about what transpired. These fantasies have been granted wide circulation on huffingtonpost.com, Alternet.org, thenation.com and Blumenthal's own blog. Among many other gross misrepresentations, Blumenthal has "reported" in his columns that I was the "godfather" behind the ABC miniseries *Path to 9/11*, a film I was unaware of until it was completed and didn't see until it was aired.

In honor of my Columbia appearance, Blumenthal created his own video and wrote his own column—"The Demons of David Horowitz." The flavor of his reporting is suggested in this description: "Pacing the stage like a drunken circus clown impersonating some bygone demagogue, and standing beneath a massive image of a woman being shot in the head, Horowitz launched into a long, frenetic rant about his own persecution at the hands of a shadowy liberal conspiracy."[15] The woman being shot in the head was a Muslim woman accused of "fornication" being executed by the Taliban; my alleged "frenetic rant" is belied by the clips shown in Marshall's video.

As it happens, I don't enjoy having to go to campuses under armed guard any more than anyone else would. I first became fully aware of the dimensions of the campus security problem in 2001,

---

[15]Max Blumenthal, "The Demons of David Horowitz," November 6, 2007; http://www.huffingtonpost.com/max-blumenthal/the-demons-of-david-horow_b_71441.html

when I was invited to speak at the University of California, Berkeley. The chancellor (no fan of mine) assigned thirty armed guards to watch over the speech. Thirty armed guards represented the university's judgment as to the scope of the threat posed by the Berkeley left, not mine. Since then, I have been physically assaulted on a number of occasions—at Butler University, Ball State, MIT and Princeton—to the point where security officers had to step in between me and the attackers. At Butler, radicals pushed a cream pie into my face. I have been rushed on the stage in such unlikely locations as the Pacific Design Center and the Beverly Wilshire Hotel in Los Angeles—both times by members of the Revolutionary Communist Party, who were out in force during Islamo-Fascism Awareness Week. In each of these cases, I had failed to hire security and would have been beaten if members of the audience had not tackled the would-be assailants and wrestled them to the ground.

By contrast, the Islamo-Fascism event at Columbia was peaceful—a fact which is deceptively used in Marshall's video to insinuate that I am a charlatan, and that the threat of violence was fabricated as a fundraising tool. The Columbia event was peaceful *because* of the heavy security. The previous year, when such precautions had not been taken, leftist thugs at Columbia overran the stage and shut down an event at which Minuteman founder Jim Gilchrist was scheduled to speak. Gilchrist had been slandered in advance as a "racist" and "fascist," which made the attack perfectly justifiable to the progressives who staged it. Would they have returned to attack our event if security had not been present? Would any rational person on the receiving end of verbal attacks, such as those I have enumerated, be wise to hold a public event without arranging protection? Would any Jew, knowing that there are fanatics in our midst who are incited by their religion to regard us as apes and pigs, and who see violence as a ticket to heaven, wish to test their forbearance? What can Joshua Marshall be thinking when he portrays me as an alarmist who fantasizes these dangers?

In the end, this is not really about me. It is about the state of our country, and about students at our universities who are forced to face down a hostile and sometimes violent mob in order to put on these events. It is about the fact that a movement with fascist overtones has developed within the American left. It is about the emergence of a fanatical movement in Islam, really a death cult, which has declared war on the West, and whose anti-American agendas have been adopted by elements of the progressive left. As for so-called liberals who should properly be appalled at these developments on the left, Joshua Micah Marshall's videos are instructive. Instead of being alarmed at the danger posed by these threats, they focus on mocking and dismissing those who are addressing them.

To explain our agendas in organizing Islamo-Fascism Awareness Week, Robert Spencer and I wrote "Why Islamo-Fascism?" a document available on our websites.[16] Marshall ignores it. Instead, in yet another gesture of derision and contempt, he posts the following from one of his fans: "In honor of Islamo-Fascism Awareness Week I am busy rewriting all of my old history books in order to properly show that the danger of some men in caves, along with one moderate regional power are in fact a greater threat to the United States than were the Soviet Union, Nazi Germany, the secessionist Confederacy, and even the Redcoats from our founding days."[17] Well, who would have regarded Hitler as a threat when he was writing tracts in Bavarian beer halls? And of course the Islamo-Fascists are way ahead of that. There have been more than 9,000 terrorist attacks since 9/11, including the murders of Western infidels such as Theo Van Gogh, whose crime was attempting to warn others. A petition is currently being circulated by leftist professors, like Eric Foner at Columbia, which among other things condemns its president for criticizing the Iranian president Mahmoud Ahmadinejad when he was a guest at the school.[18]

---

[16]See Chapter 3 in this volume.

[17]http://talkingpointsmemo.com/

[18]"Columbia University Faculty Action Committee Statement of Concern," *New York Sun*, November 12, 2007; http://www.nysun.com/article/66314

There have been (and will be) no such faculty petitions to condemn the campus radicals who mounted a hate campaign against conservative students and the speakers they invited to discuss the threat from Islamo-Fascists like Ahmadinejad. And therein lies the problem for our country.

12

Encounter With the Enemy
in Milwaukee

B efore I spoke at the University of Wisconsin's Milwaukee campus last night, I was given a tour of the Student Union, which houses the offices of student clubs funded by mandatory student fees. Outside the office of the Muslim Students Association, a flyer was posted that was part of its campaign against my appearance. It was titled "Getting to Know David Horowitz" and featured a section headed, "Who is David Whorowitz [sic]?" At the top of the flyer was an anti-Semitic caricature of a Jew in the classic style of Nazi posters from the 1930s, which have become ubiquitous in the Arab world. The Jew in the caricature was standing in a garbage can with the cover on his head, dressed in a Nazi uniform, with an armband marked "H" for "Horowitz." The caption read, "Horowitz Awareness Week. Bring your white sheets and brown shirts and COME ON DOWN! Flaming crosses and Stars of David will be supplied to those who arrive early." This is one of the central tropes of the Muslim Students Association campaign on college campuses across the country: Jews are Nazis.

On the side of the garbage can, one can read a series of slanders about me that have been given wide currency by left-wing academics: "Muzzling Academics, Blacklisting, Hate Mongering, Race Baiting, Spying." The flyer describes me as an "Israeli apologist and Judeofascist," and claims I ran an ad in the university newspaper "alleging that a UWM student group, the Muslim Students

May 13, 2008, http://archive.frontpagemag.com/ReadArticle.aspx?ArtId=30832

Association, is an extremist organization engaged in violent *jihad.*" What the ad actually said was that the Muslim Students Association was created by the Muslim Brotherhood and is part of a network that supports the Islamic *jihad.* The motto of the Muslim Brotherhood is: "Allah is our objective, the Qur'an is our constitution, the Prophet is our leader, *jihad* is our way and death for the sake of Allah is the highest of our aspirations." There are more than 150 affiliated chapters of the Muslim Students Association on college campuses across the country, all funded by student-activities fees and by undisclosed outside sources. At the University of Pennsylvania, the Muslim Students Association boasts a $50,000 annual budget. Of this total, $20,000 comes from student fees. By contrast, College Democrats and College Republicans at the University of Pennsylvania receive no student funding.

This spring, as part of our efforts to make students aware of the dangers of the *jihad* against the West, we submitted a "Declaration Against Genocide" to one hundred chapters of the Muslim Students Association on campuses across the country, including the one at the University of Wisconsin, Milwaukee. The declaration asks its signers to condemn the terrorist organizations Hezbollah and Hamas, and to repudiate a call to genocide that Muslims attribute to the prophet Muhammad. The request to condemn Hamas is particularly difficult for members of the Muslim Students Association, since Hamas is an organization created by the Muslim Brotherhood. Equally difficult, no doubt, is the request to repudiate the call to genocide that has been attributed to the Prophet. This call is posted verbatim on the university website of the Muslim Students Association at the University of Southern California: "The Prophet, prayer and peace be upon him, said: The time [of judgment] will not come until Muslims will fight the Jews and kill them; until the Jews hide behind rocks and trees, which will cry: O Muslim! There is a Jew hiding behind me, come on and kill him!"

We gave the Muslim Students Association chapters more than a month to respond to our request, but not a single one out of the hundred we approached did so. We then drew up an ad which described the MSA as a group that "postures as just another campus religious and cultural organization, and gets special privileges for being that, but is in fact a radical political group that was founded by members of the Muslim Brotherhood, the godfather of Al-Qaeda and Hamas, to bring the *jihad* into the heart of American higher education."

We based our characterization in part on a study of 18 campus chapters of the MSA, which regularly sponsored anti-American and anti-Semitic speakers from such prominent points of the network as the Council on Islamic Relations, the Islamic Society of North America and the Muslim American Society. We published the study in a footnoted pamphlet called "The Muslim Students Association and the *Jihad* Network," and submitted the ad to student newspapers on 17 campuses. Of the 17 papers we contacted, 7 rejected it on grounds ranging from "unnecessarily offensive" (Columbia) to "encourages discrimination" (Michigan State). Three papers didn't respond. Of the seven that published the ad, three—the *Daily Nexus* at the University of California Santa Barbara, the *Daily Collegian* at Penn State and the *Post* at the University of Wisconsin, Milwaukee—were immediately attacked as "Islamophobic" and "racist" and accused of having caused Muslims to fear for their safety. This attack on a free press was abetted by leftwing faculty such as Michael Bérubé, a literature professor at Penn State. In the Penn State ad, we referred to the fact that the Penn State MSA had invited an imam to campus who blamed the United States for the attack on the World Trade Center and called for gays to be killed. Bérubé is a member of the national council of the American Association of University Professors; but instead of decrying the attempts to abridge freedom of the press on the campus, or expressing dismay at the imam's remarks, he attacked me as a campus provocateur.

Before I arrived at the University of Wisconsin, members of the MSA had torn down 2,000 flyers posted to advertise my event, and surrounded students who were distributing our pamphlet, screaming, "cancel the speech." Their efforts at intimidation so alarmed campus security that university officials ordered metal detectors and a security force of more than a dozen burly officers and staffers for the event. I didn't count how many individuals had to be ejected during my remarks, but there were many. Typically, the complaint of the Muslim Students Association was that my ad "endangered" the safety of Muslim students and should have been suppressed for that reason. In fact the conservative students who organized my event were mainly dressed in suits and ties and were exceptionally polite. They did not shout back or rant, as the Muslim students and their progressive supporters did; nor had the conservatives ever torn down posters or obstructed speakers for Muslim Students Association events.

A week from today I will be at the University of California Irvine to confront another branch of the *jihad* network. The Muslim Student Union there is an affiliate of the Muslim Students Association and an open supporter of the terrorist religious party Hamas, even wearing Hamas armbands at campus events. For a recent UC Irvine graduation, the MSU demanded and won the right to wear green sashes over their graduation gowns with the word *"shahid"* or "martyr" to honor suicide bombers who kill Jews. In 2006, the UC Irvine Muslim Students Union held a week of events called "Holocaust in the Holy Land." This year, the Muslim Student Union is hosting Norman Finkelstein and other Hezbollah and Hamas supporters to coincide with the 60th anniversary of the creation of Israel or what the MSU and the MSA call "the Nakba"—the catastrophe. On that anniversary, the MSA is holding "Nakba" commemorations at other campuses across the country, including the University of California Santa Barbara, where I will be speaking as well.

The agenda of the Muslim Brotherhood network is the destruction of the Jewish state. I am calling my speeches at UC Irvine and UC Santa Barbara "Campus Support for the Next Holocaust"—a provocative title, to be sure, but an accurate one.

13

The Hazards of Speaking

For a conservative, the hazards of speaking on a college campus are more extensive than one might think. Once the security guards are in place—as they inevitably must be—the risks of being physically attacked or shouted down by raucous protesters become lesser problems than those generated by the hostile environment a conservative normally encounters. These include destruction of flyers advertising the event, failure of the campus newspaper to publicize it and failure of professors to recommend or require student attendance, as they regularly do for radical speakers. Equally troublesome is the mindset of a community constantly browbeaten by left-wing propaganda or the relentless intimidation to which the student organizers are subjected by left-wing activists, who label anyone who disagrees with them "racist." All these factors conspire to institutionalize falsehoods such as "Israel is occupying stolen Arab lands," "Israel is an apartheid state," or "the Jews control American policy." When I spoke at Central Michigan University last week, for example, my speech competed with another event that had been organized by faculty members specifically for the purpose of diverting attention and attendance from mine. The counter-event featured a once-deported Muslim professor—now readmitted on a visa—who argued that 9/11 was an Israeli plot. While these extremist views are acceptable to the Michigan faculty, reasonable statements by a

---

October 24, 2008, http://archive.frontpagemag.com/ReadArticle.aspx?
ArtId=32780

visiting conservative are derided as extreme and offensive; this can seem plausible to students who may never encounter an adult with conservative views during their four years on campus.

In this environment, the campus press becomes the most hazardous land mine for a conservative visitor. As a result of changes made twenty and thirty years ago, independently owned campus newspapers draw on institutional support from universities, which give them exclusive distribution rights and allow them to bear the names of traditional campus newspapers, associating them with the university community. This arrangement allows university administrators to wash their hands of responsibility for the journalistic contents of the papers while providing them with a captive campus audience. On my campus visits, I have occasionally had competent student reporters cover my events, and I have had honest but incompetent student reporters garble my remarks. But I have also had ideologically hostile campus reporters do so with political intent. The resulting caricatures have provided useful fodder for the many leftists gunning for me on the Web. The fact that this ammunition comes with the apparent imprimatur of venerable collegiate institutions magnifies its damage. It is this hazard to one's reputation as a public intellectual that presents the most troublesome risk to a conservative who is imprudent enough to accept an invitation to come to a university to speak.

A case in point is the recent visit I made to Brown University during the third Islamo-Fascism Awareness Week in the fall of 2008. My speech was "reported" in *The Brown Daily Herald*, with which I have a long history. In 2001, its liberal editors published an ad of mine called "10 Reasons Why Reparations for Slavery Is a Bad Idea and Racist Too." The editors then stood up courageously when the campus left attacked them and destroyed an entire edition of the paper in retaliation. The leftists then threatened to repeat the vandalism every day until the editors paid them money, gave them a free full-page ad and agreed to have their representatives form a committee that would oversee the editorial content of the paper from then on. When Brown's president gently reminded these youthful totalitarians that a free press was one of the pillars of American democracy, sixty Brown professors signed an open letter condemning the president for her remarks and defending the vandals.[1]

This history is a necessary background to *The Herald*'s report on my more recent appearance. The assault began with the story's headline "Horowitz Lambastes Islam in Near Empty MacMillan [Hall]."[2] These seven words contain one damaging lie and one misleading half-truth. The half-truth is the statement regarding the poor attendance that evening. As I have already pointed out, there is not a level playing field for conservatives at Brown or any university. Brown has one visible conservative faculty member in its entire liberal arts program, and thus only one professor who might encourage his students to come to this event or spring to my defense when the event was attacked. But this professor did not attend. Nor did I expect him to attend. It would be imprudent for him to be associated with me in any way, a fact we both understand. Consequently we have never met, although I have spoken at Brown twice. Since this is a normal situation on university campuses, my usual speaking audience is a couple of hundred students.

My last talk at Brown had been an exception to this rule; some 600 students attended. It was my first visit to Brown after the reparations controversy. I had had to wait three years to be invited because the heads of the college Democrats and the International Socialist Organization had threatened violence if I came, which caused the College Republicans to rescind their original invitation.

---

[1]This episode is recounted in my book, *Uncivil Wars: The Controversy Over Reparations for Slavery*, Encounter, 2001. See also volume 6 of this series, *Progressive Racism*.

[2]Ben Schreckinger, "Horowitz Lambastes Islam," *The Brown Daily Herald*, October 23, 2008; http://www.browndailyherald.com/2008/10/23/horowitz-lambastes-islam/; Ben Schreckinger, "David Horowitz Speaks with The Herald," *The Brown Daily Herald*, October 17, 2008; http://www.browndailyherald.com/2008/10/17/david-horowitz-speaks-with-the-herald/

Because of this history, and the wounds the left's response had inflicted on the university's reputation, the president of Brown, Ruth Simmons, attended my speech along with the diversity provost and the dean of students who introduced me, while asking somewhat sarcastically if he could omit "the laudatory" items in my bio.

My appearance during Islamo-Fascism Awareness Week was an entirely different occasion, and *The Herald*'s headline was accurate in regard to the small number of students that turned out. This was the half-truth. The other half was the fact that the event had been scheduled on the night of the sixth game of the playoffs between the Boston Red Sox, the home team for New England, and the Tampa Bay Rays. The schedule for my speech had been set before Boston unexpectedly beat Anaheim in the semi-finals, and couldn't be changed. This distraction, coupled with the lack of support from Brown faculty or the campus paper, kept the attendance at our event low, a not insignificant context that was omitted by the *Herald* reporter. The lie in the headline was the claim that I attacked Islam as a religion, and therefore all Muslims. I did say that Islam had problematic elements, in particular the genocidal call by its prophet to "kill the Jews."

This call, in fact, was the focus of our Islamo-Fascism Awareness Week and therefore an inevitable subject of my talk. In my discussion of this *hadith*, however, I went out of my way to say I was not condemning or attacking or "lambasting" Islam as such. "There are both good Muslims and bad Muslims," I said repeatedly, "just as there are good Christians and bad Christians, good Jews and bad Jews." I went further. I pointed out that at a speech I gave at the University of Virginia the night before (attended by about 200 students) there were 30 or so Muslim students in the audience, who identified themselves when I asked for a show of hands of the Muslims in the room. I did this after a Muslim student questioned whether Muhammad had ever said such a thing. When I inquired further, the student said she had never heard of this famous *hadith*. I then asked for a show of hands indicating whether any of the Muslims had heard of this *hadith*. None of them said they had. Thus as in all religions, I noted, there are degrees of observance and knowledge which make generalizations a perilous undertaking, and which explains how there are adherents who can be well-meaning and "good" despite doctrines that may be bad.

This prophet's statement calling for a genocide of the Jews is not incidental to the Islamo-fascist *jihad*. It is written into the Hamas charter and is obviously a motivating force behind the agendas of Hezbollah, Hamas, the Muslim Brotherhood and the Iranian regime. I specifically used this episode provided by the Muslim students present during my Virginia talk as a "teaching moment," to illustrate the fact that there were Muslims who were innocent of the malign *jihadist* agendas. I repeated for the Brown students my belief that the majority of Muslims were most likely innocent of those agendas, and not part of the *jihad*. I could have saved my breath, given that the *Herald* headline would be read by thousands of members of the Brown community compared to the fifty who actually heard what I said.

14

Wilders at Temple

In October 2009, we launched a third "Islamo-Fascism Awareness Week" with events scheduled at Temple and Columbia universities, featuring the Dutch politician Geert Wilders. Wilders was under indictment for producing a 15-minute film about the Islamic *jihad*. The Muslim Students Association at Temple appealed to the administration to shut down the event, and issued a statement by its president Monira Gamal-Eldin that said: "*We condemn* Temple University for being the first university in the United States to allow Mr. Wilders to address their population and hope that the administration realizes the reputation and ideologies they are fostering not only to the Temple community, but to the world. The decision to allow Mr. Wilders to share his viewpoints is a danger not only for the public safety of Muslims and the honor of the core principles of Islam, but also for academic integrity and objectivity on campus. *We strongly urge* that his invitation be rescinded immediately in order to foster appreciation of free speech that is not based on hatred and discrimination." (emphases in original)

We issued our own statement defending the event, which read in part: "The Temple administration should reject this attack on the First Amendment rights of all members of the Temple community. It is not surprising that the Muslim Students Association would seek to shut down the free speech of Dutch parliamentarian

October 19 2009, http://frontpagemag.com/2009/david-horowitz/the-hate-campaign-at-temple-by-david-horowitz/

Geert Wilders, who has been an outspoken critic of Islamic terrorists and Islamic attacks on Jews and other religions. Assaults on the First Amendment and efforts to censor critics of radical Islam are, in fact, typical of the tactics used by the Muslim Students Association, the Council on American-Islamic Relations (CAIR) and the Muslim American Society, all groups which support the *jihad* against the West and are part of the network created by the Muslim Brotherhood, which is the parent organization of the terrorist groups Al-Qaeda and Hamas. The faculty advisor for Temple MSA is presently a member of the Muslim Brotherhood."[1]

Everywhere one looks these days, America's most basic freedom is under attack by the *jihadists* and the international left. The infamous UN Human Rights Commission, which includes the worst human-rights violators on the planet, has passed a resolution paving the way for an Islamic-sponsored measure against religious defamation, which includes any attempt to link Islamists to terrorism.[2] At home, Democrats have attached a "hate crimes" amendment to the new defense appropriations bill, which would make speech considered bigoted a thought-crime. Radio talk-show host Rush Limbaugh has been banned from owning a National Football League team, on grounds that he is a conservative and conservatives are hateful. At Temple University, the Muslim Students Association is attacking students who have invited one of the most important international figures in the fight against

---

[1] For the full texts of both statements cf: David Horowitz, "The *Jihad* Is Joined At Temple University As Muslim Students Try To Shut Down Wilders Event," *FrontPageMag.com*, October 15, 2009; http://frontpagemag.com/2009/david-horowitz/the-jihad-is-joined-at-temple-university-as-muslim-students-try-to-shut-down-wilders-event/

[2] "UN Human Rights Council Resolution 16/18—Report on the First Meeting of Experts," U.S. Department of State, April 19, 2012; http://www.humanrights.gov/wp-content/uploads/2012/04/1618First-MeetingReport.pdf; "Islamophobia: A Definition," *Islamophobia Watch*, Runnymede Trust, 1997: "4) Islam is seen as violent, aggressive, threatening, supportive of terrorism and engaged in a 'clash of civilizations,'" http://www.islamophobia-watch.com/islamophobia-a-definition/

Islamic terrorism, on grounds that his speech is going to be "hateful." I myself was recently scheduled to speak next Friday at St. Louis University, a Catholic college, but was banned by administrators when supporters of the *jihad* claimed that my speech would insult Muslims.

The pattern is self-evident. First, smear those who disagree with you as "hate-mongers," silence them as untouchable, and then—if the hate-crime legislation movement continues to roll— put them in jail. Perhaps the most disturbing aspect of the attempts to shut down the Temple appearance of Geert Wilders was the role played by three Temple University administrators in charge of student activities programs. At a meeting last week, they pressured the student organizers from Temple University Purpose to close down their event.[3] Temple University Purpose is an organization created "to advocate for justice and equality for oppressed and under-represented populations," which would presumably include Muslim women oppressed by *sharia* and peaceful Muslims oppressed by the Taliban, Hamas, and other radical Muslim groups. Its mission is "to provide an open forum in which conventional and unconventional views are exchanged and challenged." And that is why it is under attack—first from the Muslim Students Association, which supports the Islamic jihad against the West and therefore does not want the views of Geert Wilders heard; and then, most disturbingly, from the Temple administrators in charge of student activities at the school. These administrators told Temple University Purpose leader Brittany Walsh that Wilders did not have free-speech rights at Temple or in America "because he is a foreigner." In a courageous response, Walsh wrote the following:

"[You] stated in our meeting that Mr. Wilders is not an American citizen and therefore the First Amendment does not apply to him. The American Bill of Rights is not written to confer rights on

---

[3]https://www.facebook.com/login.php?next=http%3A%2F%2Fwww.face book.com%2Fgroups%2F86304743708%2F

Americans as to what they can do, but rather these rights are conceived as limitations on government. The Bill of Rights says Congress shall make no law abridging free speech and not once claims this only applies to American born citizens, but rather to all of mankind. Freedom of Speech has proved an essential tool in providing a medium for progressive social change in the United States; i.e.: Civil Rights Movement, Women's Equal Rights Movement, Vietnam War protests, and even the Equal Human Rights Movement occurring right now in the U.S. advocating on behalf of the LGBT community. Throughout world history, we have witnessed the devastation caused when individuals are deprived of this right to advocate on behalf of themselves. Many men and women have sacrificed their life or suffered severely to allow you and [me] to be free; thousands are still doing so today.

"Furthermore, I would never dream of telling the Muslim Students Association that they may not practice their religion or espouse their beliefs, but I expect that same respect and consideration to be extended to all individuals and/or groups. As was stated previously in our meeting, regardless of how I may, or may not, feel about what Mr. Wilders believes, I do believe it is his right to say it. Temple University Purpose will defend Mr. Wilders, and anyone else for that matter, against institutions and communities who attempt to silence them. The Right to Freedom of Speech is a fundamental right upon which this country was founded. Our founding fathers found that tyrants will always seek to silence those in opposition in an effort to squash non compliant beliefs and felt it to be of vital importance that men and women alike are protected from future governments, mob rule, and tyrants who seek to steal their voice. All of this being said, it would be a disservice to the Temple community, hypocritical of TUP's mission, and a disrespect to all of those who have sacrificed for our right to invite Mr. Wilders to Temple, to rescind his invitation. The Temple community is being provided with a rare opportunity to have an open forum with a highly intelligent, though controversial, politician. Moreover, it is my hope that the community will come together, let their voices be heard, and participate in this educational experience being provided for them. Temple University Purpose plans to go ahead with the event on the 20th of October and hope we may do so with your support."

I hope the Temple administrators will be persuaded by this eloquent statement and will attend the Wilders event and give courageous students like Brittany Walsh and her colleague Alvaro Watson their support. And that every American reading this will understand the gravity of the battle that has been joined.

15

The Most Basic Right

This is a month in which the president of the United States has co-sponsored a UN resolution with Egypt to ban speech that defames religion; in which the Democratic Party has placed an amendment on a defense appropriations bill to make anti-gay speech a thought-crime; and in which the White House has launched an all-out attack on the Fox News Channel because it didn't like what Fox commentators were saying. Instead of reacting with appropriate horror at this assault on a free press, a leading "liberal" pundit, *Time* columnist Joe Klein, has called Fox's behavior "seditious," helping to provide a framework in which any criticism of government would be a "hate crime."

How deeply entrenched is this totalitarian virus in our national culture? A recent column in the Temple University press indicates that it is already an integral element in the curriculum of our schools. The column, authored by a student named Josh Fernandez, is a condemnation of the recent appearance at Temple by the Dutch parliamentarian Geert Wilders. Wilders is under indictment in the Netherlands for defaming Islam with a fifteen- minute film, *Fitna,* which explains why so many atrocities have been committed in its name. Under pressure from Islamic totalitarians, legislators in other European countries are already well on their way to outlawing free speech.[1]

November 2, 2009, http://frontpagemag.com/2009/david-horowitz/the-totalitarians-among-us-by-david-horowitz/

[1]David Swindle, "In Honor of Geert Wilders: Fitna," *FrontPageMag.com,* October 19, 2009; http://frontpagemag.com/2009/david-swindle/in-honor-of-geert-wilders-fitna/

The Temple column was part of a concerted effort by the Muslim Students Association and Temple leftists to stop Wilders from speaking. Three Temple administrators participated in this effort, telling the students who sponsored the event, "foreigners don't have free speech rights in America." Under this university pressure, the College Republicans withdrew from its sponsorship and the Temple student government condemned it.

The Fernandez column began by quoting Wilders: "'I know that some of you here were very much against me speaking tonight. To those who opposed me coming here, I would to like to quote the very famous British author George Orwell,' Wilders said in his opening, 'If liberty means anything at all, it means the right to tell people what they do not want to hear.'" Indicating that he didn't understand a word of what he had just quoted, Fernandez offers this perfectly Orwellian rejoinder: "It's not that Temple students didn't want Wilders to exercise his right to 'tell people what they do not want to hear,' but they didn't want to hear hateful rhetoric. ..." Free speech is precisely the freedom to speak what is objectionable—or hateful—to others. The difference between a free society and a fear society, as Natan Sharansky has observed, is that in a free society you can speak your mind in public and not worry about whether the government will come after you for having said it.[2] In a sense, this is the only freedom we have because, without it, the party who controls the state will outlaw its opposition. Under Stalin, the hate crime was being "anti-Soviet."

Fernandez continues: "Wilders claims to make a distinction between 'the [Muslim] people [whom he supports] and the ideology' of Islam [which he condemns], but when he spouts hateful statements, such as 'Western culture is far better than the Islamic culture, and we should defend it,' he counteracts his alleged distinction." How quickly hate speech becomes standing up for the freedoms your country enjoys, which Islamic totalitarianism

---

[2]Natan Sharansky, "Defending Identity: Its Indispensable Role in Protecting Democracy," PublicAffairs, 2008

denies. And this in the city of Philadelphia, the birthplace of American liberty!

After picketing the Wilders event to discourage students from attending, a cohort of campus leftists came inside to heckle the speech, and at one point succeeded in interrupting it. Wilders addressed the hecklers directly. "I am defending gays and women," he said, "from the attacks of the Islamists. I am doing your work for you. You should be supporting me." Confounding his critics for the moment, Wilders was able to continue his speech. But when he finished and the question period was over, the row of leftists stood up and chanted, "Racist, Sexist, Anti-gay, Geert Wilders Go Away!" as though they had heard nothing he said.

America's first and most fundamental freedom is under attack. The attack originates with Islamic *jihadists* and the totalitarian left, but it is being supported by useful fools and the seriously confused. The events at Temple University should be a wake-up call to all Americans.

16

Jew-Hatred at USC

I want to thank the College Republicans for being brave enough to invite me, and I want to thank all of you who are actually here to listen. It used to be a pleasure for me to speak on a college campus like USC. The last time I did so, I was able to stroll onto the campus and walk over to the statue of Tommy Trojan, where College Republicans had erected a platform for a rally to support our troops in Afghanistan after 9/11. Now I can't set foot on this campus—or any campus—without being accompanied by a personal bodyguard and a battalion of armed campus security police to protect me and my student hosts.

Sheer prudence forces me to take these measures because I have been demonized by the campus left at virtually every school I've visited in the past decade, and I've been physically assaulted at several. USC officials regard the threats against this event seriously enough to have assigned twelve armed officers to watch over the proceedings. The police are not here to protect you from me. They are here to protect me and my student hosts from the members of the USC Progressive Alliance, Students for Justice in Palestine and the USC Muslim Student Union who are responsible for the threats, and who have incited hatred towards this event and its

---

Speech given at USC, November 4, 2009 and edited for publication, January 15, 2010; http://frontpagemag.com/2010/david-horowitz/the-anti-semitic-jihad-on-campus-my-night-at-usc/; A video of my speech can be found at: http://www.youtube.com/watch?v=kG4cYcXgibo (Part I); http://www.youtube.com/watch?v=vSakQMB573M (Part II); http://www.youtube.com/watch?v=yfhPiPxSo-M (Part III)

speaker. These are the tactics favored by fascists—and when I use that word I mean it literally. I don't use it the way the left does, as an epithet for anyone they happen not to like.

The attacks on this event and those organizing it are part of a national hate campaign the left has organized against me and others who share my views. It can be tracked on numerous websites over nearly a decade and is evidenced in the common themes of slander and abuse that are directed towards us. The left's campaign against me is a response to my opposition to its anti-American, anti-democratic and anti-Semitic agendas. Consequently I accept their attacks as features of the battlefield I have set foot on. They are signature methods of leftist "argument." Now the College Republicans on this campus have been caught in the crossfire. These students pay the same tuition as the political thugs who are assailing this event and who are supported by the USC campus newspaper, which has slandered them. They do not deserve to be treated this way. Nor should a university administrator who has joined their pack lend legitimacy to modes of discourse that violate the ethical standards of the institution he represents.[1]

As part of its attacks on our event, the USC Progressive Alliance put out a flyer containing gross fabrications and slanders against the students hosting it. The flyer's headline read, "Hate Muslims? So Do We." The authors presented it as a document issued by College Republicans. In fact, the College Republicans had nothing to do with the flyer, while the sentiments expressed in it are reprehensible to them. This isn't even an original deception. Two years ago, an identical flyer was posted all over the George Washington University campus when I spoke there during

---

[1]This refers to a statement by USC's vice president for Student Affairs, Michael L. Jackson, which appeared in a full-page ad he placed at his own expense in the campus newspaper, which he oversees as part of his university functions. The statement condemns my appearance at USC. I discussed this administrative intervention in an article titled, "Censorship and Libel at USC," *FrontPageMag.com*, January 14, 2010; http://frontpagemag.com/2010/david-horowitz/censorship-and-libel-at-usc-by-david-horowitz/

an Islamo-Fascism Awareness Week. That flyer also bore the forged signature of the student group sponsoring my speech. When the president of the university became aware of the poster, he was so outraged that he sent emissaries to the dorm rooms of the leaders of the Young America's Foundation, which was the sponsoring group. The president's emissaries arrived at eight in the morning and summoned the students to his office, where he threatened them with expulsion. The students explained that they had absolutely nothing to do with the offensive poster and didn't hate Muslims. But the president was adamant. That night he convened a campus meeting to deplore the attack. As you are aware, there is a new religion of diversity on college campuses, which is based on the idea that there are endangered human species who need to be protected—all of them conveniently championed by the left as groups that are oppressed. In fact the only oppressed and persecuted groups on college campuses are those under attack from the left—campus conservatives, Christians and Jews.

At the meeting the president had called, he told the hundreds of gathered students and faculty that the posting of the flyer attacking Muslims was a terrible thing in the history of the university, and he would severely punish whoever was found to be responsible. The unforeseen result was that the leftist who had created the flyer and posted it around campus had pangs of guilt that his prank might have hurt the feelings of Muslim students. He stepped forward to confess that he was the author. Instead of the dire consequences promised the conservative students when they were suspected of being responsible, the radical culprit was given a slap on the wrist, a $25 fine or the equivalent of a campus parking ticket.

In point of fact, far from being under duress, Muslim students are everywhere coddled on college campuses, where they are showered with special privileges—generous student funding, special access to university administrations, and the opportunity to target political opponents with slanderous attacks that would not be tolerated from any other group. At the University of California

Irvine, to take one example among many, members of the Muslim Student Union have been allowed to harass Jewish students, wear Hamas armbands praising suicide bombers over their graduation robes, and hold prayer services in the administration building of a state institution.

The current flyer distributed at this university by the USC Progressive Alliance characterizes me as a person hostile to all believing Muslims: "In the past, Horowitz has said, 'While having the body of the human being, a Muslim who unquestioningly follows the Koran behaves like a soulless beast.'" This is a total fabrication. Who actually talks like this except Ayman Zawahiri and Osama bin Laden? Yet this invented quote is presented as a view that I hold in order to justify the left's attack on College Republicans for having invited an "Islamophobe" and "racist" to campus. Another campus organization and notorious supporter of the terrorist attacks on Israel, USC Students for Justice in Palestine, posted a defamatory statement on Facebook with a list of repellent opinions I am alleged to hold. These inventions also appeared in a letter to *The Daily Trojan*. Not only did *The Daily Trojan* print this scurrilous attack, it refused to print the point-by-point rebuttals of the fabricated statements I submitted to them. The letter to *The Trojan* was signed by half a dozen officially recognized leftist organizations and five USC faculty members. Among other canards in the list was the accusation that "Horowitz has previously asserted that African-Americans owe American society a debt for having been enslaved for hundreds of years." Who in his right mind would say anything like that? I certainly didn't.

There were no quotation marks around the statement attributed to me, but this malicious claim is by no means original. It is a statement that has been circulated on the Web by other leftist groups since I published an ad in 40 college newspapers back in 2001 opposing a leftist campaign to make Americans pay reparations for slavery. I was not against the idea of reparations for slavery. I was against the idea of reparations for slavery 137 years after 350,000 Union soldiers gave their lives to abolish slavery and at a time when no one alive was a former slave or slaveholder. As someone who marched in civil rights demonstrations before the parents of any of the students in this room were born, I thought reparations a bad and divisive idea—bad for Americans in general and for the descendants of slaves in particular.[2]

If you have studied American history, you know that the waves of immigration that brought to these shores the ancestors of more than 80 percent of Americans alive today took place beginning in 1880—seventeen years after the Emancipation Proclamation. The real purpose of this reparations campaign was to stigmatize the descendants of immigrants whose ancestors had nothing to do with slavery, while requiring them to pay reparations to African Americans who had never been slaves, including millionaires like Jesse Jackson and Oprah Winfrey, the richest woman in America. In other words, the reparations movement was a divisive campaign to isolate African-Americans and incite resentment. That was the political reality I opposed.

The ad I wrote contained ten reasons for which I thought the reparations proposal a bad idea. Unfortunately, one can't conduct a public exchange of ideas with leftwing activists, since they are a species of religious fanatics who regard opponents as immoral, indecent and unworthy of an intellectual response. Their self-righteousness inspires them to rant and chant and defame their opponents, and try to shut them up. These intimidations succeed in driving more moderate voices off the field of contentious battles, and keep them from standing up for the principles of a liberal discourse. The ad I wrote originally appeared as an article in *Salon.com*, a leftwing magazine for which I was a regular guest columnist. Not a single one of my leftist editors thought the article or any of its statements racist, although the left has been throwing this slander in my face ever since.

---

[2] My 2001 campaign against the reparations movement is documented in Volume VI of this series, *Progressive Racism*, and in my book *Uncivil Wars: The Controversy Over Reparations For Slavery*, Encounter, 2001.

What I said in the ad was that if Americans living today were beneficiaries of the slave economy, *as the proponents of reparations were claiming,* then everyone living would be a beneficiary, blacks and whites alike. I also said that while the ancestors of African-Americans were brought here in chains while the ancestors of others came voluntarily, the fact is that Africans whose ancestors were not brought to America as slaves are on average thirty times poorer than African-Americans today, have a one-in-three chance or more of getting AIDS, and live under horrible tyrannies. I also said that African-Americans alive today, like all Americans, owe a debt to this country for their prosperity and freedom. This is quite different from the moronic statement that African-Americans owe America a debt for having once made them slaves.

Why is the left attacking me now? Because I have organized a week of protest against campus organizations that support the war being waged by Hamas, Hezbollah and Iran against the Jews and the Jewish state.[3] Among these organizations are Students for Justice in Palestine, the USC Progressive Alliance and the Muslim Student Union, which is an affiliate of the national Muslim Students Association.

I will share with you now my actual views about Muslims as opposed to the slander that I hate them. I will spell out these views now, but I assure you it won't make any difference to those who are attacking me. My certainty stems from the fact that I've taken pains to explain these views every time I've spoken on a campus, including my dozens of appearances during Islamo-Fascism Awareness Week, and there are plenty of video records of these appearances on the Internet, and yet the same attacks are made against me every time I appear. Islamo-Fascism Awareness Week is not a protest against Muslims. In fact, the first Islamo-Fascism Awareness Week, which was held two years ago, was specifically

---

[3] The official theme of the fourth Islamo-Fascism Awareness Week was "Stopping the Campus War Against Israel and the Jews."

organized to protest the oppression of Muslim women in Islamic countries. In case you weren't aware of it, in Muslim countries there are 140,000 adolescent girls whose genitals are sliced off every year without anesthetic. That was one of the obscenities we were protesting. At Columbia University, where one of our events was held, we projected onto a giant screen the photo of a Taliban soldier holding an AK–47 to the head of a Muslim woman in a *burqa*. On YouTube there is a video of this incident where you can see the soldier actually blow the poor woman's head off. Why would he do that? Because she had been *accused* of fornicating, of having illicit, un-Koran-approved sexual relations. Being a woman, she was not allowed to testify in her own defense. To prove her innocence she would have been required to produce four males to testify that she had been raped. Otherwise, they would blow her head off. Does anybody here find that offensive? But if you were to say that out loud from a university platform, as I have, the left would be all over you claiming that you hate Muslims and are a racist and an Islamophobe. No I don't, and no I am not. I am defending that Muslim woman against the Taliban soldier. Students for Justice in Palestine and the Muslim Students Association, by contrast, are busy raising money and organizing support for the persecutors of Muslim women.

Here are my views concerning Muslims: There are good Muslims and bad Muslims, just as there are good Christians and bad ones, good Jews and bad Jews. Most Muslims are like everybody else; they want peace, and are law-abiding. Probably their religion is very personal to them, and doesn't involve efforts to convert and subordinate or kill others. There is a difference between religious institutions and the religion of individuals. Many Catholics do not follow church doctrine on birth control and abortion, for example. The Ku Klux Klan is a Protestant Christian organization, but most Protestants and their churches would condemn the Ku Klux Klan. One of my concerns regarding organized Islam is that I don't see a comparable readiness to condemn Jew-hatred or the genocidal incitements regularly made by individuals and governments speaking in the name of Islam against the existence of the Jewish state. There are hateful sayings in the Gospels against Jews—for example, that the Jews are cursed. But the Christian churches have distanced themselves from those passages.

The Koran is rife with hateful comments against the Jews, statements much more troubling than those in the Gospels. Jews are referred to as apes and pigs ...

[At this point, members of Students for Justice in Palestine who were in attendance stood up as if on command. Some remained standing with their backs turned towards me in protest while others marched out.]

For those of you who've never seen a demonstration in a university lecture hall, this is what it looks like. Everybody who has turned a back towards me will be ejected, and we will just pause until that can be accomplished. Ushering them out is an appropriate intolerance and disrespect for the intolerant and disrespectful.

The focus of tonight's event at USC is the posting of a particularly troubling *hadith*, or saying of the Prophet Muhammad, on the official USC website. This *hadith* is a specific call for Muslims to exterminate the Jews: "The Day of Judgment will only come when Muslims fight the Jews and kill them. When the Jews hide behind the rocks and the trees and the rocks and the trees cry out, 'Oh Muslim, there is a Jew hiding being me, come and kill him.'" That saying was posted by the USC Muslim Student Union on the official USC website and remained there until a complaint was lodged by my organization, acting through the Wiesenthal Center and a concerned trustee. Responding to the complaint, the USC's provost had the *hadith* removed. The USC Muslim Student Union and the Council on American-Islamic Relations immediately protested the removal as religious persecution. This is a prime example of what I mean by the troubling responses of organized Islam regarding the hateful and even genocidal proclamations associated with its religion.

There are about a thousand sayings of the prophet among the *hadith*. They were collected 200 years after the prophet's death.

Accordingly, a modern person might entertain the thought that there could have been an error in transcription along the way. In fact, there is a commission in Turkey whose mission is to examine the authenticity of the *hadiths* and discard those that are deemed inauthentic. Is it too much to hope that this hateful saying attributed to the prophet might be regarded as inauthentic? It probably is. Turkey is presently a virulently anti-Jewish state, and it is doubtful that the authorities would have the decency to do so.

The reason we organized this event is that the hateful, genocidal saying of the prophet is back on the official USC website today. It is back even though it violates USC's code of ethics, which are presumably binding on all faculty and students. The USC "Principles of Community" state: "As a scholarly community, we aspire to create an environment in which racism, sexism, ageism, xenophobia and homophobia do not go unchallenged ... we speak out against hatred and bigotry wherever and whenever we find them." At present, hatred and bigotry of Muslims against Jews appears to be exempt from the code. This expression of hate was restored to the USC website by an organization calling itself the Center for Muslim-Jewish Exchange.

One of the statements attributed to me in the literature protesting this event is absolutely correct. I am reported to have said, "Muslim Student Union groups in the United States are supporters of terrorist activity abroad, part of the network founded by the Muslim Brotherhood and Hamas, and funded by Saudi money." I did say that, and the statement is true. The national Muslim Students Association presents itself as a cultural organization on campuses across the country, but it is in fact part of the Muslim Brotherhood network. At Temple University, where we held an event recently, the faculty adviser for the Muslim Students Association is a member of the Muslim Brotherhood. I have met several members of the Muslim Students Association on campuses where I have appeared. They are generally well spoken and appear civil when you talk to them. But that impression lasts only until you start probing their actual beliefs. For example, when I gave a talk at the University of California Santa Barbara last year, there were about fifty members of the Muslim Students Association in the audience, some with signs.[4] Throughout my hour-long lecture I paused periodically to ask them if they were willing to condemn the terrorist organizations Hezbollah and Hamas, both of which claim to speak in the name of Islam. The official Hamas charter contains the very *hadith* I have mentioned, calling on Muslims to kill the Jews as a religious requirement for their redemption. Not one member of the Muslim Students Association in the audience at my talk was willing to condemn Hamas or Hezbollah.

When I had finished and the question-and-answer period began, the first person to speak was the president of the Muslim Students Association. So I said to him, "Before you ask your question, let me put one to you: Will you condemn Hezbollah as a genocidal, terrorist organization?" His response to this question was that it was too complicated for a yes or no answer. So I said, "Let me put it to you this way. I am a Jew, and the head of Hezbollah has said he hopes that we Jews will all gather in Israel so he won't have to hunt us down worldwide. Are you for that or against it?" He would not answer. This shocked my conservative student hosts. It was a revelation to them that a well-spoken Muslim student, with whom they had had many civil encounters, would not condemn a genocidal threat directed against Jews by a Muslim terrorist. Indeed, not one of the fifty members of the Muslim Students Association was willing to do so.

It is teaching moments like this that make me willing to subject myself to the indecencies of coming to a campus like USC and being called a racist, having my reputation shredded and my name dragged through the mud. As many as 20,000 individuals on this elite university campus have read a claim, printed under the

---

[4]A video of this speech is available here: http://www.youtube.com/watch?v=O-BsElcG6hA (Part I); http://www.youtube.com/watch?v=lvVYuJOvizw (Part II); http://www.youtube.com/watch?v=VmHnpINmrɪk (Part III)

authority of USC's vice president of Student Affairs, that David Horowitz thought it was a good idea to have slavery, and that blacks should be grateful for their ancestors having been enslaved. I hope most people would suspect there might be something fishy about these statements attributed to me, but it's not something I can count on. My purpose in enduring these attacks is to teach the students who come to hear me two important lessons. The first is for Jewish students. As Jews in this country we are facing real enemies who will pretend to be for peace and justice. In order to disarm us, they will go through the charade of engaging in civil exchanges with members of Jewish organizations who are deluded enough to think they can persuade people who want to kill Jews that maybe they're mistaken; that we are really nice people who don't deserve such a fate. I want these Jews not to make the mistake their forebears made with the Nazis who, they also thought, were too civilized to want to exterminate them.

My second purpose is to alert Americans to what may be the most important battle of our lifetime, which is the battle we are having on this very campus for freedom of speech. What is at stake in this conflict at USC—and on campuses across the country—is the ability to assert that there are Muslims who have a religious hatred for others and who consider it a religious obligation to make war on them. Of course there are also Muslims who dissent from these views, who find the genocidal sayings of the prophet hateful and who would condemn the Muslim oppressions of women and gays and Christians. But so far, not many have had the courage to speak up. Where are the Muslim organizations condemning genital mutilation? Where are the Muslim organizations condemning the genocidal war against the Jews? Hitler hid the Final Solution from the German people because he thought they were too civilized to embrace it, that they might object to the idea of exterminating a whole people. Mahmoud Ahmadinejad and Hassan Nasrallah shout it from the rooftops. The very call to destroy the Jewish state—echoed on campuses across the country—is an act of genocide in the dictionary meaning of the word. If they were calling for the destruction of the only black state in existence this would be obvious to everyone, even to university communities. But on today's campuses, the call to eliminate the Jewish state is greeted with silence and even support.

There are 57 Muslim countries, but not one Muslim government has denounced Iran's call to wipe Israel and America from the face of the earth. That tells me as an American and a Jew that Islam itself is part of the problem. There were lots of good Germans but, in the end, they didn't make a damn's worth of difference to the six million Jews who perished in the Holocaust. I don't know how many good Muslims there are, but it doesn't matter if they remain silent while their co-religionists conduct a war against the rest of us. What matters is how many of them are going to actually stand up and oppose Hamas, Hezbollah and Iran. So far the Muslim Students Association, the largest Muslim student organization in America, has refused to do just that.

Just a few years ago, a Danish cartoonist drew a picture of Muhammad with a lit bomb on his turban. It was a satirical gibe at Islamists who use the Koran to justify murder. Millions of Muslims rioted all over the world in protest, destroying property and killing innocent people. Their protests were not against those who use the Koran to conduct suicide bombings against innocent civilians. They were protesting the satirical cartoon as a blasphemous act. This was a massive show of force designed to intimidate critics of Islam's holy war against the West. And it was successful. Western papers did not dare to print the cartoons. Years later, Yale University Press published a book about the cartoons but, fearful of reprisals from *jihadist* Muslims, Yale did not include a single one of the cartoons that inspired the protests in the text. The assault on freedom of speech in America, which is most advanced on college campuses, is greater today than at any time within living memory, thanks to the efforts of the political left, their liberal protectors, and the Islamic *jihadists* who have established a base in this country and on campuses like USC.

The Muslim Students Association, whose members have helped to organize the protest against this talk, is part of the Muslim Brotherhood Network and of the Brotherhood's plan to destroy American civilization. How do we know this? We know it because, during the 2007 trial in Texas of the Holy Land Foundation, a Muslim charity that was funding Hamas, the FBI seized Brotherhood documents describing its network and plan.[5] The organizations named in the document as tasked with carrying out the plan included the Muslim Students Association, the Council on American-Islamic Relations, the Muslim American Society, and the Islamic Society of North America. Members of these groups not only enjoy privileged access to university administrations on campuses across America, but to the administration in the White House as well.

The organized smear campaign designed to intimidate the sponsors of tonight's event and cause them to cancel it is a campaign familiar to every campus where speakers with views like mine appear. Speakers such as Robert Spencer, Nonie Darwish, Wafa Sultan, Daniel Pipes and Walid Shoebat are accompanied by armed guards when they appear in university settings; this because of the threats posed by the Muslim Students Association, Students for Justice in Palestine and their leftist allies, the Progressive Alliance being only one of many. No critic of the Islamo-Fascist war against the West is permitted a civil platform on a college campus today. That is the reality.

A few weeks ago, I was in Philadelphia and New York to host the Dutch parliamentarian Geert Wilders at two campus events. Wilders is now the head of the third-largest party in the Netherlands, and could be elected prime minister in the next elections. In the Netherlands, freedom of speech is even more endangered than it is here. Criticizing Islam can be a crime in the Netherlands and in other parts of Europe; Wilders is currently under indictment for

---

[5] http://www.discoverthenetworks.org/groupProfile.asp?grpid=6181

"insulting Islam" and could be sent to jail for his offense. In Pakistan, the crime of blasphemy is punishable by death. How did Geert Wilders insult Islam? He made statements to the effect that, while the majority of Muslims are peace-loving and law-abiding, Islam itself is a problem, and its militant adherents a threat—because of Islam's oppression of non-Muslims, women and other minorities, and its incitements to war against infidels in general and Jews in particular. Some will object that all religions contain problematic proclamations by their founders. In the Old Testament, for example, God tells Moses to destroy the Amalekites, every man, woman and child. But there are no Amalekites in the world today. It is an entirely different story when Muhammad calls for the extermination of the Jews and infidels who refuse to submit to Allah, and leaders of Islam generally refuse to distance themselves from these proclamations. So there is in fact a problem; but to say so, as Geert Wilders did, is an actionable offense.

In America, the campaign to suppress critics of Islamic bigotry and violence is a national campaign orchestrated by the Muslim Brotherhood, the organization that spawned Al-Qaeda, Hamas, and all the terrorist ideologies of Islam. Every spring, Muslim Students Associations hold *Nakba* protests on campuses across the country. What is a *Nakba* protest? It is a protest against the very existence of the Jewish state. It is held on the day of Israel's birth. In Arabic, *nakba* means "catastrophe." To protest the very existence of an ethnic state is a genocidal incitement. The *Nakba* protests are fueled by genocidal lies. The most prominent of these is that Israel exists on occupied land—land that belonged to the Arabs and was stolen from them. There is no basis for such claims. There is no Arab land that is being occupied. For 400 years prior to the creation of the state of Israel, the Palestine Mandate was controlled by the Ottoman Turks and then by the British victors in World War I. The Turks are not Arabs but they *are* Muslims, and it is a sin for Muslims to surrender any territory that has been part of Islam to the infidel. That is the source of the Fatah refusal—and now the Hamas refusal—to recognize the Jewish state. It is also the source of Al-Qaeda's refusal to recognize the sovereignty of a non-Jewish nation, Spain, whose territory also once belonged to Islam. There are not two rights contending in the Middle East. There is the state of Israel, and then there is the Islamic crusade to drive all non-Muslim peoples from what was once the Muslim *ummah* or—failing that—to make them submit to Muslim rule. In other words, there is one side that wants to eliminate the other side. That is the one issue you can't negotiate—the desire to end your existence. That is the nature of the conflict in the Middle East, and that is why there is no peace.

In closing, let me revisit the issue that confronts us: the issue of free speech—the right of critics of Islam to make themselves heard. In America, the right of free speech is not a right you can put in your pocket or withhold from others. It is a limit on what *government* can do. The First Amendment says that government shall make no laws abridging the right of free speech. It is the cornerstone of our democratic system. Every other freedom we have comes from our right to speak freely, to disagree with orthodox views. Once you remove that right—once you ban events that feature Geert Wilders or David Horowitz, once you outlaw opinions that you find offensive—you have outlawed democracy itself, which is the right to disagree and therefore to oppose the power of the government or the majority. If we lose the right to disagree and be heard, then sooner or later there will be only one politically correct authority, and one politically correct party, the party in power. If people are allowed the power to suppress speech they don't like, they will have no trouble finding the moral justification for doing so by calling it hate speech or whatever the current fashion will support. No matter what views you hold, or what you think of anything else I have said today, you need to defend this right because this is all you have. If you don't have this right, you don't have any other.

The final thought I want to leave you with is that you must continue the battle that has begun on this campus. The groups that attempted to shut down this speech need to be disciplined.

This is not behavior appropriate to a university. This is a threat to the fundamental principles on which a university is based. All the groups that were involved in these attacks are officially recognized student groups. They have applied for official recognition and have received privileges, including money to fund their own events. Every one of them understands there are obligations involved in receiving recognition, and that they are subject to university scrutiny. What the university now needs to do is to tell all student organizations: "If you attempt to obstruct a speaker who has been invited by another student group, or if you slander USC students or their guests, you are going to be put on probation—or suspended—and lose your privileges." It's that simple. It's how a university must function.[6] The students who sponsored this talk are paying the same tuition as the students who assaulted them. They are going to be here when I'm gone. They did not deserve to be called racists, or to have their safety threatened, as they did this week. No university should tolerate, let alone encourage, behavior like this. It is a deplorable fact that the University of Southern California currently does.

In closing, I want to thank you for being a good audience, and particularly those of you who disagree with me and stayed to the end. And I want to thank again the very brave College Republicans, who invited me and suffered these indignities with me, and stood up through it all.

---

[6]Unfortunately, no disciplinary action was taken by the university as a result of this episode.

17

St. Louis University's
Inverted Values

L ast week, I was in Washington, where I visited with three U.S. senators and three representatives, including the House Whip. I was meeting Eric Cantor for the first time, but all the others had appeared at events I had hosted, or had provided blurbs for my political books. Jon Kyl, the Minority Whip in the Senate, invited me to address the Republican Senate leadership lunch on my next trip to Washington. I mention this because, while I was in Dulles airport waiting for my return flight, I received a call from my office informing me that a speech I had been invited to give at St. Louis University two weeks later was likely to be cancelled because university administrators regarded me as unfit to address their students.

St. Louis University is a Catholic school. The administrator in charge, Dean Scott Smith, told the student whose group had invited me that "Horowitz would never be allowed to speak on a platform alone at St. Louis University. He could be invited only if there was another speaker on the program to oppose his point of view." Moreover, Smith added, while my speaking fee had to be paid by the College Republicans, my designated opponent would have his fees and expenses paid by the university. In other words, St. Louis University would not allow its own resources to be tainted by such an unwelcome visitor. This was the second attempt by the St. Louis students

---

January 29, 2010, http://frontpagemag.com/2010/david-horowitz/st-louis-us-inverted-values/

to invite me, and for the second time Dean Smith had thrown a road-block in front of their invitation. In October, he had said I could not speak unattended because I would "insinuate that all Muslims are fascists," something I have never done. In fact, there are videos of my speeches all over the Web in which I say just the opposite. While St. Louis administrators apply restrictions to critics of radical Islam, no such rules are invoked for Holocaust deniers or supporters of genocidal communist regimes. Both Norman Finkelstein and Angela Davis have been invited as stand-alone speakers at St. Louis University, without being required to have anti-communists or defenders of Israel on stage to refute them.

I decided to call Smith's bluff by agreeing to his terms and suggesting that I debate Cary Nelson, the well-to-the-left president of the American Association of University Professors, on the subject of academic freedom. I called Nelson and he agreed. Smith was not appeased because he was aware that Nelson had responded by saying that St. Louis University was a "university in name only" and obviously didn't respect the First Amendment. So Smith asked the student host, Dan Laub, why the subject had changed from Islamo-Fascism to academic freedom. Why indeed! I responded by proposing that the title of the debate should be "Academic Freedom and Islamo-Fascism." Curve ball. Smith came back with a new caveat. There would have to be a third speaker, a sort of caretaker for Nelson and me to put our discussion in the framework of "Catholic Values." What Catholic Values had the communist Angela Davis or the atheist Norman Finkelstein expressed when they spoke there alone?

It gets worse. This weekend Dean Smith and the Catholic administrators at St. Louis University hosted a three-day conference put on by the Muslim Students Association. The conference dealt with religious themes such as why veiling women, or restricting their inheritance rights to half that of men, or requiring their submission to their husbands, represents "the perfection of our religion."[1]

---

[1] https://docs.google.com/document/pub?id=1PosmNoPUmCRXpoDHN-wbmPs5lmpdNnioooLSFVRichb8

18

A Disgraceful Evening
at Cooper Union

On Sunday C-Span aired a Cooper Union panel with Tariq Ramadan, grandson of the founder of the Muslim Brotherhood and until recently banned from America for funding terrorists and aiding their networks. On the platform were Jacob Weisberg of *Slate*, the moderator; George Packer, who provided the only illuminating moment in the proceedings; and Joan Wallach Scott, a notorious academic enabler of Ramadan and terrorist Sami al-Arian, and a professor at Princeton's Institute for Advanced Study. Also present was Dalia Mogahed, an Islamist and sometime advisor to President Obama.[1]

Ramadan claimed to be a democrat but kept attacking the Iraq war, which had brought democracy to millions of Muslims, as "illegal." Mogahed and Scott deflected questions from Weisberg about the oppression of women in Islam, an international scandal, by talking about economic inequality and joblessness among Muslim immigrants in Europe, and the oppression of women in the Catholic religion—an instance of moral equivalence brought to a new low. Weisberg asked Ramadan about a statement he had made calling for a "moratorium" on the stoning of women for alleged infidelity. Here Ramadan introduced a word he was to use

April 20, 2010, http://frontpagemag.com/2010/david-horowitz/a-disgrace-ful-evening-at-cooper-union-2/
[1]http://www.discoverthenetworks.org/individualProfile.asp?indid=2428

throughout the evening: "contextualization," or the verbal equivalent of a fog machine. If you contextualized "stoning," you could forget the barbarity of it and simply see it as a cultural oddity, which needed to be reconsidered and treated with tolerance. Instead of expressing outrage at the practice of stoning, the feminist professor, Joan Wallach Scott, thought the moratorium proposal a good idea, raising progressive hypocrisy to new heights.

The discussion got interesting when Packer brought up the fact that Ramadan's grandfather had declared the Hitlerite grand mufti of Jerusalem a hero, while helping him avoid being tried as a war criminal after the Holocaust. Ramadan contextualized this, saying his grandfather would not support a Nazi except as a "nationalist" and only supported the mufti because he opposed Zionism. Precisely. "Kill the Jews" is what the Palestinian cause and the Muslim Brotherhood are about; it's why they both seek to destroy the only democracy in the Middle East and the only state that is tolerant towards others.

Packer held his ground manfully but neglected to mention that Ramadan's grandfather had *Mein Kampf* translated into Arabic in the thirties. He also didn't say that the war against Israel, as conducted by the Brotherhood and its offspring Hamas, is a war against the Jews in precisely the sense that the Nazis conducted a war against Jews. In fact, the mufti—Ramadan's grandfather—was leading a genocidal campaign against Palestinian Jews in the Twenties, well before Hitler got his Final Solution off the launching pad. Joan Wallach Scott seconded Ramadan's contextualization throughout the discussion, even when it came to rationalizing the murder of her own people.

When it was over I took a shower.

19

The Anti-Israel Jihad at UCLA

I hope we're in for a civil, intellectual evening tonight. But since this is a university, and I have a lot of experience with universities, my expectations aren't high. You can't get a good education if they're only telling you half the story. Everybody understands this. If you watch a court TV show and there is only a prosecutor commenting on the case, with no defense attorney, you know you're not getting the whole story. That is true with all controversies in human affairs: all the really important questions are controversial and require the contest of differing viewpoints in order to assess them properly. So I have to begin by telling you that, if you're in a liberal arts program at this university, you are not getting a good education.

The conservative students I talked to earlier today can only identify three or four conservatives out of hundreds of faculty members in the liberal arts division. As at other universities, the course curricula and reading lists at UCLA are thoroughly one-sided, and reflect the same ideological mentality that has purged conservatives from its faculty. In the nation outside the university, the division between self-identified conservatives and so-called liberals (I don't really like to refer to intolerant people as "liberal") is fairly balanced. But university faculties are practically conservative-free. How does that happen? Well, it happens as a result of the largest, longest and most successful blacklist in the history of this

Speech given at UCLA on May 11, 2011; http://frontpagemag.com/2011/frontpagemag-com/confronting-the-anti-israel-jihad-on-campus/

country. I attended Columbia University as a Marxist during the McCarthy era. McCarthy never had the kind of ability to persecute Marxists inside the university that faculty Marxists are able to exercise against conservative students today. That is because, with rare exceptions, the senator was never able to penetrate the university community, which was hostile to him and his agendas.

Closely related to what should be an academic principle of presenting two sides to controversial issues is the principle of free speech. One of the problems facing our nation is that people take for granted the privileges and rights that they have as Americans. There is no more important American right than the right of free speech. Every single right you enjoy is dependent on it. If you don't have the ability to express your dissent, if you can be effectively silenced and driven from the public square, then you can't defend any of your other rights. The inevitable result is a one-party system and a closed society. Free speech today is under systematic, nation-wide attack on our college campuses. It is under attack by the political left—by people who call themselves progressives and are always whining that they are the victims of McCarthyites and witch-hunters. In fact, it is they who are the McCarthyites and witch-hunters, demonizing their opponents and seeking to drive them from the discussion.

Tonight's event is occurring under a cloud of intimidation— determined efforts to prevent it from taking place. A speech by one individual to 300 people in a single room, on a campus with a population of 45,000, is apparently too great a threat for the progressive witch-hunters, who have sought to shut us down. The Muslim Students Association, Students for Justice in Palestine and their willing accomplice, Jewish Voice for Peace, have joined in a campaign to vilify and demonize me, claiming that I am unfit to speak on their campus.[1] But I am not their prime target, because

---

[1] Jewish Voice for Peace is a left-wing organization that supports the Israeli Apartheid weeks, along with the campaign to divest from Israel and boycott Israeli goods; http://www.discoverthenetworks.org/printgroupProfile.asp?grpid=7600

I come to campus and then leave. Their real targets are the students who have sponsored me, and who will still be part of this community when I go. The opponents of what you are about to hear tonight intimidated other groups from inviting me in the first place and then tried to prevent the College Republicans, who did invite me, from holding the event this evening, and also from putting up the "Palestinian Wall of Lies" I created to refute the genocidal propaganda displayed on this campus during "Palestine Awareness Week."[2]

One of the threats against me was serious enough that the campus police notified the person I have hired to provide my personal security. I don't go to a university campus anymore without a bodyguard because I have been physically attacked on several occasions when I have spoken on university campuses. Moreover, there is such hatred directed at me, usually accompanied by made-up quotes designed to portray me as a "racist" and "Islamophobe," that I have to take seriously the possibility that some deranged individual or group might want to act on that hatred and cause me bodily harm. And this is true for many a conservative speaker. On the other hand, it is not true for any leftist. Leftists do not feel the need to bring bodyguards to campus, and university administrators do not feel the need to provide the kind of campus security detail you can see here tonight. So you can judge for yourself who is threatening whom, and to whom the label "fascist" might be appropriately applied.

This past weekend, students on the UCLA campus were addressed by a speaker I happen to have known when I was still a leftist—a Jew who not long ago traveled to Lebanon to meet with Hassan Nasrallah, the terrorist head of Hezbollah. Nasrallah has led tens of thousands of Shi'as in chants of "Death to America! Death to Israel!" and has said that he hopes that all the Jews would gather in Israel so he won't have to hunt us down globally. The

---

[2]http://www.wall-of-truth.org/

UCLA speaker, who had traveled to Lebanon to kiss the ring of this fanatical Jew-hater, had just written an article saying that Barack Obama is a murderer, that Obama murdered Osama bin Laden, and that if anybody should be assassinated it should be George W. Bush, because he's a much greater monster than Osama bin Laden. Of course, the Jew I'm referring to is Noam Chomsky, who lost his mind thirty or forty years ago—a mishap that hasn't prevented him from becoming a progressive icon and the most widely cited intellect in the academic community today.

Nobody attacked the Chomsky event. There was no attempt by campus conservatives to intimidate the left-wing groups who invited and supported a terrorist-worshipping, self-declared enemy of America and vitriolic attacker of Jews. In fact, his talk was promoted in the campus paper, the *Daily Bruin*, as mine was not, and he was celebrated as an academic star by the same paper after his speech. The point is that Chomsky was allowed to come to campus undisturbed and to say whatever was on his degenerated mind. And that is a proper attitude on a university campus, which should be an arena for the exchange of ideas however misguided. By contrast, in my case there was such hateful name-calling, and such outrageous intimidation of the students who invited me, that only one campus group was willing to do so. More than one group was privately supportive of my publicly expressed views; but only one had the courage actually to invite me, and stand in the line of fire. That group is the Bruin Republicans, and I thank them for their fortitude. My organization also asked UCLA students to put up the "Palestinian Wall of Lies" we have created to refute the "apartheid" claims that are made against Israel. Our intention was to apprise UCLA students of the facts so that they would be able to understand the genocidal intentions of the Palestinians and their supporters. The plan to put up the wall was also the focus of such threats and attacks that Jewish groups on this campus would not support it.

A more tolerant campus atmosphere would be encouraged if I were invited to speak by university faculty. I've given approximately 400 speeches on university campuses, yet on only three occasions have I been invited by members of university faculties. Three out of 400. I assure you this experience is not exceptional or unique among conservative speakers. Campus leftists and their "liberal" enablers should be ashamed of themselves for working so assiduously to deny their students the opportunity to hear the other side of these important debates. We should never forget that leftists are aspiring totalitarians and active intimidators, and should not continue to be surprised by these behaviors.

I understand why the left seeks to suppress and silence its opponents. It does so out of fear that it is unable to answer the arguments that conservatives bring to the table. The left does not want to be in a room with anyone who is ready to point out that those very leftists—self-proclaimed champions of women and gays and minorities—are acting in solidarity with Islamic Nazis who oppress women and are determined to cleanse the world of gays and Jews.

This explains why the Muslim Students Association and Students for Justice in Palestine, and their progressive allies like Jewish Voice for Peace, hate and fear me. It is because I have exposed them as agents of the Muslim Brotherhood, supporters of Hamas, and willing accomplices to the genocidal agendas of the Palestinian cause. The Muslim Brotherhood supported Hitler, spawned Al-Qaeda and created Hamas. Its founder, Hassan al-Banna, said in 1948 that, if the Jews created a state, Muslims would push them into the sea. Its spiritual leader today, Yusef Qaradawi, says that Muslims will finish the job Hitler started—in so many words: "Throughout history, Allah has imposed upon the [Jews] people who would punish them for their corruption. The last punishment was carried out by Hitler. By means of all the things he did to them—even though they exaggerated this issue—he managed to put them in their place. This was divine punishment for them. Allah willing, the next time will be at the hands of the believers." This pledge of Nazi faith was made on Al Jazeera TV for an audience of millions of Qaradawi-adoring Muslims.

During "Palestine Awareness Week" on this campus, Hamas supporters erected an "Israeli Apartheid Wall" covered with lethal lies about the Jewish homeland, beginning with the claim that Israel is an apartheid state. In fact, Israel is the only country in the Middle East that is *not* an apartheid state. Most of the Arab countries of the Middle East exclude Palestinians, which is why the Palestinian refugee camps are still filled 63 years after the 1948 war. There were 800,000 Jewish refugees from Arab states as a result of that war, but they have all been re-settled in Israel. The head of the Palestinian Authority, Mahmoud Abbas, has said that no Jew will be allowed to live in the Palestinian West Bank. But there are more than a million Muslim Arabs who are citizens of Israel, with more rights than Arabs in any Arab state. Israel is the only place in the Middle East where an Arab who is gay can live without fear, and the only place where he can march in a Gay Pride parade. There are 57 Muslim countries but not one in which gays can hold a parade. Calling Israel an apartheid state, when the reality is so starkly opposite, can have only one purpose: to inflame the ignorant and the fanatic, and incite them to collaborate in the destruction of the Jewish state.

The UCLA students who supported these lies during Palestine Awareness Week, and who have opposed tonight's event, are accessories to the genocide of the Jews that Hamas and Hezbollah and the Muslim Brotherhood are openly planning. Why is there no outrage from UCLA faculty and administrators? Why are there no adult voices on this campus, saying that these are lies and that this is just wrong? That it violates every precept of diversity and tolerance and respect for the "other" that is professed by this academic community? Muslims are protected on this campus; blacks are protected on this campus; Hispanics are protected on this campus; but not Jews. When they go to classes, Jewish students have thrust in their faces an Apartheid Wall accusing other Jews of stealing a whole country, of being racists and oppressing an entire people. Confronting Jewish students on this "apartheid wall" is a worshipful image of Sheikh Yassin, leader of Hamas, personally responsible for the murder of more than 350 Jews solely because they were Jews. They were not soldiers; they were not policemen; they were Jews.

I want to read some of the statements recently made by Hamas leaders, now part of a unity coalition representing all Palestinians. If there is anybody here from Jewish Voice for Peace who wants to explain these quotes, or how they, as Jews, could embrace a movement that lives by them, be my guest. The head of Hamas, Mahmoud al-Zahar, recently said: "There is no place for you Jews among us and you have no future among the nations of the world. You are headed to annihilation." The speaker of the Hamas-controlled Gaza parliament said this: "Be certain that America is on its way to disappear. Make us victorious over the infidel people. Allah take hold of the Jews and their allies, Allah take hold of the Americans and their allies, Allah count them and kill them to the last one and don't leave even one." That's everybody in this room, in case you didn't get his point.

Keep in mind that Hitler hid the Final Solution from the Germans because he thought they were too civilized to accept it. Ahmadinejad shouts it from the rooftops. Where is the Palestinian leader who has condemned it? Where is the Palestinian leader who recognizes the right of the Jewish state to exist? Where is the Palestinian who stands up for Jewish rights and Jewish survival the way hundreds of thousands if not millions of Jews in Israel, the United States and Europe stand up for Palestinians?

Hamas is the sworn enemy of all Americans, and the sworn enemy of all Jews. Yet there are Americans and Jews on this campus who support Hamas. How would you describe the statements I have just quoted, which promise the extermination of Americans and Jews? These are the statements of Nazis. Enshrined in the Hamas charter is the vow to obliterate Israel and exterminate its Jews. Yet this is the party supported on this campus by the Muslim Students Association, Students for Justice in Palestine, Jewish Voice for Peace, and by the progressive left generally.[3] It is because

---

[3]"Selected Documents Regarding Palestine," http://www.thejerusalem-fund.org/www.thejerusalemfund.org/carryover/documents/charter.html

I am determined to confront these Jewish and Muslim and leftist students with the evil they have embraced that I am hated and feared by them; that they distort what I have said in the past and slander me to prevent others from hearing the truth. The Muslim Students Association has described me as saying that all Muslims are Nazis. This is a lie. I have said that Hamas Muslims and Hezbollah Muslims and PLO Muslims are Nazis, and I stand by that. When I made these same charges at Brooklyn College earlier this spring, using the identical quotes, the first words in response to my speech, from the members of the "Palestinian Club" who came to protest, were: "You want to lynch all *Muslims.*"[4] Note that these so-called Palestinians did not identify themselves as Palestinians but as Muslims. That is the reality of the conflict in Middle East. It is not about establishing a Palestinian state; it is about purging the Muslim *ummah* of its Jews. In Orwellian fashion, the agents of a genocidal movement to exterminate the Jews claim the mantle of victims, and slander the victims and their defenders as persecutors: *Islamophobe! Racist!*

This is the charge being made against me now at UC Santa Barbara, where I am scheduled to speak in two weeks.[5] *Horowitz says all Muslims are Nazis. He is a threat to Muslim students on this campus. He should not be allowed to speak.* Three years ago, when I spoke in Santa Barbara, thirty members of the Muslim Students Association were in the audience. Throughout my speech, I asked them if they would condemn Hamas as a genocidal terrorist organization. Not one of them would, including their president, to whom I put the question directly. The Muslim Students Association president said, "That's too complicated a question for a yes/no answer." So I said, "Let me put it to you this way: I am a Jew. The

---

[4]David Horowitz, "Opposing the Palestinian War Against the Jews," *FrontPageMag.com*, March 25, 2011; http://frontpagemag.com/2011/ david-horowitz/opposing-the-palestinian-war-against-the-jews/
[5]Christina Lavingia, "Board Denies Funding for David Horowitz Event," *The Daily Nexus*, May 3, 2011; http://www.dailynexus.com/2011–05– 03/board-denies-funding-david-horowitz-event/

head of Hezbollah has said he hopes that we Jews will all gather in Israel so that he doesn't have to hunt us down globally. For it or against it?"[6] He would not answer. Last May, I spoke at UC San Diego and was confronted by a young woman who was a member of the Muslim Students Association. You can see our exchange on YouTube.[7] She answered the question more honestly than the Santa Barbara MSA president. She said, "For it."

If the statements by Palestinian leaders that I quoted are not what they actually said, my critics would have a legitimate argument. Unfortunately for all the progressives in this room, these quotes are not my versions of what they said. They are what they said, what they believe, and what they are fighting for.

I recently placed an ad in *The New York Times* with this headline: "The Palestinian Case Against Israel Is a Genocidal Lie." When I submitted the same ad to the UCLA *Daily Bruin,* whose editor is a Muslim, the paper refused to print it. What the *Daily Bruin* did not want members of the UCLA community to see is the refutation of the claim that Israel occupies Palestine or that the Palestinians have any right to Israel's land. These are genocidal lies.

Israel was not created on any land that belonged to Arabs, let alone "Palestinians." Israel was created on land that belonged to the Turks for 400 years before the birth of the Jewish state. Four hundred years is longer than America has been in existence. The Arab claim has less justification than the claim of the Iroquois to New York. If one is going to roll back the map 400 years, why not 1,000 or 2,000? The land that is Israel today was owned by the

---

[6] A video of this speech is available here: http://www.youtube.com/watch?v=O-BsElcG6hA (Part I); http://www.youtube.com/watch?v=lvVYuJOvizw (Part II); http://www.youtube.com/watch?v=VmHnpINmr1k (Part III)

[7] "The Palestinian Wall of Lies," http://www.youtube.com/watch?v=khVqSsLq8cM&feature=player_embedded; "David Horowitz at UCSD 5/10/2010," http://www.youtube.com/watch?v=8fSvyvourTE; See the chapter, "Genocidal Acts at UC San Diego," in the second part of this volume.

Turks; and the Turks are not Arabs, nor are they Palestinians. How many people under the age of 25 in this room know that Israel was created on land belonging to the Turks? I see by your hands that there are about ten. Out of more than several hundred. Some education you are all getting at this university. For those of you new to this history, the Turks could not prevent the transfer from taking place because they had chosen the wrong side in World War I and were defeated. One of the rules of war is that, when you lose, the victors get to redraw the map. This also applies to aggressors in war. After World War II, the entire region of East Prussia—the industrial heartland of Germany—was taken from Germany and given to Poland. That was because the Germans had invaded Poland three times in a century. Twelve million Germans were removed from Prussia—from the homes and lands they had occupied for nearly a thousand years. That was their punishment for being aggressors, like the Arabs. The Arab states bordering Israel launched not one but three wars of aggression against the Jewish state. By all the laws of international warfare, the Jews had every right to expel all the Arabs from the West Bank and Gaza and annex these territories. In fact they didn't. The Jews were more merciful than the Allies in World War II—or more foolish.

There were other nations created out of the ruins of the Turkish Empire, Arab nations—Syria, Iraq, Lebanon and Jordan. Jordan's population is 70 percent made up of the same people who live on the West Bank and in Gaza, Palestinian Arabs. But they are ruled by a Hashemite minority. Where are the calls for the liberation of the Palestinians of Jordan? There are none. Nobody calling for the liberation of "Palestine" is interested in the self-determination of Palestinians. Their first priority is getting rid of the Jews. "From the River to the Sea, Palestine Will Be Free." The Jordan River is the eastern boundary of Israel, the Mediterranean Sea is the boundary to the west. In other words, Palestinian freedom as defined by the Arabs is synonymous with Israel's destruction. Who can fail to understand this?

The word "Palestine" itself is not Arabic. It is Latin. The Romans gave the region around the Jordan River the name "Palestine" as a humiliation for the Jews whom they conquered nearly 2,000 years ago. The name referred to the Philistines, who were the Jews' enemies. They were not Arabs. There were no Arabs in the region until 500 years later. Throughout the subsequent two thousand years, there has never been a political entity or state or country called "Palestine." The idea of such a country was invented in 1964, fifteen years after Israel's birth. In 1948, when Israel was created, there was no Arab people self-identified as "Palestinians." The Palestinian national identity was invented in 1964 with the creation of the Palestine Liberation Organization. In 1964, the West Bank and Gaza were occupied territories. After the 1948 Arab war against Israel, Jordan annexed the West Bank and the so-called Palestinian homeland disappeared from the map. The same thing happened to Gaza, which was annexed by Egypt. But if you read the PLO's founding charter you will not see a single reference to the fact that Jordan had swallowed the West Bank and Egypt the Gaza Strip. The PLO charter is not about liberating so-called Palestinians; it is about getting rid of "Zionists," i.e. the Jews. The only reason the West Bank is not still part of Jordan and Gaza part of Egypt is because the 1967 Arab war of aggression against Israel was repulsed; and the victor, Israel, did not annex these areas and expel the Jew-hating aggressors, but maintained them as "territories" awaiting a peace treaty that the Arabs never signed.

The famous "Palestine Mandate" refers to a geographical region, not an ethnicity, not a people. It is a term like "New England," and Palestinians are like New Englanders. The "Palestine Mandate" was a portion of the Turkish Empire promised to the Jews. In the end, they were only given a tiny sliver of the Mandate, less than 10 percent of the land, more than half of which was an arid desert. But even that 10 percent was too much for the xenophobic, Jew-hating Arabs and Muslims of the region, who could not tolerate any Jewish state in their midst. The Palestinian cause is not about Palestinians. If it were, there would be a liberation movement in Jordan and protests against the bans on Palestinian immigration to other Arab states. It is about pushing the Jews into the sea. That is why there has been no peace in the Middle East; why the Arabs rejected the creation of a Palestinian state on the West Bank and Gaza in 1948; why they rejected the offer of 98 percent of what they claimed to be asking for from Israel in 2000. The terms were intolerable to them in both cases because they included a Jewish state, however tiny—in fact, less than 0.02 percent of the entire landmass of the Middle East. The Muslim-Arab Middle East must be *Judenrein*. That is the true agenda of the Arabs.

I'm confident, by the way, that even though this event is being videotaped, absolutely nothing that I say will be reported accurately on this campus, or by progressive sites on the Internet. My remarks will be twisted to portray me as a racist and Islamophobe in order to bury the truth about the Arab-Muslim war to exterminate the Jews of the Middle East. I am confident of this because a speech I gave earlier this year at Brooklyn College was filmed by the Palestinian Club, which then doctored it and posted it on YouTube with the endearing title: "Horowitz Spreading Hate at Brooklyn College."[8]

The doctored film was shown by a member of the Muslim Students Association to the legislative council at UC Santa Barbara to persuade them not to allocate funds to the College Republicans who had invited me to speak. Another member of the Muslim Students Association accused me of saying that "all Muslims are

---

[8]"David Horowitz spreading hatred of Palestinians, Arabs and Muslims @ Brooklyn College," http://www.youtube.com/watch?v=IaTtj9Mc000; The undoctored version can be found at "David Horowitz Mugged by Jewophobes in Brooklyn," http://www.youtube.com/watch?v=ys_EmqwZ_Qg. My account of this event can be found in the second part of this volume, the chapter titled, "It's Time For Jews to Stand Up For Themselves."

Nazis." Here is the context they omitted: At Brooklyn College I read the same Hamas quotes I read here. Those were not included in the Palestinian Club's film, which presented only my statement that "they" were Nazis—"they" being the Hamas leaders who made them. The film was edited to make it seem as if I had said "all Muslims are Nazis," which I did not. I was then quoted in the film as saying that the Palestinians were "sick," as though I regarded them as sick merely because they were Palestinians. What I actually said was: "Progressives justify Palestinians' support for organizations with Nazi agendas by claiming that they're 'oppressed.' But even if they were oppressed, that is no excuse for embracing Nazism. People have been oppressed for thousands of years, yet there has never before been a people that has strapped bombs to its own children, told them to blow themselves up along with other children who are Jews, and if they do so, they will go to heaven. Moreover, if they are lucky enough to be male, they will be rewarded with 72 virgins. *That* is sick."

Suicide bombing in the Palestinian territories is a national, government-sanctioned, encouraged and honored cult. There are no visible dissenters from the cult. This is the message they don't want to hear, the reality they don't want to face. It interferes with the fiction they want to sell to others—that Israel is a racist state and should be destroyed. Part of the problem, certainly on this campus, is that Jews are not standing up for themselves the way they need to. It is disgraceful that the Jewish community at UCLA (not to mention people who regard themselves as enlightened, progressive and liberal) failed to say that the Israeli Apartheid Wall is a violation of the very spirit of diversity and tolerance that the University of California claims to represent. What kind of respect is it to call a nation, which is one of the most tolerant societies on the face of the earth, an apartheid state? That is the defamation of a people pure and simple, and a prelude—given the grim realities of the Middle East—to genocide.

In closing, let me say that the threat I mentioned at the outset of this talk, reported by the campus police, was from the Afrikan

American Students Union (spelled with a "k" no less). Why did they threaten me? They explain their animus in the leaflet they distributed here tonight, which focuses on something I said ten years ago during my campaign against reparations for slavery 137 years after the fact: "As a result of America's efforts to realize the ideals of equality and freedom, blacks in America are now the freest and richest black people anywhere on the face of the earth, including all of the nations that are ruled by blacks." This is the truth, even if the Afrikan American Students Union is desperate to deny it. I forgive students for making these kinds of errors. I don't forgive their professors, who have failed to educate them about these basic facts of their American citizenship and have also failed to inculcate respect for those who disagree with them. Professors who do not provide students with contending opinions on controversial issues, and don't provide them with materials that will allow them to think for themselves, are derelict in their duty as teaching professionals. I have waged a long and futile campaign to defend the academic freedom of students, who have a right not to be subjected to political speeches in the classroom and a right to have professors present them with both sides of controversial issues, thus teaching them how to think rather than what to think. That is the problem at this university on the matter of the Middle East, and on all matters that affect our social and political futures. Students are being told what to think by leftists who have effectively excluded conservatives from their academic faculties, and have converted their classrooms into political soapboxes. And that has got to stop.

Thank you. You've been a very civil audience.

20

Fear and Loathing in Santa Barbara

"Speaker David Horowitz Causes Controversy ...
UCSB Students Fear 'Islamophobia'"

That is the headline in one of the many stories that appeared in the campus papers at the University of California, Santa Barbara, attacking my scheduled appearance at the college tonight.[1] Ponder it for a moment. A speaker is coming to the university to disagree with its reigning orthodoxy, and fear strikes the student body. And these are supposed to be members of an elite university community. Since these attacks began as soon as my talk was announced, I titled it, "Infantile Disorders at UCSB: Why the Muslim Students Association and Students for Justice in Palestine Are Afraid of David Horowitz."

When the very brave College Republicans went to the student legislative council to appeal for funds for my speech, they were confronted with a five-hour-long frenzied effort to intimidate them into disinviting me. The anti-Horowitz barrage included numerous lies about what I had said in a speech the year before on the same campus—despite the fact that all my remarks were read-

May 26, 2011, http://frontpagemag.com/2011/david-horowitz/speaker-david-horowitz-causes-controversy-ucsb-students-fear-islamophobia/
[1] Amanda Garcia, "David Horowitz Causes Controversy at A.S., UCSB Students Fear 'Islamophobia'," *The Bottom Line,* May 4, 2011; http://thebottomline.as.ucsb.edu/2011/05/speaker-david-horowitz-causes-controversy-at-associated-students-ucsb-students-fear-islamaphobia

ily accessible in a video on the Internet.[2] The council members were also shown a doctored video of a speech I gave earlier this year at Brooklyn College, which was edited to make me look irrational and bigoted.[3]

Naturally, the student council members who opposed my appearance said they were all for free speech, but opposed mine because it would make students feel "unsafe." In other words, if speech unsettles your assumptions, suppress it. In fact, the only real threat to student safety surrounding my event comes from my opponents and their political allies. That's why the university is providing security for the event. Conservative students do not threaten the events of leftists. Yet, in one Alice-in-Wonderland moment, a Muslim student at the council meeting claimed to belong to a "marginalized" group.[4] This same student, according to the paper, represented a campus coalition representing "60–80 diverse ... student groups" that were planning to boycott my event on grounds that my presence would make them feel unsafe. Really. The only students on the Santa Barbara campus who can reasonably feel unsafe are the College Republicans who have been attacked as "Islamophobes" and "racists" for inviting me, and who are not supported by any campus authority.

In the end, the council couldn't deny minimal funding for the event, since—as they had to be reminded—it is still against the law for them to discriminate on the basis of political viewpoint. However, their on-the-record statements were evidence of their political intent, and the Foundation for Individual Rights in Education has

---

[2]"David Horowitz: 'Infantile Disorders at UCSB: Why the Muslim Students Association Is Afraid of David Horowitz'," http://www.youtube.com/watch?v=-uchzoKR3xI

[3]"David Horowitz on the 'Israeli-Palestinian Conflict: Myths and Facts' (Brooklyn College)," http://www.youtube.com/watch?v=Nq38Qu_IiRM& feature=player_embedded See also "It's Time for the Jews to Stand Up for Themselves" in the second part of this volume.

[4]Maane Khatchatourian, "UCSB Hosts Horowitz," *The Daily Nexus*, May 26, 2011; http://www.dailynexus.com/2011–05-26/ucsb-hosts-horowitz/

put them on notice that they will face a legal challenge unless they repair the damage they have done to free speech.[5] Having failed to suppress my speech, the council then funded an event created for the occasion by my opponents, to be held at exactly the same time as my scheduled speech. The proposed event was initially to be called a "Workshop Against Hate," its sole purpose being to stigmatize me and my student hosts as bigots. In the course of receiving their funding, the organizers decided on the less provocative title, "Respect Coalition." Two of the organizing members of this coalition are the Muslim Students Association and Students for Justice in Palestine, organizers of "Israeli Apartheid Walls" and protests on campuses across the country. The very title of their walls and weeks are hateful lies, since by no stretch of the imagination is Israel an apartheid state. It is precisely for pointing out such uncomfortable truths that I, and the students who invite me, are the campus targets of their hate campaigns.

---

[5]Adam Kissel, "UC Santa Barbara Student Government Tries to Derail David Horowitz Event, Lies About It," *Foundation For Individual Rights In Education*, May 26, 2011; http://thefire.org/article/13226.html

21

Totalitarians Within

On May 11, 2011, I spoke to a student audience at UCLA for about an hour. The speech was videotaped and recorded on audio; *Frontpage Magazine* posted both the video and an edited transcript. We are now posting an unedited transcript for reasons I will make clear.[1] On May 24, the Undergraduate Students Association at UCLA, by a 10–0 vote, passed a resolution proposed by the Muslim Students Association declaring that "UCLA is a UC Campus Against Islamophobia."[2] I don't know that my appearance was the sole trigger for this resolution; but it didn't surprise me to find that, among the numerous "Whereas" clauses in which the justifying reasons for the resolution are stated, I am the only individual mentioned. Since student governments are proving grounds for future politicians, it is a moment to reflect on what is in store for the nation if these university elites repeat their gains in the world beyond the campus.

Here is how the Muslim Students Association formulated the concept of *Islamophobia* for the resolution: "Islamophobia is defined as ideologies, beliefs, and actions that perpetuate inaccurate and xenophobic views toward the culture and practice of Islam and the personification of its followers, such as being seen as

May 31, 2011, http://frontpagemag.com/2011/david-horowitz/the-totalitarians-within/
[1] "David Horowitz at UCLA: Transcript," *FrontPageMag.com*, May 30, 2011; http://frontpagemag.com/2011/dashton/david-horowitz-at-ucla-transcript/
[2] http://www.facebook.com/pages/UC-Against-Islamophobia/170198249702653

monolithic, seen as a separate and 'other' culture that does not share common values, seen as inferior to the West, seen as violent, aggressive, and supportive of terrorism, seen as sexist and oppressive of women, seen as a political ideology used for political advantage, anti-Muslim hostility, and exclusionary or discriminatory practices against Muslims from mainstream society . . "[3]

"Islamophobia" is manifest in statements about Islam that are "inaccurate"—but by whose standard? Islamophobia includes statements reflecting the view that Islam "does not share common values"—as, for example, a belief in the separation of church and state? Islamophobia is manifest in attitudes that regard Islam as "inferior to the West" or describe Islam "as sexist and oppressive of women." In other words, no more noticing that, in Islamic doctrine and *sharia*-governed countries, women are consigned to a second-class status that renders them the virtual chattels of males. Islamophobia is the opinion that Islam is a political ideology. Can anyone say that it is not a political ideology in Iran, Saudi Arabia, Pakistan or Gaza?—to name just a few sovereignties where the lines between politics and religion are invisible. To do so, one would have to not notice that Hezbollah (the "Party of God") or the Muslim Brotherhood, which is now the most powerful political party in Egypt, are actually political. Nor can one link Islamic beliefs—codified by a warrior named Muhammad, who urged his followers to slay infidels and cut off their heads—to terrorists who invoke Muhammad as an authority when slaying infidels by cutting off their heads.

My speech at UCLA is adduced in the resolution as evidence of the Islamophobia directed against Muslims on the UCLA campus: "Whereas, On Wednesday May 11th controversial speaker David Horowitz made false allegations on campus against the Muslim Students Association and the Afrikan Student Union, and further instilled hate against Muslims by stating that "Islam is a sick, sick

---

[3]Ibid.

culture ..." There are two footnotes attached to this clause, as if there were some actual connection to my appearance at UCLA on May 11.[4] One of the footnotes cites a column by a UCLA Muslim, Asra Ziauddin, which identifies the "Wall of Lies"—a statement I had made against the slanders of "Palestinian Awareness Week" at UCLA—as Islamophobic. During that week, campus activists had claimed—among many other blatant falsehoods aimed at demonizing Jews—that Israel is an "apartheid state." My response was that Israel is not only not an apartheid state, it is the only real democracy in the Middle East. To this Ziauddin countered: "Myth—Israel [is] the only democracy in the Middle East. Fact: This democracy only works for Jewish citizens." Actual Fact— Israel's democracy works for 1.4 million Arabs who are Israeli citizens as well. To prove his fallacious point, Ziauddin writes: "Six million Palestinian refugees have not been granted the right of return." I don't for a moment believe that Ziauddin's invented figure "six million" is a coincidence, but there is no such right of return, except in the minds of Palestinian revanchists.

The second footnote refers to the claim that I said, "Islam is a sick, sick culture." The footnote is a link to the audio version of the hour-long speech I gave at UCLA. But the audio refutes the claim and provides a way to measure the brazen character of the lies the Muslim Students Association gets away with on the UCLA campus. There is only one passage in the speech that refers to "a sick, sick culture." As it happens—and it is not really coincidental—this passage refers to a speech I made at Brooklyn College, which had been distorted by the Palestinians who produced a doctored video of my appearance, called "Horowitz Spreading Hate at Brooklyn College."[5] What I said was this. People have been

---

[4]Asra Ziauddin, "Understanding Israel-Palestine Requires Grasp of Myths, Facts," *Daily Bruin,* May 18, 2011; http://web.archive.org/ web/20110521044836/http://www.dailybruin.com/index.php/article/20 11/05/understanding_israelpalestine_requires_grasp_of_myths_facts# comment4519

oppressed for thousands of years, horribly oppressed. Enslaved. Massacred. And yet, in thousands of years of recorded history, there has never before, *never* been a people that has strapped bombs onto its own children, told them to go ahead and blow up other children, and if they do, they're going to go to heaven. Moreover, if they're lucky enough to be male, they're going to be rewarded with 72 virgins. That is sick. That is a sick death-cult.[6]

Quite obviously, what I was talking about in my Brooklyn College speech was the Palestinian culture of death, framed by the Hamas version of Islam. So what my UCLA Muslim critics are actually saying is that Hamas's death-cult version of Islam is actually Islam. I didn't say this, the Muslim Students Association did. If the UCLA student government, which passed this resolution without opposition, were an actual government, you can bet they would pass an Islamophobia law that would put me in jail—or worse. Bear in mind that these are students at one of the top dozen schools in America, and there doesn't seem to be an adult around to teach them what a democracy is—or what a totalitarian concept like "Islamophobia" portends.

5"David Horowitz spreading hatred of Palestinians, Arabs and Muslims @ Brooklyn College," http://www.youtube.com/watch?v=IaTtj9Mco00
6"David Horowitz at UCLA: Transcript," May 30, 2011, http://frontpagemag.com/2011/dashton/david-horowitz-at-ucla-transcript/

PART II

The Middle East Conflict

I

Why Israel Is the Victim

The Gaza Strip is a narrow corridor of land 25 miles long, about twice the area of Washington, D.C. It is situated between Israel and the Mediterranean Sea, and has a southern border with Egypt. When the UN created Israel in 1948 out of the ruins of the Turkish empire, eight Arab countries launched an attack on the newborn nation with the stated goal of destroying it. The attackers included Egypt, whose tanks came through the Gaza land bridge. In its defensive war against the invaders, Israel emerged triumphant but chose not to occupy Gaza, which was then annexed by Egypt.

Nineteen years later, in May 1967, the Egyptian dictator Gamel Abdel Nasser massed hundreds of thousands of troops on the Israeli border with Gaza and closed the Port of Eilat in an attempt to strangle the Israeli state. On June 5, Israel struck back and, in a "Six-Day War," vanquished the Egyptian armies and drove them out of the Gaza strip. After the war, Israel refused to withdraw its own armies from Gaza and the West Bank because the Arab invaders refused to negotiate a formal peace treaty. A few thousand Jews settled in Gaza. By 2005 they numbered 8,500, a tiny community compared to the 1.4 million Palestinian Arabs. While they lived in Gaza, the Jewish settlers were in constant danger—particularly after the formation of one of the world's leading terrorist

Originally published Wednesday, January 09, 2002, http://archive.frontpagemag.com/Printable.aspx?ArtId=23620. Preface on Gaza added in 2013.

organizations, Hamas, whose stated goal was and is the destruction of Israel and the establishment of an Islamic state "from the River to the Sea"—in other words, in all of Israel.

In September 2000, following Yasser Arafat's rejection of the Oslo peace process, the Palestinians launched an *Intifada* which consisted of unrelenting terrorist attacks on Israeli civilians. The attacks were carried out by Hamas, Palestinian Islamic Jihad, and the al-Aqsa Martyrs Brigade, an arm of the Palestinian Authority; it lasted four years until Israel built a fence along its borders, which all but stopped them. Having built the security fence, the Israeli government announced it was withdrawing its military forces from the Gaza Strip as a gesture of peace. As part of its withdrawal, it removed all the Jews living in Gaza, since they could no longer be protected from their Arab neighbors. This unilateral withdrawal was completed in August 2005.

Forget for a moment the geopolitical rationale for the withdrawal from Gaza and consider why the Jewish settlements in Gaza were an issue for the Arabs. Palestinian Arabs, and all the Arab states of the Middle East, are determined not to live alongside Jews and want to dismantle the Jewish state. They hate Jews so ferociously that they have conducted a permanent war against them since the creation of Israel in 1948. There is not an Arab state or Arab-controlled piece of territory in the Middle East that will allow Jews to live in it. This is why the Arab states rejected the two-state solution the UN offered them in 1948, which would have created a Palestinian state on the West Bank and in Gaza. The Arabs wanted to destroy the Jewish state more than they wanted to create a Palestinian one. In contrast to the hostility of all Arab states to Jews, Israel has welcomed Palestinian Arabs to its communities as citizens of the Jewish state. There are more than a million Arabs living safely in Israel, where they enjoy more citizen rights than Arabs living in any Arab country, or for that matter Muslims living in any Muslim country. If Arabs treated Jews half as well, there would be no Middle East "problem." But the ethnic cleansing of the Jews has always been the primary objective of the opponents of the Jewish state—first Arab nationalists and now Muslim *jihadists* whose ambition is a Muslim republic throughout the Middle East with no competing nationalities, cultures or religions. In rejecting a two-state solution in 1948 and 2001, Palestinian Arabs have shown that they want to kill Jews more than they want an independent state.

The tiny Jewish population that had settled in Gaza created an agricultural industry, constructing greenhouses and irrigation systems that produced fruits, vegetables and flowers. As a result of this industry, while the Jews represented less than 1 percent of the Gaza population they produced nearly 20 percent of its gross domestic product.[1] If the Palestinian inhabitants of Gaza weren't consumed by ethnic hatred, they would have done everything in their power to import more Jews rather than agitate to get rid of the few who created this wealth. With 50,000 Jews living in Gaza, still a small minority in a population of 1.4 million, the Arabs there could have doubled their economy.

When the Israeli government removed the Jews of Gaza, there remained the problem of what to do with the greenhouses and irrigation systems they left behind. A Jewish philanthropist in America stepped forward to solve the problem. Mortimer Zuckerman, the publisher of *U.S. News and World Report*, raised $14 million to buy the greenhouses from their Jewish owners and give them at no cost to the Palestinians of Gaza. It was a gesture of peace, an effort to encourage the Palestinians to look on the withdrawal as a step in the process of ending the sixty-year war. The Palestinian response to this peace offering was swift and unambiguous. On the day the Israeli troops left, Hamas, which was now the elected government of Gaza, looted and destroyed the greenhouses and irrigation systems and began firing rockets into Israeli schoolyards and towns on the border.[2]

---

[1]http://city-journal.org/2009/19_3_jewish-capitalism.html
[2]http://abriefhistory.org/?p=1337; http://www.theatlantic.com/international/archive/2011/09/why-would-israel-give-up-territory-after-gaza/244995/

The withdrawal from Gaza is an emblem of the entire Middle East conflict. This is not a conflict of right versus right. It is a conflict instigated and sustained by the refusal of the Arab and Muslim inhabitants of the Middle East to live as neighbors alongside a nation that is non-Arab, non-Muslim, and democratic. The cause of the conflict is that the Arabs hate Jews more than they love peace.

The Jewish Problem and Its "Solution"

Zionism is a national liberation movement identical in most ways to other liberation movements that leftists and progressives the world over—and in every case but this one—fervently support. This exceptionalism is also visible at the reverse end of the political spectrum: In every other instance, right-wingers oppose national liberation movements that are under the spell of Marxist delusions and committed to violent means. But some right-wingers make an exception for the "liberation movement" that Palestinians have aimed at the Jews. The unique opposition to a Jewish homeland at both ends of the political spectrum identifies the problem that Zionism was created to solve.

The "Jewish problem" is just another name for the fact that Jews are the most universally hated and persecuted ethnic group in history. The Zionist founders believed that hatred of Jews was a direct consequence of their stateless condition. As long as Jews were aliens in every society they found themselves in, they would always be seen as interlopers; their loyalties would be suspect and persecution would follow. This was what happened to Captain Alfred Dreyfus, whom French anti-Semites falsely accused of spying and who was put on trial for treason by the French government in 1896. Theodor Herzl was an assimilated, westernized Jew, a Viennese journalist who witnessed the Dreyfus frame-up in Paris and was inspired to create the Zionist movement. Herzl and other Zionist founders believed that if Jews had a nation of their own, this very fact would "normalize" their condition in the community of nations. Jews had been without a state since the beginning of the Diaspora, when the Romans expelled them from Judea on the west bank of the Jordan River, some two thousand years earlier. The Zionists believed that once the Jews obtained a homeland—Judea itself a logical site—and became again like other peoples, anti-Semitism would wither on its poisonous vine and the Jewish problem would disappear.

In the 1920s, the British and French victors in World War I created the states that now define the Middle East out of the ashes of the empire of their defeated Turkish adversary.[3] In a region the Ottoman Turks had controlled for four hundred years, Britain and France drew the boundaries of new nations—Syria, Lebanon, Transjordan and Iraq. Previously, the British had promised the Jews they could establish a "national home" in the geographical area known as the Palestine Mandate. But in 1921, the British separated 80 percent of the Mandate, named it "Transjordan" and gave it to the Arabs. Transjordan was created for the Arabian monarch King Abdullah, who had been defeated in tribal warfare on the Arabian Peninsula and lacked a seat of power. Abdullah's tribe was Hashemite, while the vast majority of Abdullah's subjects were Arabs. What was left of the original Palestine Mandate—between the west bank of the Jordan River and the Mediterranean Sea—had been settled by Arabs and Jews. Jews, in fact, had lived in the area continuously for 3,700 years, even after the Romans had destroyed their state in Judea in 70 AD. Arabs became the dominant local population for the first time in the 7th century AD as a result of the Muslim invasions. These Arabs were largely nomads who had no distinctive language or culture to separate them from other Arabs, and were ethnically indistinct from the Arabs of Transjordan. They did not refer to themselves as "Palestinians" then or in all the time since, they made no attempt to create an independent state west or east of the Jordan River, and none was ever established.

---

[3] Mitchell G. Bard, "Myths and Facts: A Guide to the Arab-Israeli Conflict—Israel's Roots," http://www.jewishvirtuallibrary.org/jsource/myths3/MFroots.html

While the Jews waited for a portion of the Mandate they had been promised, the pressure for a homeland dramatically increased with the Nazi Holocaust, which targeted Jews for extermination and managed to murder six million; in part because no country, not even England or the United States, would open its borders and allow Jews to enter freely. In 1948, the United Nations voted to partition the remaining portion of the original Mandate to make a Jewish homeland possible. Under the partition plan, the Arabs were given the Jews' ancient home in Judea and Samaria—now known as the West Bank—as well as the "Gaza Strip" on the border with Egypt. The Jews were then allotted three slivers of disconnected land along the Mediterranean. Sixty percent of the land allotted to the Jews was the arid Negev desert, and the entire portion represented only about 10 percent of the original Palestine Mandate. Out of these unpromising parts, the Jews created a new state, Israel. At this time, the idea of a Palestinian nation, much less a movement to create one, did not even exist.

At the moment of Israel's birth, Palestinian Arabs lived on roughly 90 percent of the original Palestine Mandate—in Transjordan and in the UN partition area. There were also 800,000 Arabs living in Israel itself. But while Arabs became Israeli citizens, Jews were legally barred from settling in the thirty-five thousand square miles of Transjordan, which eventually was renamed "Jordan." The Arab population around the Jordan River had actually more than tripled since the Zionists first began settling the region in significant numbers in the 1880s. The reason for this increase was that the Jewish settlers had brought industrial and agricultural development with them, which attracted Arab immigrants to what had previously been a sparsely settled and economically destitute area. If the Palestinian Arabs had been willing to accept this arrangement by which they received 90 percent of the land in the Palestine Mandate—and under which they benefited from the industry, enterprise and political democracy the Jews brought to the region—there would have been no Middle East conflict. But they were not.

Instead, the Arab League, representing five neighboring Arab states, declared war on Israel on the day of its creation. Five Arab armies invaded the three slivers of land with the aim of destroying the infant Jewish state. During the fighting, according to the UN mediator on the scene, an estimated 472,000 Arabs fled their homes—some to escape the dangers of war, others driven out in the heat of war. They planned on returning after what they assumed would be the inevitable Arab victory and the destruction of the Jewish state. But the Jews—many of them recent Holocaust survivors—withstood the attack. The five Arab armies were repelled.

Yet there was no peace. Even though their armies were beaten, the Arab states were determined to carry on their campaign of destruction and to remain formally at war with Israel. After the defeat of the Arab armies, the Palestinians who lived in the Arab area of the UN partition did not attempt to create a state of their own. Instead, in 1950, Jordan annexed the entire West Bank and Egypt annexed the Gaza Strip. There were no Arab protests over these annexations, because the people who lived in the West Bank and Gaza did not think of themselves as a separate people but as Arabs.

Refugees: Jewish and Arab

As a result of the annexation and the continuing state of war, the Arab refugees who had fled the Israeli slivers did not return. There was a refugee flow into Israel, but it was a flow of Jews who had been expelled from the Arab countries. All over the Middle East, Jews were forced to leave lands they had lived on for centuries. Although Israel was a tiny geographical area and a fledgling state, its government welcomed and resettled six hundred thousand Jewish refugees and made them citizens. At the same time, the Jews resumed their work of creating a new nation. They annexed a small amount of territory to make their state defensible, including a land bridge to Jerusalem.

In the years that followed, the Israelis made their desert bloom. They built the only industrialized economy in the entire Middle

East. They built the only liberal democracy in the Middle East, and they treated the Arabs who remained in Israel well. To this day, the very large Israeli-Arab minority has more rights and privileges than any other Arab population in the entire Middle East. This is especially true of the newly minted "Palestinian" Arabs who lived first under Yasser Arafat's corrupt dictatorship, and then under the Palestinian Authority, which inherited his totalitarian rule.

The Arab Wars Against Israel

The present Middle East conflict is said to be about "occupied territories"—the West Bank of the Jordan and the Gaza strip—and Israel's refusal to relinquish them. But this claim ignores the actual history of the conflict. During the first twenty years of the conflict, Israel did not control the West Bank or the Gaza Strip. When Jordan and Egypt annexed the West Bank and the Gaza strip after the 1948 war, there was no Arab outrage. When the PLO was formed in 1964, the Palestinians did not protest the annexations of Gaza and the West Bank by Egypt and Jordan. Their war was the Arab war against the Jewish state.

In 1967, Egypt, Syria and Jordan—whose leaders had never ceased to call for the destruction of Israel—massed hundreds of thousands of troops on Israel's borders and blockaded the Straits of Tiran, closing the port of Eilat, Israel's only opening to the East. This was an act of war. Because Israel had no land mass to defend itself from being overrun, it struck the Arab armies first and defeated them, as it had in 1948. In repelling these armies, Israel came into control of the West Bank and the Gaza strip as well as the oil-rich Sinai desert. Israel had every right to annex these territories captured from the aggressors. This was a time-honored ritual among nations; it was precisely how Syria, Lebanon, Iraq and Jordan had come into existence themselves. But Israel did not do so. On the other hand, Israel did not withdraw its armies or relinquish its control. The reason was that the Arab aggressors once again refused to make peace and declared themselves still at war, a threat no government could ignore. By this time, Israel was a country of two to three million surrounded by declared enemies whose combined populations numbered over a hundred million. Geographically, Israel was so small that at one point it was less than ten miles across. No responsible Israeli government could relinquish a territorial buffer while its hostile neighbors were still formally at war. This is the reality that frames the current phase of the Middle East conflict.

In 1973, six years after the second Arab war against the Jews, the Arab armies again attacked Israel. The attack was led by Syria and Egypt, abetted by Iraq, Libya, Saudi Arabia, Kuwait and five other countries that gave military support to the aggressors, including an Iraqi division of eighteen thousand men. Israel again defeated the Arab forces. After this war, Egypt—and Egypt alone—agreed to make a formal peace. The peace was signed by Egyptian president Anwar Sadat, who was later assassinated by Islamic radicals for this "betrayal," paying for his statesmanship with his life. Sadat is one of three Arab leaders assassinated by other Arabs for making peace with the Jews.

Under the "Camp David Accords" that Sadat signed, Israel returned the entire Sinai with all its oil riches to the Egyptian aggressor. This act demonstrated once and for all that the solution to the Middle East conflict was ready at hand. It only required the willingness of the Arabs to agree.

The Arabs still claim that Jewish settlements in the West Bank are the obstacle to peace. But the Arab settlements in Israel—they are actually called "cities"—are not a problem for Israel; so why should Jewish settlements be a problem for Arabs? They are a problem because the Arabs do not want Jews to live on Arab lands, as their leaders have said in so many words. The Middle East conflict is not about Israel's occupation of the territories; it is about the refusal of the Arabs to make peace with Israel, or to live side by side with Jews, and therefore their desire to destroy the Jewish state. This desire is encapsulated in the word all Palestinians—"moderates" and extremists—use to describe the creation of Israel. They call the birth of Israel the "nakba," the catastrophe.

Self-Determination Is Not the Agenda

The Palestinians and their supporters claim that the Middle East conflict is about the Palestinians' yearning for a state and the refusal of Israel to accept their aspiration. This claim is clearly false. The Palestine Liberation Organization was created in 1964, sixteen years after the establishment of Israel and the first anti-Israel war. The PLO was created at a time when the West Bank was not under Israeli control but was part of Jordan. The PLO, however, was not created so that the Palestinians could achieve self-determination in Jordan, which at the time comprised 90 percent of the original Palestine Mandate. The PLO's express purpose, in the words of its own leaders, was to "push the Jews into the sea." The official "covenant" of the new Palestine Liberation Organization referred to the "Zionist invasion," declared that Israel's Jews were "not an independent nationality," described Zionism as "racist" and "fascist," called for "the liquidation of the Zionist presence," and specified that "armed struggle is the only way to liberate Palestine." In short, "liberation" required the destruction of the Jewish state. The covenant did not call for the liberation of the West Bank from Jordanian rule or the liberation of Gaza from Egyptian control.

For thirty years, the PLO covenant remained unchanged in its call for Israel's destruction. Then, in the mid-1990s, under enormous international pressure following the Oslo accords, PLO leader Yasser Arafat agreed to revise the PLO covenant. As a *quid pro quo* for accepting the existence of Israel, Arafat was allowed to return to the West Bank from his Tunisian exile and create an armed "Palestinian Authority." However, his words of peace meant nothing. No new covenant was drafted or ratified by the PLO to recognize the existence of the Jewish state in return for Israel's concessions. Even at the time he signed the agreement, Arafat assured Palestinians that his agreement to revise the PLO charter was purely tactical and did not alter the Palestinians' ultimate goals. Arafat gave this assurance in a speech to the Palestine Legislative Council, calling on Palestinians to remember the

Prophet Muhammad's Treaty of Hudaybiyah.[4] In that treaty, Muhammad entered into a ten-year peace pact with the Koresh tribe. The treaty was purely tactical. Two years after signing it, when Muhammad had mustered enough military strength, his armies overwhelmed the Koresh, who surrendered without a fight. Arafat was signaling that whatever he might say to win a tactical peace at Oslo, the war against Israel would go on.

Even during the early years of the Oslo peace process, it was clear that the PLO's goal was Israel's destruction. The Palestinians' determination to destroy Israel was abundantly clear in their newly created demand of a "right of return" to Israel for "five million" Arab "refugees." The figure five million refugees is more than ten times the number of Arabs who actually left the Jewish slivers of the British Mandate in 1948. Moreover, a poll of Palestinian refugee families in the West Bank, conducted by the Palestinian Center for Policy and Survey Research in the spring of 2003, revealed that only 10 percent of those questioned said they actually wanted to return.[5] In addition to its absurdity, this new demand has several aspects that reveal the Palestinians' genocidal agenda for the Jews. The first is that the "right of return" is itself a calculated mockery of Israel's law guaranteeing Jews a "right of return" on which Israel itself is based. The Israeli law reflects the fact that no country would provide a refuge for Jews fleeing Hitler's extermination program during World War II. It is only because the world turned its back on the Jews, when their survival was at stake, that the state of Israel grants this right to every Jew who asks for it.

But there is no genocidal threat to Arabs, no lack of international support militarily and economically, and no Palestinian

---

[4]"Treaty of Hudaybiyyah," http://en.wikipedia.org/wiki/Treaty_of_Hudaybiyyah

[5]"Results of PSR Refugees' Polls in the West Bank/Gaza Strip, Jordan and Lebanon on Refugees' Preferences and Behavior in a Palestinian-Israeli Permanent Refugee Agreement—January-June 2003," *Palestinian Center for Policy and Survey Research*, July 18, 2003; http://www.pcpsr.org/survey/polls/2003/refugeesjune03.html

"diaspora," although the Palestinians have cynically appropriated the very term to describe their self-inflicted quandary. The fact that many Arabs, including the Grand Mufti of Jerusalem, supported Hitler's "Final Solution" to exterminate the Jews only serves to compound the insult. It is further compounded by the fact that more than some 90 percent of the Palestinians now in the West Bank and Gaza have never lived a day of their lives in territorial Israel. The claim of a "right of return" is thus little more than a brazen expression of contempt for the Jews, and for their historic suffering. More importantly, it is an expression of contempt for the very idea of a Jewish state. The incorporation of five million Arabs into Israel would render the Jews a permanent minority in their own country, and would thus spell the end of Israel. That is why the Arabs have made it a fundamental demand. It is just one more instance of the bad faith the Arab side has manifested through every chapter of this tragic history.

Possibly the most glaring expression of this bad faith is the Arabs' deplorable treatment of the Palestinian refugees and refusal for half a century to relocate them, or to alleviate their condition, even during the years they were under Jordanian rule. While Israel was making the desert bloom, relocating six hundred thousand Jewish refugees from Arab states and building an industrial democracy, the Arabs were busy making sure that their refugees remained in squalid camps in the West Bank and Gaza, where they were powerless, without rights, and economically destitute. Despite economic aid from the UN and Israel itself, despite the oil wealth of the Arab kingdoms, the Arab leaders have refused to undertake the efforts that would liberate the refugees from their miserable camps, or to make the economic investment that would alleviate the refugees' condition. There are now twenty-two Arab states providing homes for the same ethnic population, speaking a common Arabic language. But the only Arab state that will allow Palestinian Arabs to become citizens is Jordan. And the only state the Palestinians covet is Israel.

The Policy of Resentment and Hate

The refusal to address the condition of the Palestinian refugee population is a calculated Arab policy to keep the Palestinians in a state of desperation, in order to incite their hatred of Israel for the wars to come. Not to leave anything to chance, the mosques and schools of the Arabs generally, and the Palestinians in particular, preach and teach Jew-hatred every day. Elementary school children in Palestinian Arab schools are taught to chant "Death to the heathen Jews" and to aspire to be martyrs as they are learning to read in their classrooms.[6] These twin policies—deprivation of the Palestinian Arabs and hatred of the Jews—are carried out without protest from any sector of Palestinian or Arab society. That, in itself, speaks volumes about the nature of the Middle East conflict.

There are plenty of individual Palestinian victims, as there are Jewish victims, familiar from the nightly news. But the collective Palestinian grievance is without merit. It is a self-inflicted wound, the product of the Arabs' intransigence, xenophobia, bigotry, exploitation of their own people, and inability to co-exist with those who are not Arabs or Muslims. While Israel is an open, democratic, multi-ethnic, multicultural society that includes a large enfranchised Arab minority, the Palestinian Authority is an intolerant, mono-cultural, undemocratic and monolithic police state.

As the repellent attitudes, criminal methods and dishonest goals of the Palestine liberation movement should make clear to any reasonable observer, its present cause is based on Jew-hatred, on resentment of the modern democratic West, and on little else. Since there was no Palestinian nation before the creation of Israel, and since Palestinians regarded themselves simply as Arabs, with their land as part of Syria, it is not surprising that many of the chief creators of the Palestine Liberation Organization did not even live in the Palestine Mandate before the creation of Israel, let alone in the slivers of mostly desert that were allotted to the Jews.

---

[6]http://www.palwatch.org/main.aspx?fi=846

While the same Arab states that claim to be outraged by the Jews' treatment of Palestinians treat their own Arab populations far worse than Arabs are treated in Israel, they are also silent about the disenfranchised Palestinian majority that lives in Jordan. In 1970, Jordan's King Hussein massacred thousands of PLO militants. But the PLO does not call for the overthrow of Hashemite rule in Jordan and does not hate the Hashemite monarchy. Only Jews are hated. It is an increasingly lethal hatred and a majority view. During the Second *Intifada*, 70 percent of Arabs in the West Bank and Gaza said they favored the suicide-bombing of women and children if the targets were Jews. There is no Arab "Peace Now" movement, not even a small one, whereas in Israel the movement demanding concessions to Arabs in the name of peace is a formidable political force. There is no Arab spokesman who will speak for the rights and sufferings of Jews, but there are hundreds of thousands of Jews in Israel, and all over the world, who will speak of "justice" for the Palestinians. How can the Jews expect fair treatment from a people that collectively does not even recognize their humanity?

A Phony Peace

The Oslo peace process begun in 1993 was based on the pledge of both parties to renounce violence as a means of settling their dispute. But the Palestinians never renounced violence; in September 2001 they officially launched a new *Intifada* against Israel, effectively terminating the peace process. During that process, in the years between 1993 and 1999, there had been over 4,000 terrorist incidents committed by Palestinians against Israelis, and more than a thousand Israeli civilians killed as a result, more than had been killed in the previous 25 years. By contrast, during the same period, Israelis were so desperate for peace that they reciprocated these acts of murder by conceding to the Palestinians in the West Bank and Gaza a self-governing authority and a 40,000-man armed "police force," while offering them 95 percent of the territory their negotiators demanded. This Israeli generosity was rewarded by

Arafat's rejection of the offer and the launching of suicide bombings in crowded discos and shopping malls, an outpouring of Palestinian Jew-hatred and a renewed war.

The Palestinians broke the Oslo accords precisely because of Israeli generosity—because the government of Ehud Barak had offered to meet 95 percent of their demands, including turning over parts of Jerusalem to their control, a possibility once considered unthinkable. These concessions confronted Arafat with the one outcome he did not want: peace with Israel, peace without the destruction of the Jewish state. Arafat rejected the Israeli concessions, accompanying his rejection with a new explosion of anti-Jewish violence, which he named "the al-Aqsa *Intifada*," after the mosque on the Temple Mount. He gave his renewed aggression the name of a Muslim shrine to create the illusion that the *Intifada* had been provoked not by his unilateral destruction of the peace process, but by then hard-line opposition leader Ariel Sharon's highly publicized visit to the site. Months afterward, the Palestinian Authority itself admitted the *Intifada* had been planned months before Sharon's visit as a follow up to the rejection of the Oslo accords. In the words of Imad Falouji, the Palestinian Authority's communications minister, "[The uprising] had been planned since Chairman Arafat's return from Camp David, when he turned the tables on the former U.S. president [Clinton] and rejected the American conditions."[7] The same conclusion was reached by the Mitchell Commission, headed by former U.S. Senator George Mitchell, whose purpose was to investigate the events: "The Sharon visit did not cause the al-Aqsa *Intifada*."[8]

In an interview he gave after the new *Intifada* had begun, Faisal Husseini—a well-known "moderate" in the PLO leadership—described the Oslo peace process as a "Trojan horse," designed to

[7]Mitchell G. Bard, "The 'al-Aqsa Intifada'," http://www.jewishvirtuallibrary.org/jsource/myths/mf19a.html

[8]"The Mitchell Report," May 4, 2001, http://www.jewishvirtuallibrary.org/jsource/Peace/Mitchellrep.html

fool the Israelis into letting the Palestinians arm themselves inside the Jewish citadel in order to destroy it. "If you are asking me as a Pan-Arab nationalist what are the Palestinian borders according to the higher strategy, I will immediately reply: 'From the river to the sea'"—in other words, from the Jordan to the Mediterranean, the whole of Israel with not even the original slivers left.[9]

Moral Distinctions

To understand the Middle East impasse, one should pay attention to the moral distinction between the combatants as revealed in their actions. When a deranged Jew goes into an Arab mosque and kills the worshippers—which happened once—he is acting alone and is universally condemned by the Israeli government, by Jews in Israel and everywhere. But when an Arab suicide bomber wades into a crowd of families with baby-strollers leaving evening worship, or enters a disco filled with teenagers or a shopping mall crowded with women and children and blows them up—which has happened frequently—he is someone who is supported by the Palestinians *as a people*. He has been trained and sent by a component of the PLO or the Palestinian Authority; he has been told by his religious leaders that his crime will get him into heaven, where he will pleasure himself with 72 virgins; his praises will be officially sung throughout the Arab world; his mother will be given money by the Palestinian Authority; his Arab neighbors will come to pay honor to his household for having produced a "martyr for Allah;" and his government will call him a national hero. The Palestinian liberation movement is the first such cause to elevate

---

[9]David Remnick, "In a Dark Time," *The New Yorker*, March 18, 2002, p. 51; http://www.newyorker.com/archive/2002/03/18/020318ta_talk_remnick; "The Case Against Arafat: The Campaign By Yasir Arafat and the Palestinian Authority to Destroy Israel," introduction by Ambassador Jeanne Kirkpatrick, published by the Zionist Organization of America, 1992, p. 5

the killing of children—both the enemy's and its own—into a religious calling. Even Hitler didn't think of this.

It is not only the methods of the Palestine liberation movement that are repellent. The Palestinian cause is itself corrupt. The "Palestinian problem" is a problem created by the Arabs themselves, and can only be solved by them. The reason there are Palestinian "refugees" is that no Arab state, except Jordan, will allow them to become citizens. The organs of the PLO and Palestinian Authority, despite billions in revenues, have left them to stew in refugee camps for sixty years. In Jordan, Palestinians already have a state in which they are a majority but which denies them self-determination. Why is Jordan not the object of the Palestinian "liberation" struggle? The only possible answer is that it is not ruled by the hated Jews. If a nation-state is all the Palestinians desired, Jordan would be the solution. So would an agreement to settle 95 percent of the land one had demanded. But the Palestinians want to destroy Israel. This is a morally repulsive goal. It is the Nazi virus revived. Despite this, the Palestinian cause is generally supported by the international community of nations. It is precisely because the Palestinians want to destroy a state that Jews have created—and because they are killing Jews—that they enjoy international credibility and otherwise inexplicable support.

In the end, it is this international resistance to the cause of Jewish survival, the persistence of global Jew-hatred, that refutes the Zionist hope of a solution to the "Jewish problem." The creation of Israel is an awe-inspiring human success story. But the permanent war to destroy it undermines the original Zionist idea. More than fifty years after the creation of Israel, the Jews are still the most hated ethnic group in the world. Islamic radicals want to destroy Israel, and so do Islamic moderates. Hatred of Jews is taught in Islam's mosques; in Egypt and in other Arab countries *Mein Kampf* is a bestseller; the anti-Semitic forgery, the "Protocols of the Elders of Zion," is promoted by the government press throughout the Arab Middle East; and Jewish conspiracy theories abound, as in the following statement from a sermon given by the Mufti of Jerusalem, spiritual leader of the Palestinian Arabs, in the al-Aqsa Mosque on July 11, 1997: "Oh Allah, destroy America, for she is ruled by Zionist Jews...."[10]

For the Jews in the Middle East, the present conflict is a life-and-death struggle; yet every government in the UN, with the exception of the United States and sometimes of Britain, Australia and Canada, regularly votes against Israel in the face of a terrorist enemy who has no respect for the rights or lives of Jews. After the Al-Qaeda attack on the World Trade Center, the French ambassador to England complained that the whole world was endangered because of "that shitty little country," Israel.[11] This caused a scandal in England, but nowhere else. All that stands between the Jews of the Middle East and another Holocaust is their own military prowess and the support of the United States. Even in the United States, however, one can now turn the TV to channels like MSNBC and CNN to see the elected prime minister of a tiny democracy equated politically and morally with terrorists and enemies of the United States, such as the leaders of Hamas. During the first Gulf War, Israel was America's firm ally, while Arafat and the Palestinians were Saddam Hussein's staunchest Arab supporters. Yet the next two U.S. administrations—Republican and Democrat alike—strove for evenhanded "neutrality" in the conflict in the Middle East, and pressured Israel into a suicidal "peace process" with a foe dedicated to its destruction. Only after September 11 was the United States willing to recognize Arafat as an enemy of peace and not a viable negotiating partner. And now the

[10]"Senior Palestinian Official Calls for Destruction of America and Labels it a Terrorist State," *Israel Ministry of Foreign Affairs*, September 14, 1997; http://www.mfa.gov.il/mfa/mfa-archive/1996–1997/pages/senior%20palestinian%20official%20calls%20for%20destruction.aspx
[11]Daniel Bernard (diplomat), http://en.wikipedia.org/wiki/Daniel_Bernard_(diplomat); "'Anti-Semitic' French Envoy Under Fire," *BBC News*, December 20, 2001, http://news.bbc.co.uk/2/hi/1721172.stm

pendulum has swung back, with the ascension of Barack Obama to the presidency.

In terms of the "Jewish problem" that Herzl and the Zionist founders set out to solve, it is safer today to be a Jew in America than a Jew in Israel. This is part of why I, a Jew, am an unambivalent, passionate American patriot. America is good for the Jews, as it is good for every minority that embraces its social contract. But the tragic history of the attempt to establish a Jewish state in the Middle East is also why I am a fierce supporter of Israel's survival, and why I have no sympathy for the Palestinian side in this conflict. Nor will I have such sympathy, until the day comes when I can look into Palestinian eyes and see something other than death desired for Jews like me.

2

Our Enemy Is One

Israel and America are in greater danger than ever before. Israel is fighting for its survival against an enemy that is determined to destroy it—an enemy that has the tacit support of most of the world's governments. Every man, woman and child in America has been targeted for death by religious fanatics armed with modern weapons, including weapons of mass destruction; yet, in its efforts to eliminate the threat, the U.S. is only reluctantly supported—if at all—by the rest of the world.

As we confront these dangers, Americans need to understand that, in radical Islam, America and Israel are facing the same enemy. Yasser Arafat and the Palestine Liberation Organization invented the suicide bombing of innocent civilians, created the first terrorist training camps, and are hand-in-glove allies of Al-Qaeda and Saddam Hussein. Palestinian terrorists were part of the Al-Qaeda team that bombed the World Trade Center in 1993, killing six and wounding a thousand, and the Khobar Towers in 1996, killing 19 American servicemen.

One month after the second World Trade Center attack, an editorial in the official newspaper of the Palestinian Authority compared Rudy Giuliani to Adolf Hitler: "New York Mayor Rudolph Giuliani hides his first name, chosen for him by his Italian father, so as not to remind Jewish voters of the infamous Rudolph Hitler.

March 20, 2002, http://archive.frontpagemag.com/Printable.aspx?ArtId=
21323

This is why he prefers to shorten it to Rudy."[1] Two months later, on December 28, 2001, a sermon delivered in the al-Aqsa Mosque on the Temple Mount, and broadcast over the Palestinian Authority's official Voice of Palestine radio, declared: "The infidel countries, led by the United States, invented the excuse and justification for their dirty war against Islam and Islamic movements all over the world, following the attack against it. The U.S. used, in its criminal aggression against Afghanistan, the most destructive bombs there are ... Do the Muslims of today know how to realize Allah's path, and to turn only to Allah? Not to turn to the evil United States, or to Europe so filled with hatred toward Islam and Muslims?"[2] And on Pearl Harbor Remembrance Day 2001, Yasser Arafat's official "Voice of Palestine" broadcast another sermon at the al-Aqsa Mosque, delivered by Mohammed Hassin, which said in part: "The 'Mongolians' and 'Crusaders' are raising their heads and enlisting armies to fight the Islamic nations in an oppressive campaign, under the label of 'terrorism,' which the infidels are attaching to the Arabs and Muslims for the purpose of realizing their imperialist interests, and to spread their control over the Muslim countries and their resources."[3]

This small sampling of the available evidence captures a truth that every American must grasp. Islamic radicals from Pakistan to Palestine, including government agencies in Iraq and Iran, have summoned Muslims to a holy war against the modern, tolerant, democratic, Judeo-Christian, secular West. They hate us, and they have targeted us for who we are. This is a war whose outcome cannot be negotiated. It will be resolved only by the defeat of radical Islam or the destruction of the West.

In this battle, Israel is a frontline nation whose very survival is now at stake. This tiny nation has been the target of a fifty-year

---

[1]"The Case Against Arafat: The Campaign By Yasir Arafat and the Palestinian Authority to Destroy Israel," introduction by Ambassador Jeanne Kirkpatrick, published by the Zionist Organization of America, 1992
[2]Ibid.
[3]Ibid.

holy war by the Arab states, which surround and vastly outnumber it. The war against Israel is as much a prelude to the war against the West as the Spanish Civil War was to World War II. Palestinian propaganda and the Western media misrepresent this war as though it pitted an Israeli Goliath against a Palestinian David, or at best as a conflict between two irrational neighbors. But there is no moral equivalence here. The West Bank and Gaza were annexed by Jordan and Egypt fifty years ago with no Arab complaints. Israel has absorbed a million Jewish refugees from Arab lands and the Soviet Union with no complaints. The 3.7 million seething refugees who live in abject poverty on the West Bank, and who have received more than a billion dollars in aid from Israel and the rest of the world, are refugees only because the Arab states have rejected them and kept them in poverty so they can be cannon-fodder for their campaign to push the Jews into the sea. The "Palestinian problem" is entirely a creation of the Arabs themselves, a product of their refusal to live side by side with non-Arabs and infidels they think they can destroy.

The attacks of September 11 signaled the determination of radical Islam to extend to the United States a war it began in 1948, when Hassan al-Banna, the pro-Hitler leader of the Muslim Brotherhood, called on Muslims to push the Jews "into the sea." The war against America was begun with the taking of hostages by the revolutionary government of Iran in 1979, and then with the Iranian-inspired attack by Hezbollah on the American marine barracks in Lebanon in 1983. To defend themselves, Americans must first recognize that war has been declared on their country. To understand the nature of that war, they must also recognize that the defense of Israel is a defense of their own frontier.

3

The Palestinians' True Cause

Holed up in his besieged and battered Ramallah headquarters, Yasser Arafat has called for "millions of martyrs to march to Jerusalem ... this is our destiny ... this is the path I have chosen."[1] With these words, the Palestinian leader announced his real agenda for anyone who did not understand it before. This agenda is manifest in the suicide bombings that target Jewish babies, in the maps that erase the state of Israel, in the rejection of the 1999 peace offering that included 95 percent of their negotiating demands, in the never-abandoned 1964 liberation manifesto that called for the obliteration of Zionist Israel. It is manifest in the models set by their spiritual leaders, the Grand Muftis of Jerusalem—the current one who calls for the destruction of America and the Jews, and the one from the past who, during the Nazi Holocaust, joined Adolf Hitler and planned his own death camp for the Jews of the Middle East. It is clear for all those who want to see. The goal of Arafat and the Palestinian leadership is now, and has always been, the elimination of Jewry from their midst.

The seed of the Palestinians' genocidal mania is rooted in Islam. It began its metastasis more than a hundred years ago, when the first Zionist settlements signaled that an oppressed people, huddled on the fringes of the Turkish empire, was about to assert

---

April 3, 2002, http://www.salon.com/2002/04/04/israel_35/
[1]"Arab Television Channels Interview Arafat," *MEMRI*, March 31, 2002; http://www.ourjerusalem.com/opinion/story/opinion20020402.html

itself. Jews, in fact, had been living continuously in the region of the Jordan for 3,000 years. For 2,000 years they had been a stateless minority, easily and frequently abused. But once the Jews began to assert and defend their presence in a world that regarded them as infidels, they immediately became the targets of an Islamic *jihad*—a permanent holy war whose goal was their destruction. The struggle in the Middle East is not now, and has never been, about land. Israel occupies a minuscule fraction of 1 percent of the Arab Middle East and less than 10 percent of the entire Palestine Mandate—a geographical area, not a political entity and certainly no nation, when the Jews' right to a piece of it was granted. It was just a 10 percent portion of the defeated Turkish empire governed by the British victors after the World War I, who then allotted 90 percent of it to the Arabs.

Present-day Jordan, a nation created by Britain, occupies 80 percent of the original Palestine Mandate. Nearly 70 percent of its inhabitants are still Arabs of the Palestine region, yet Jordan is not the target of a Palestine liberation movement. How is this possible? It is possible because the Hashemites who rule Palestinian Jordan, and are a minority within Jordan, are Muslims and not Jews. The Middle East War is not about land and not about injustice to "Palestinians." It is a religious war—a *jihad*—against the Jews. In 1949, Jordan annexed the West Bank—the center of the alleged current territorial dispute—and held it for eighteen long years, up to the 1967 Arab aggression against Israel. Jordan and the other Arab states lost their war of aggression. The Jewish victors retained control of the West Bank because the Arab states refused to make peace and recognize Israel; and Israel refused to return the land to their declared enemies lest they use it as a staging area for a third war against them. Not once in all the previous eighteen years had there been an audible complaint from the Palestinians or their "liberation" organization or the other Arab states about the injustice done to the Palestinian inhabitants. Not once was there an outcry that Jordan had annexed the Palestinian "nation." That is because there was no such nation. Palestinians considered themselves Arabs and Muslims. "Palestinian" is a remote after-thought inspired by Arabs' ethnic hatred of Jews, and desire to push them into the sea.

Zionist settlers first began arriving in the already existing Jew-ish communities of Palestine in the 1880s. They were hoping to end the persecution, which was a result of their stateless condition and their expulsion two thousand years earlier from their home-land in Judea and Samaria, today known as the West Bank. At the time of the Zionists' arrival, Palestine was a sparsely occupied, barren desert, controlled by the Ottoman Turks as it had been for nearly four hundred years. Not only was there no Palestinian nation, there were hardly any Arabs at all. This is how the Ameri-can writer Mark Twain described what he saw when, in the 1880s, he visited the place that is the site of such bloodshed today: "Of all the lands there are for dismal scenery, I think Palestine must be the prince. The hills are barren ... The valleys are unsightly deserts fringed with a feeble vegetation that has an expression about it of being sorrowful and despondent ... It is a hopeless dreary heartbroken land ... Palestine sits in sackcloth and ashes ... Over it broods the spell of a curse that has withered its fields and fettered its energies ... Nazareth is forlorn ... Jericho ... accursed ... Jerusalem ... a pauper village ... Palestine is desolate ... A silent, mournful expanse. We never saw a human being on the whole route ... Even the olive and the cactus, those fast friends of a worthless soil, had almost deserted the country."[2]

Of this barren land, the Jews were granted three slivers amounting to 10 percent of the whole. More than half of their allotment was the Negev desert; but within a generation the Jews made the slivers bloom. Even today, over a century later, the boundary between Israel and Syria is still referred to as the "green line," symbolizing the difference between the Israeli side, which under the care of the Jews has become fertile ground, and the

---

[2]Mark Twain, "The Innocents Abroad," Chapter LVI, 1869; http://classi-clit.about.com/library/bl-etexts/mtwain/bl-mtwain-innocents-56.htm

Arabs' side, which is still an arid desert. On their portion, the Jews also built the only industrial and democratic nation in the entire Middle East. The industrial productivity and civic tolerance of the Jews, in the state they created, have given birth to an Arab citizenry inside Israel of more than one million people, more prosperous and privileged than the citizens of any Arab country. Unlike their Arab brethren, the Arab citizens of Israel vote in free elections and are themselves elected to the Israeli parliament. Their status provides an eloquent contrast to the intolerant and hate-filled Arab world that surrounds and threatens the Jewish state. As Israeli citizens, Arabs have more rights, privileges and opportunities than the inhabitants of any Arab state or kingdom in the Middle East. At the same time, the so-called Palestinian refugees of the West Bank are barred even from becoming citizens in 21 of the 22 Arab nations, which is why they are still "refugees." This is because the Arabs want them to be miserable and destitute, and available as cannon fodder for their war against Israel. In contrast, the 600,000 Jewish refugees who fled or were expelled from Arab countries after the 1948 war have been fully resettled in Israel, where they are productive citizens who desperately want peace.

What is the crime of the Jews, that they should not have been welcomed into this unpromising desert from the very beginning? What is the crime of the Jews, that their infant state should have been attacked by five Arab armies on the day of its creation? What is the crime of the Jews, that these Arab states should have continued their war for 50 years without a peace in sight? What is the crime of the Jews, that these Arabs should make Jewish women and children the targets of their suicide bombers, and that their leader should call for millions more suicidal "martyrs" to destroy Israel once and for all? Their crime is that they are Jews. Their crime is that they are heathens in the empire of Islam. Islam divides the world into *Dar al-Islam*, the "house of Islam," and *Dar al-Harb*, the "house of war," which is the house of infidels who must convert to Islam or be put to the sword. Perhaps there is a moderate Islamic society that rejects this alternative and has found a way to live peacefully with unbelievers who are its neighbors. But such an Islamic society does not exist as a political force in the Arab and Muslim Middle East today. That is why even three barren slivers were too much to allow the Jews. That is why the creation of a minuscule state in the middle of a desert provoked a genocidal war. Israel is *Dar al-Harb*, while Jordan is *Dar al-Islam*. That is why the annexation of the entire West Bank by the kingdom of Jordan meant nothing to the Palestinian Muslims who inhabited it. That is why peace cannot be made with the Jews. They are infidels who live in the house of war.

Arafat, the Palestinian Authority, Hamas, Hezbollah, Islamic Jihad and the al-Aqsa Martyrs—along with the governments in Saudi Arabia, Iraq, Syria and Iran who support their terror and their genocidal agendas—are the Nazis of the Middle East. There will be no peace until they are defeated or destroyed.

4

The Next Twist of the Knife

During the first Gulf War, Saddam Hussein's most vocal and intense allies were the Palestinians and their terrorist authority. Yet the first postwar act of the Bush Administration was to pressure the Israelis into a "peace process" with people whose only desire was to destroy them. The same scenario seems to be developing now with the so-called "Road Map to Peace." There are two causes of the Arab-Israeli conflict. The first is Arab racism, which rejects any ethnic presence that is not Arab in its neighborhood; the second is Islamic bigotry, which leads to the same rejection. In 1922, the Arabs were awarded 90 percent of the Palestine Mandate—a territory in which no country existed and which had been promised by its British rulers to the Jews. Jews were forbidden to live in this Arab portion of the mandate—a concession by the British to Arab racism. At the same time, because the Jews were a tolerant and democratic people, nearly a million Arabs were assimilated into the tiny portion allotted to the state of Israel in 1948, and were given more rights than Arabs anywhere else in the Middle East. The Arab response to this compromise was a seven-nation military assault on the new Jewish state, which was comprised of recent survivors of the worst genocide in human history. From the outset, then, the Middle East conflict was a war of xenophobic backwardness and ethnic barbarism,

April 13, 2003, http://archive.frontpagemag.com/Printable.aspx?ArtId=18711

waged against a persecuted people who intended no harm to their neighbors and sought only peace.

For the next fifty years, the Arab states waged continuous warfare against the Jews with the intention of driving them into the sea. Even the current "peace movement" conducted by pro-Arab leftists in America is filled with voices calling for the "liberation of Palestine from the river to the sea"—in other words, the elimination of the Jewish state. The Palestinian Authority and its present leadership (including its newly elected, Holocaust-denying premier) is a terrorist entity with openly displayed genocidal intentions. Sixty-three percent of the Palestinians are on record supporting the blowing up of their own children for the purpose of blowing up Jews, especially women and children, and defenseless civilians.[1] Why would anyone think that such people are capable of making a durable peace? Why should the Jews, who were allies of America in its war against Iraq, be called on to make concessions to Saddam's Palestinian allies?

If terror is rewarded by American and British pressure on Israel, why should the Palestinians *not* resort to terror again at the first disappointment of their ambitions? This is how the Oslo peace process failed; it is why any peace process that is not preceded by drastic reforms of the Palestinian Authority, and a renunciation of violence, will also fail. The criticism of the Jews is that they have built settlements in the West Bank. Notice that there is no similar criticism of the Arabs for forbidding Jews to live in the lands that Arabs control. Why are Jewish settlements in the West Bank—the historic homeland of the Jews—a problem for Arabs? Why is it outrageous for Jews to want to live in someone else's country? The answer is that the Arabs are racists who reject any Jewish presence in their own lands. This was the cause of the Middle East conflict in 1948, and it is the cause of the Middle East conflict today.

---

[1]Mitchell G. Bard, "Online Exclusives," http://www.jewishvirtuallibrary.org/jsource/myths/mf24.html

5

Hunt Down the Terrorists

The premise of the Road Map to Peace—imposed on the parties to the Middle East conflict by the United States, Britain, the EU and Russia—is that the conflict cannot be solved by military means. As the terrorist attacks of the last few days should make clear to everyone, the premise is wrong. The Middle East conflict can *only* be solved by military means.

As President Bush said after the bombing in Jerusalem, "It is clear that there are those in the Middle East who hate peace." We know who they are because they have declared themselves: Hamas, Islamic Jihad, Hezbollah and Yasser Arafat's al-Aqsa Martyrs Brigade (and thus the Palestinian Authority). There can be no peace with someone who wants to kill you. The terrorist entities on the Palestinian side of the conflict want exactly that. The Road Map powers have put Israel in an impossible position. No government in the world can fail to respond when its civilians are murdered. The regrettable statement by President Bush, condemning Israel's wholly justified military response to Hamas's military attack, shows that the Road Map powers do not want Israel to protect itself or disarm the terrorists. If that is the case, it is morally incumbent on the Road Map powers to do it themselves. Only that way can real peace negotiations begin.

President Bush needs to assemble a coalition of the willing once again, insert a military force into the West Bank and the Gaza

---

June 12, 2003, http://archive.frontpagemag.com/Printable.aspx?ArtId= 17738

Strip, hunt down the Palestinian terrorists and bring them to justice. The entire reason for the so-called Israeli occupation of the West Bank and Gaza has been to protect Israel's citizens from being murdered by a determined enemy. Israel has failed to accomplish this objective because the rest of the world, and particularly its most important ally, the United States, has prevented it from doing what is necessary—specifically, from demilitarizing these zones of terror. Since the Muslim Middle East (with the exception of Jordan and Egypt) is formally at war with Israel, and has been so for 55 years, this is probably impractical in any case. Israel would have to go to war with Iran, for example, to close down Hezbollah and Hamas. However, what Israel cannot do the United States, Britain, the EU and Russia most certainly can. This is what the War on Terror is about. It is a war to defend the West against radical Islam. It will not be won until the Islamic regimes that support this war, most particularly the regimes in the West Bank, Gaza, Syria and Iran, are changed by any means necessary.

The Palestinian Authority, which despite being a terrorist state is supposed to be a party to the peace process, cannot be changed or reformed from within. It is a corrupt terrorist police state. Any internal challenge to the terrorists who run it will be ruthlessly suppressed. Many Palestinians genuinely interested in peace have been assassinated over the years for that very reason. It is therefore both counterproductive and morally unconscionable for the United States and other powers to equate Israeli responses to Palestinian terror with the terror itself, and pretend that there are two parties interested in peace. Yet that is what the present "peace process" entails. It is an unworkable process. The sooner it is terminated, the better for the sake of humanity and above all for the prospects of peace. The only peace process that will work is one that first disarms and disables the enemies of peace.

6

Censor the Message

Our Freedom Center is currently running a campaign to put an ad in as many college newspapers as possible, pointing out that the War on Terror is seamless, that the Islamic radicals who want to destroy the state of Israel are the same radicals who want to destroy us.[1] This is crucial for understanding the War on Terror because the principal way our enemies seek to divide us and sap our will to resist is by arguing that our policies are a "root cause" of the attacks against us. Many who do not support the terrorists nonetheless accept the argument that the attacks on us are caused by our support for the state of Israel; and that Israel's policies, in turn, are the cause of the attacks against it. This is the argument, for example, made by Pat Buchanan and the paleo-conservatives at *The American Conservative*. It is the principal argument of campus leftists who exploit the distorted version of history that has already been inflicted on students by faculty Islamists and radicals intent on turning them against the war in Iraq—which is also America's war to defend itself against the Islamic *jihad*.

The ad reads as follows:

Israel Is the Canary In the Coal Mine
The war between Arabs and Jews is not the cause of the War on Terror, as apologists for Muslim radicals claim; it *is* the War on Terror.

November 23, 2004, http://archive.frontpagemag.com/Printable.aspx? ArtId=10450
[1]The ad was sponsored by the David Horowitz Freedom Center.

Twenty-five years ago, there were two non-Islamic democracies in the Arab Middle East: Israel and Lebanon. This was too much for Islamic radicals, Syrian irredentists and Palestinians who joined forces to destroy Lebanon and make it a base for terror.

The goal of the post-Oslo *Intifada* is not to establish a Palestinian state alongside a Jewish state. Its goal is an Islamic *ummah* extending "from the Jordan to the sea." That is why Oslo was rejected by Arafat, even though Barak and Clinton offered him an independent state on virtually all of the land Palestinians claimed in the West Bank of the Jordan. That is why the very birth of Israel is referred to by all the present Palestinian leadership as the "Nakba"—the "catastrophe." To Islamic radicals at war with the West, the very creation of Israel is a catastrophe.

American apologists for Arab aggression are also apologists for Islamic aggression. In their eyes, Arab terror in the Middle East has a root cause in the policies of Israel, whom terrorists refer to as the "little Satan." For apologists of the Islamic terror of 9/11 and the Zarqawi terror in Iraq, *jihad* is not a self-generating creed but has a "root cause" in the policies of "the Great Satan," which is us.

Peace in the Middle East and peace in the war with Al-Qaeda and Zarqawi will come only when the terrorists surrender or are defeated.[2]

Thus far our office has been able to place this ad in 15 papers, while four have already rejected it for political reasons. These are the *Daily Californian* (Berkeley), *The Battalion* (Texas A&M), *The Exponent* (Purdue), and *The Maroon* (University of Chicago). None of these papers would provide a reason why the ad was rejected. That is because the real reason is intimidation by pro-terrorist groups on campus. When I spoke to the editor of the Texas A&M *Battalion*, it was apparent to me that she had no quarrel with the text of the ad and no reason for not running it. She kept referring to the "editors'" disapproval, ignoring the fact that she was the

---

[2]David Horowitz, "Help Stop the Anti-Israeli Divestment Campaign," February 10, 2003; http://archive.frontpagemag.com/readArticle.aspx?ARTID=19822

editor-in-chief. When I called Robert Wagner, who is the "General Manager of Student Media" at Texas A&M, he also provided no argument against running the ad; he simply told me that the paper had a right to reject it.

In fact, the paper at Texas A&M shouldn't have such a right. As part of a state institution, the *Battalion* should be subject to the First Amendment, which means that its editorial decisions about whether to run political ads must be viewpoint-neutral. Unfortunately, universities long ago dealt with campus leftists' political censorship by washing their hands of the problem. Papers like the *Battalion*, the *Daily Californian* and most other college papers are quasi-independent of the universities whose names they bear and whose offices they use; so they can escape the protections of the First Amendment. As private institutions, Purdue and the University of Chicago are also exempt.

When asked the reason for the rejection of the ad, the editor of the Chicago *Maroon* said to our staffer it wasn't "appropriate" for her paper. "She said that she won't put her reasons for the rejection in writing as I asked her to do, because we 'know the ad is controversial.' She said she doesn't want to deal with the repercussions of publishing the ad. She said that people come screaming and yelling at her when she publishes anything like this. She said that we don't have to hear them but she does, and that people threaten to stop others from advertising in their paper, and that bottom-line she is not going to run the ad." This is a form of terror, albeit non-violent. In this issue of Frontpagemag.com, we are running another story about a similar campaign of intimidation conducted by Palestinians against College Republicans on the San Francisco State campus. As at Texas A&M, the administration at San Francisco State is in near perfect collusion with the intimidators on their campus. This situation will only change with the active involvement of the public, including the trustees and alumni donors and concerned legislators.

It would be helpful if alumni and other concerned citizens phoned the university administrations to protest this censorship.

These incidents serve to confirm the central message of the Freedom Center: The War on Terror begins at home. Our troops are risking their lives for us in Fallujah. It is time for the rest of us to support them by taking on the forces that support our enemies in the United States.[3]

---

[3]Ten years later this situation remains unchanged, if not worse.

7

The First Terrorist People

The Palestinian Nazi Party has won the elections in Gaza. This party, Hamas, calls for the obliteration of the Jewish state (in so many words) and the killing of Jews because they are Jews (in so many words); it cites the Prophet Muhammad's damnation of the Jews and incitement to murder Jews as its authority for these goals. Hamas is a party of Islamic fanatics whose hero is Osama bin Laden and who have launched a global *jihad* against the United States and the West. With the vote in Gaza, in record numbers, the Palestinian people have joined *en masse* the Axis of Evil.[1] They are the self-declared enemies of Jews, of America and of civilized values, and should be treated as such. The Palestinians have declared with this vote they want no peace. They should be given none.

The defeated Fatah Party—the "moderate" party in the eyes of the official West—is the creation of the terrorist Yasser Arafat. Its charter also calls for the destruction of Israel. Its leadership has been dedicated to terror since helping to found the Palestine Liberation Organization in 1964, itself a creation of the Egyptian dictator Gamal Abdel Nasser and the Soviet KGB. Its leader, Mahmoud Abbas, is a Holocaust denier and was instrumental in the kidnapping and execution of the Israeli Olympic team in Munich in 1972. He has been Arafat's accomplice in terror ever since. The father of

January 26, 2006, http://archive.frontpagemag.com/Printable.aspx?ArtId=5772
[1] So named by President Bush after 9/11, and including Iraq, Iran and North Korea

Palestinian nationalism himself, the Grand Mufti of Jerusalem, Haj Amin al-Husseini, was a fanatical devotee of Adolf Hitler who served the Nazi cause in Berlin during the Second World War and infused Palestinian nationalism with the Jew-hatred that has inspired it ever since.

The Palestinians are the first people in the history of humanity to embrace terror and genocide as a way of life. Palestinian schools train kindergarteners and first graders to aspire to murder innocent Jews by blowing themselves up alongside them, telling these children that if they are fortunate enough to have male genitalia they will go to heaven and be rewarded with 72 virgins to attend their every whim. Palestinian parents murder their own children by telling them to kill Jewish children so that Allah can receive them. This is the sickest culture on the face of the earth, and the fact that it is supported by progressives in Europe and America reveals the moral sickness of those who support the Palestinians in the name of "social justice."

At the core of the Palestinian sickness is a hatred for the West and Israel for the crimes of being successful, democratic, tolerant and non-Muslim. And at the core of *that* sickness is self-hatred— self-hatred for the thousand-year failure of Arab Muslim culture to compete with the West and for the absolute bankruptcy of the Palestinian cause, despite billions in aid contributed by Europe, Israel, and the United States, whose sole purpose was to help a people consumed by their own emotional poisons. A large portion of the aid, of course, was stolen in transit by their corrupt and homicidal leaders, who buried the loot in Swiss bank accounts or used it to buy weapons of mass murder and spread destruction, which is the only contribution that the Arabs of the Palestinian mandate have made to the world since their national aspirations were first announced half a century ago.

8

Gaza: Moment of Truth

Americans need to take a hard look at what is going on in the Middle East, because it provides the clearest picture possible of the war we are in. On one side are Al-Qaeda, Hamas, Hezbollah, Syria and Iran and their allies—Russia, France, Greece, and the UN majority. On the other is the only democracy in the land of Muslim and Arab terror. The origins of this latest front in the War on Terror are crystal clear: the desire of the Muslim terrorists—the elected majority among Palestinian Arabs and the occupying Shi'ite army in Lebanon, backed by Syria and Iran—to destroy Israel and push the Jews into the sea. The war reveals the impossibility of a Palestinian state and the necessity of a civilized occupying force in a region populated by a people who have been brainwashed in an ideology of hate. Their self-government is a crime waiting to happen.

There were 8,500 Jews living in Gaza until recently. They were so creative that, while representing less than 1 percent of the population, they accounted for 10 percent of its gross annual product. Productive and law-abiding as they were, their existence in Gaza required an Israeli army presence to protect them, so uncontrollable is the genocidal hatred of Palestinians for Jews. The Israeli army in Gaza was also necessary to prevent Palestinians from lobbing rockets into Israeli schoolyards across the border. Eventually, the Israeli leadership made a decision to capitulate to Arab Jew-hatred and

Written at the onset of the second Lebanon war, Friday, July 14, 2006; http://archive.frontpagemag.com/Printable.aspx?ArtId=3569

uproot the Jews living in Gaza, also withdrawing the forces that protected Israel from being attacked by Arab criminals. In the months that followed, the Arabs did nothing to improve their new homeland, which they now controlled completely. Instead, they elected genocidal terrorists to govern them. They destroyed the horticulture industry the Jews had created. They lobbed more than eight hundred rockets into Israel. During all this mayhem no word of condemnation for the Gaza aggressors came from the UN, France, Russia or the rest of the Jew-despising, terrorist-appeasing and terrorist-supporting international community. This encouraged the Hamas army command, based in Syria, to authorize a further aggression, a tunnel into Israel and the kidnapping of an Israeli soldier, Gilad Shalit. For good measure, ordinary Palestinians in the West Bank murdered an 18-year-old Jewish hitch-hiker for the crime of being a Jew. Still no condemnation of the Palestinians from France, Russia or at the UN; and this encouraged Iran's terrorist army, Hezbollah, to initiate another aggression, this time from the north.

The goal of the United States and Israel and all freedom-loving, civilized people in this war must be the destruction of the Hamas and Hezbollah leadership, their military infrastructure and capabilities. If there were a UN worthy of the name, it would expel Syria and Iran from its body, and would send a Security Council armed force to the West Bank and Gaza to institute an occupation whose duration should not be less than a generation. During this occupation, the hate schools of the West Bank and Gaza should be reformed so that the children of Palestinian Arabs are taught basic rules of civilized behavior—tolerance instead of hatred, condemnation of suicide bombers instead of reverence for them as martyrs, and such common decencies as regarding monsters like Samir Kuntar—a terrorist who killed a father in front his child and then bashed the child's head in with his rifle. The Palestinian Authority honors Kuntar as a hero and role model for Palestinian children.[1]

---

[1]Yossi Klein Halevi, "Battle Plans," July 13, 2006; http://jewishworldreview.com/0706/halevi_war.php3

The world will not be a safe place until the present regimes in Gaza, the West Bank, Syria and Iran are gone. This is a war all Americans should support.

9

Jihadist *Fellow Travelers*

It is in the nature of Stalinism for its adherents to make a certain kind of lying—and not only to others but first of all to themselves—a fundamental part of their lives. It is always a mistake to assume that Stalinists do not know the truth about the political reality they espouse. If they don't know the truth (or all of it) one day, they know it the next, and it makes absolutely no difference to them politically. For their loyalty is to something other than the truth. And no historical enormity is so great, no personal humiliation or betrayal so extreme, no crime so heinous that it cannot be assimilated into the 'ideals' that govern the Stalinist mind, which is impervious alike to documentary evidence and moral discrimination.

HILTON KRAMER

[NOTE: The "Second Lebanon War" began on July 12, 2006, when guerillas from Hezbollah—Arabic for "Party of God"—crossed into Israel and attacked an Israeli Defense Force patrol, killing three men and capturing two others.]

At the outset of Iran's proxy war to obliterate the state of Israel, the editors of *The Nation*—the oldest and most influential magazine of the American left—published a lead feature condemning Israel as a terrorist state and blaming the

July 18, 2006, http://archive.frontpagemag.com/Printable.aspx?ArtId=3524

war on Israel's "oppressive occupation" of Arab lands. Written by a Palestinian Arab, Marwan Bishara, the article—"Israel on the Offensive"—claimed that Israel had "exploited" the kidnapping of its soldiers as a pretext for an aggressive war against Hamas and the "besieged" territories.[1] "The nature of the Israeli offensive is to punish, overwhelm and deter with disproportionate force, regardless of the suffering ..." To end this violence, according to this writer and his editors, Israel should cease its "aggression" and pursue negotiations with the forces that want to wipe it from the face of the earth.

Assuming that negotiations would lead to a prisoner exchange and the freeing of Israel's kidnapped soldiers, what exactly would this mean? Israel's kidnapped soldiers were behind internationally recognized borders protecting their own citizens from external attack. To secure the return of its soldiers, *The Nation* is suggesting Israel should release fifteen hundred Arab terrorists with blood already on their hands and murder in their hearts. Past exchanges have shown that released Hamas and PLO prisoners quickly rejoin their terrorist armies and spill more Israeli blood. This is not a "prisoner exchange." It is a proposal to replenish an army of religious fanatics sworn to genocide. And of course, in the eyes of *The Nation*, it is Israel—not Syria, not Iran, not radical Islam—that is responsible for the terrorists. "Whether we like it or not, Hamas, like Hezbollah, is mostly a by-product of an oppressive occupation."[2]

Although *The Nation* is not so bold as to call openly for the obliteration of Israel or the killing of Jews, it has made itself the mouthpiece for Islamic Nazis who do. Apologetics for fanatical Islamists has become *The Nation's raison d'être*. According to *The Nation*, if there are culprits in the War on Terror, they are America and Israel. Every argument *The Nation* advances is a slightly

---

[1] Marwan Bishara, "Israel on the Offensive," *The Nation*, July 5, 2006; http://www.thenation.com/article/israel-offensive
[2] Ibid.

modified and more civilized version of the terrorists' argument for themselves. *The Nation* is thus a fellow traveler of the new Nazism, just as surely as it was a fellow traveler of the old Stalinism. It cannot go all the way in supporting the Muslim *jihad*, but it will use all its political capital and literary skill to make the *jihad* seem as admirable as possible, and the *jihadists'* victims as deserving of their fates.

According to *The Nation* and, be it said, much of the American left, it is Israel's "occupation" that is the original sin in the Middle East conflict. Not coincidentally, this is exactly the argument the fellow-traveling left also uses to attack America's war against the terrorists in Iraq. It is America's "occupation" that needs to be ended, not the terrorists' presence. It is American imperialism that has created the Iraqi "resistance," whose terrorists, as it happens, are also orchestrated and armed by the Nazi regimes in Syria and Iran.

In point of fact, there is no Israeli occupation of Lebanon or Gaza that might have precipitated this war. Quite the contrary; it is the *lack* of an Israeli occupation of Lebanon and Gaza—of a controlling authority to enforce the peace—that has led to the present war. Israel's withdrawals from Lebanon and Gaza created the vacuum the terrorists have filled. These withdrawals, on the other hand, were successful in one sense alone: they were designed to disarm the arguments of the terrorists and their apologists, whose propaganda has now been unmasked as a cynical sham. But *The Nation* goes on repeating its lies all the same. There is no occupation of Lebanon for Hezbollah to protest. There is no occupation of Gaza for Hamas to protest. So why are they at war? The occupation that inspires their terror is the Jews' occupation of the state of Israel. *This* is what Hezbollah and Hamas cannot abide.

The Nation's current apologetics for the terrorist bloc continue a nearly one-hundred-year-old tradition of its editors' support for the totalitarian enemies of America and the West. For nearly a century, *The Nation's* editors "explained" and justified every Communist tyrant from Stalin to Castro. When terrorists slaughtered the innocent on 9/11, *The Nation*'s editors decried *American* jingoism and *America's* "empire." They opposed the overthrow of Saddam Hussein; they continue to attack the liberation of Iraq as an imperialist "occupation" and democratic America as a "terrorist state." But even in the context of this sordid record, *The Nation*'s present support for the agents of a new Holocaust marks a new moral low. Its role in this war, as in the war in Iraq, is too transparent to be defended. Its editors may not openly embrace the goal of eliminating the Jewish presence in the Middle East, and possibly can't even admit to themselves that this is the radicals' goal. But *The Nation*'s editors are nonetheless dedicated to justifying the *jihadists* who are pursuing this goal, and for that they cannot be forgiven.

10

Lebanon Is Not Innocent

In war, innocents pay a heavy price. There is no way to fight a war without collateral damage to civilians, unless the opposing armies agree to meet in a desert and let the superior force prevail. Such damage certainly cannot be avoided when the aggressor is a terrorist army that deliberately places its headquarters, its weapons depots, its missile launchers and its staging bases in the middle of large urban centers like Beirut, or in the small villages abutting the border of its victims.

Sometimes the death of innocents comes not from collateral damage but from the deliberate targeting of civilians—as is almost invariably the case with terrorist armies like Hezbollah and Hamas. In World War II, wherever the Wehrmacht went, Jews were rounded up for the slaughter. Guernica and Lidice are names of innocent towns with no military value that were deliberately destroyed by the fascists. Sometimes innocents are targeted by civilized armies for strategic reasons. The allied bombings of Dresden, Tokyo, Hiroshima and Nagasaki incinerated hundreds of thousands of civilians to break the morale of the enemy and end the war sooner, with the intention of saving millions of lives.

Critics of Israel's defensive war against Islamic terrorists are busily wringing their hands over the destruction that has been wrought on Lebanon, which they portray as innocent. They invoke these tragedies while calling on Israel to cease its fire and

---

July 24, 2006, http://archive.frontpagemag.com/Printable.aspx?ArtId= 3449

leave the Hezbollah aggressors intact to wage aggression another day. Since Israel had no role in starting this war, this is similar to blaming the Allies for the damage inflicted on Germany in World War II—and doing so while the war is in progress. Critics who make such demands in the midst of a war are aiding and abetting the aggressors.

But the very idea that Lebanon is an innocent bystander in the war against Israel is false. Lebanon is host to the terrorist aggressor, which has sworn to eliminate Israel and its Jews from the face of the earth. This is the explicit creed of both Hezbollah and its sponsor Iran—and not just in their charter or in statements made months or years ago. Iran's dictator reiterated the threat even yesterday: "Israel has pushed the button of its own destruction. The Zionists made their worst decision and triggered their extinction by attacking Lebanon."[1] *Extinction*—it's not as though this little Hitler conceals his ambitions.

Hezbollah is part of the Lebanese government, occupying two cabinet positions and seats in its parliament. This same government had previously agreed to enforce UN Resolution 1559, which calls on it to disarm all militias on its territory, most prominently Hezbollah. If the Lebanese government had met this obligation, there would be no war, and there would be no Lebanese civilian casualties. Instead the government allowed Hezbollah to build its headquarters and underground bunkers in populated neighborhoods of Beirut. It allowed Hezbollah to import 13,000 missiles from Syria and Iran and fire them into Israel's cities and towns. The 75,000-man Lebanese army has not sealed off the Syrian border and, according to reports, has allowed Syria to re-supply Hezbollah in the midst of its aggression. The Lebanese government allowed Hezbollah to build underground fortresses on its southern border from which it launched its aggression. It allowed

---

[1] Ezra HaLevi, "Iran's Ahmadinejad: Israel's Destruction at Hand," *Israel National News*, April 23, 2006; http://www.israelnationalnews.com/News/News.aspx/108152

Hezbollah to launch rockets into the towns of northern Israel to terrorize and kill innocent civilians. Israel has done nothing to provoke this attack from Lebanese territory. But in the midst of Hezbollah's aggression against Israel, Lebanon's prime minister has joined the attackers in blaming Israel for Lebanon's misery instead of its source.

It will be objected that Lebanon is helpless; that its democracy was destroyed and its territory conquered by the PLO, Hezbollah, Syria and Iran. It will be said that the Lebanese cannot resist the superior force of Hezbollah's "state within a state." But this is an argument made in bad faith. No one is helpless. When France was occupied by Germany during World War II, General de Gaulle organized the "free French" into a fighting force. The so-called "Cedar Revolution" showed that there are ways of manifesting opposition and resistance to occupiers. Even though it failed, it showed that resistance is possible. If there is resistance to Islamic terror in Lebanon today, it is as invisible as the moderates in Islam. The Lebanese army has not lifted a finger to obstruct Hezbollah's aggression, but the Lebanese prime minister has been forthright in attacking Israel. Who, watching Lebanese interviewed by reporters during the war—including the Lebanese-Americans evacuated to safety—can doubt that their hatred is for Jews and not for the Islamic killers of both the Jews and the Lebanese?

These attitudes do not make the Lebanese deserving of the war that Hezbollah and Iran have inflicted on them; but they do not make them innocent either. Hezbollah's Shi'ite fanatics are Lebanese. Over the last twenty years, Hezbollah has become an integral part of Lebanese society and Lebanon's government. All the while, Hezbollah has sworn to eliminate Israel from the face of the earth. If war has overtaken Lebanon, no one can pretend that the Lebanese didn't see it coming.

The last stand of Western imperialism is the patronizing attitude displayed by Western radicals and liberals toward Third World Muslims and Arabs. If Americans taught their children to murder Muslims as a quick pass to heaven, the left would regard this as a crime against humanity. But if Palestinians are the perpetrators of such crimes and Jews are the targets, it's a different story. In this case, terror is the only means (and therefore the understandable means) of a "desperate" people. Of course, Jews who have been told by Iran and Hezbollah that their extinction is imminent cannot be desperate.

Hezbollah's evil leader, Hassan Nasrallah, is not a victim, let alone a helpless one; nor is he stupid, or unaware of what he is doing. He knows just what his agenda is. "There is no solution to the conflict in this region except with the disappearance of Israel," he told a crowd of idolators. "I promise Israel that it will see more suicide attacks, for we will write our history with blood."[2] His supporters responded in a chorus with chants of "Death to Israel, death to America." Counseling the Israelis to lay down their arms in the face of these threats, and to negotiate with a movement that seeks their destruction, is practical support for the malignant agendas of Hassan Nasrallah and his crew. Making excuses for the Lebanese appeasement of these agendas, while directing moral outrage against the intended victims, repeats a familiar pattern among leftist critics of America and Israel. In leveling their criticism of the wars in Lebanon, Gaza and Iraq, these leftists attribute civilian casualties not to the terrorists but to their opponents; liberation and self-defense are denounced as "occupation." This is not even moral equivalence; it is sympathy for the devil.

Until the arrival of Arafat and the Palestinian terrorists, Lebanon was a Christian democracy. But Islamic radicalism could not tolerate either Christianity or democracy. This—not the presence of tiny Israel, a hundred times smaller than its current antagonists—is the root cause of the violence in the Middle East. The cause is Arab intolerance and Islamic hate. One Jewish state among twenty-two Arab states was one too many. Six million Jews

---

[2]From a December 31, 1999 speech at a Hezbollah rally in Beirut (reprinted in The Associated Press); http://israelipalestinian.procon. org/view.answers.php?questionID=410&print=true

among 300 million Arabs was too much to bear. A sliver of land amounting to less than 1 percent of the Arab land mass, which belonged first to the Ottoman Turks and then to Europeans, was an imperialist outrage. Lebanon, a country raped by the Syrian-Iranian axis and the Palestinian terrorists, has become an integral component of the plan to push the Jews into the sea. The destruction of Lebanon is a tragedy of the 58-year-long Arab-Muslim war against Israel, against democracy, and against Christianity in the Middle East. But the Lebanese today are no longer innocent.

11

Death Cult

That American progressives should have aligned themselves with the terrorists in Gaza comes as no surprise and is hardly interesting. American progressives have aligned themselves with totalitarian movements since 1917 and, indeed, since 1789. It is what they do and who they are. What is interesting are the pathetic excuses they make for 21st-century Nazis. In the December 28 issue of *The Nation*, Chris Hedges defends Jimmy Carter's latest effort to throw the Jews to the lions. In the course of feeding the anti-Jewish frenzy of the Islamic crusaders, Hedges explains the fratricidal conflict between Palestinian factions in Gaza. For those not paying attention, a highlight of this mayhem was the assassination of three Palestinian children, aged 3 to 9, who were on their way to school. The deed was done to punish their father for belonging to the wrong Palestinian terrorist group. Approximately five hundred Palestinians have been killed by other Palestinians in this feud. Hedges's explanation for this nightmare is drawn from the fertile brain of an Israeli leftist: "[The Palestinians in Gaza] are behaving as expected at the end of the extended experiment called 'what happens when you imprison 1.3 million human beings in an enclosed space like battery hens.'"

This is pretty pat. For forty years since Israel liberated Gaza from Egyptian rule, Arabs have complained about the "occupation" of their "homeland." This is one of the innumerable Arab

January 1, 2007, http://archive.frontpagemag.com/Printable.aspx?ArtId=826

lies that underpin their unworthy cause. The reason for the Israeli occupation was, first, that Gaza was a hostile corridor across which Israel was invaded three times; second, that the Arabs have been in a state of declared war against Israel since 1948; and third, that there were 7,000 Jews living in Gaza who, unlike the Arabs living in Israel, would be slaughtered if there were not Israeli troops there to protect them. Hedges and his friends, of course, reflexively overlook the genocidal ambitions of the Palestinians. In 2005, the Israelis left Gaza and evacuated the Jews—by the way, Gaza's most productive and law-abiding citizens—since Palestinians complained at the time that the occupation was the obstacle to peace. But now that it is liberated, Gaza is—a prison! This is the excuse for continuing the war against the Jews. It is also the explanation for the Palestinians' crimes against themselves. The entire Middle East will be a prison until Hamas and *The Nation*'s progressives have their way and Israel is wiped off the map.

This is only the beginning of the progressive explanation for the Palestinian assassinations of three-year-olds. In the progressive world-view, Palestinians have the brains of chickens. When cooped up by Israelis, they kill each other. Gaza is a lot bigger than the Warsaw Ghetto, where—unlike the Arabs of Gaza—five hundred thousand Jews were actually imprisoned. Yet no Jews went around killing three- to nine-year-olds. Anne Frank and her family were actually penned up like battery hens. It didn't make them assassins. Of course they didn't have a religion like Islam in which assassins—the word itself is Islam-derived—are regarded as saints. There are more than a million Arabs living in Israel— roughly the number of Arabs living in Gaza. By *The Nation*'s standards, you could say they were penned up like battery hens. Yet they don't go around killing each other. The reason is that, in Israel, they are free—as they would not be in any Arab state. And, unlike the Arabs in Hamas-run Gaza, they are not followers of a state-sponsored death cult, which teaches them to kill for Allah and especially to kill Jews. This death cult is the problem in the

Middle East, the source of the continuing conflict and the reason Palestinian factions are killing each other.

The death cult calls on its followers—the same religious fanatics that progressives have embraced—to kill and be killed for God. Here is a frenzied utterance of the late and unlamented head of Hamas, Abdel Aziz al-Rantissi, whose murderous career was mercifully terminated by Israeli forces: "We realize that Bush is the enemy of God, the enemy of Islam and Muslims. America declared war on God. Sharon declared war on God and God declared war on America, Bush and Sharon."[1] But Bush and Sharon are only the beginning. If you are in the army of God, then those who oppose you, even co-religionists, are not. During the current mayhem in Gaza, followers of Mahmoud Abbas and Fatah fired on a Hamas rally in the West Bank. This was the response, as reported by ABC: "'What a war Mahmoud Abbas you are launching, first against God, and then against Hamas,' senior Hamas leader Khalil al-Hayya told a Gaza City rally of 100,000 Hamas supporters, who fired their guns in the air and chanted 'God is Greatest.'"[2] In other words, the sickness that has consumed the Palestinians of Gaza and the West Bank is self-generated, an emanation of the death cult they have been nurturing for decades. On the other hand, if you're a progressive, blame it on the Jews. After all, that is how your genocidal friends would explain it themselves.

---

[1]"New Hamas leader: Bush is 'enemy of Muslims'," *CNN.com*, May 6, 2004; http://www.cnn.com/2004/WORLD/meast/03/28/mideast.conflict/index.html

[2]"Hamas Says Abbas Wants War," *Al Jazeera*, December 16, 2006; http://www.aljazeera.com/news/middleeast/2006/12/200852513125577 928.html

It's Munich in Annapolis

The American Secretary of State should be in Baghdad, brokering a reconciliation between Iraqi factions and locking down a victory for which nearly 4,000 Americans gave their lives. Iraq is the central front in the holy war against the West being waged by Al-Qaeda and the Islamic Republic of Iran; an American defeat in Iraq would lead to an escalation of that war to proportions that would make the current conflict seem tame by comparison.

Instead, Condoleezza Rice has been shuttling between capitals in the Middle East in an attempt to feed a piece of Jewish meat to the jackals on the West Bank, hoping that bribery and concessions will turn them into doves, and they will be willing to live side-by-side with a non-Islamic state, which is run by pigs and monkeys, whom their prophet has damned. This will not happen. The Palestinians do not want to live alongside a Jewish state in the Muslim Middle East; they want to destroy it. The Munich that Bush and Rice have prepared for Israel in Annapolis will fail because the Palestinians are terrorists whose only path is violence and whose unwavering goal is genocide. Seventy percent of Palestinians support suicide bombing and seventy percent support Hamas. The other thirty support the Islamo-Fascists of Fatah and their terrorist

November 26, 2007, http://archive.frontpagemag.com/Printable.aspx?
ArtId=28992; http://en.wikipedia.org/wiki/Annapolis_Conference

armies: the al-Aqsa Martyrs Brigade, the Popular Front for the Liberation of Palestine and Palestine Islamic Jihad.[1]

It's indicative of the bad faith of the architects of the Annapolis peace conference that they have persuaded Syria, the unindicted co-conspirator of the Axis of Evil, the destroyer of Christian and democratic Lebanon, the refuge for Saddam's bloodthirsty lieutenants, to come to the table and parley for a return of the Golan Heights so that they can begin shelling Israeli farmers again. The Annapolis Munich is a betrayal of Israel, but it is also a betrayal of America and its troops in the field as well. The armory of the terrorists in Iraq is Iran; the force behind Hezbollah and Hamas in the Middle East is Iran. The Palestinians are not the cause of the Islamic crusade against the West; they are an integral part of it. Giving them a piece of Israel in East Jerusalem will not satisfy their hunger for conquest. It will only whet their appetite for more.

---

[1]Mitchell G. Bard, "Online Exclusives," http://www.jewishvirtualli-brary.org/jsource/myths/mf24.html

13

The War Against the Jews

The unspoken truth about the fighting in Gaza—which began on December 19, 2008, when Hamas rockets broke a voluntary truce—is that this is the frontline of a much larger war that began 30 years ago with the Islamic Revolution in Iran and is now global in scope. Its agenda is the extermination of the Jews and the destruction of the West. The Islamic terrorist party Hamas makes no secret of this agenda. Its Egyptian founders and Palestinian inspirers were active followers of Adolf Hitler and enthusiasts of the Nazi Holocaust.[1] The founding charter of Hamas promises that "Islam will obliterate Israel," and memorializes the Egyptian admirer of Hitler, Hassan al-Banna, as "the martyr ... of blessed memory." The same document contains the genocidal incitement of the Prophet Muhammad to kill the Jews, to hunt them down "until they hide behind the rocks and the trees, and the rocks and trees cry out 'O Muslim, there is a Jew hiding behind me, come and kill him.'"[2]

In 2006, these Islamic Nazis took possession of the Gaza Strip, which is now *Judenrein*. Hamas has turned Gaza into a terrorist fortress, launching rockets into Israeli schoolyards, hospitals, and townships—and launching them from Palestinian neighborhoods to ensure that the maximum number of civilians on its own side

---

January 9, 2009, http://archive.frontpagemag.com/Printable.aspx?ArtId= 33658
[1] Hamas was created by the Muslim Brotherhood.
[2] "Selected Documents Regarding Palestine," http://www.thejerusalem-fund.org/www.thejerusalemfund.org/carryover/documents/charter.html

will be killed in any retaliation and become a further grievance for the cause. The terrorists will win the Armageddon they are planning, they boast, because "the Jews love life and we love death."[3]

All around the world, across Europe and throughout the United States, Muslim and secular radicals are rallying to this Nazi cause, supporting Hamas, attacking Israel and the Jews. The unholy alliance formed by Muslim fanatics and socialist radicals is the face of the terrorist future in the West. It is a coalition between the Islamic Nazis and Western progressives, for whom no party is so evil that it does not deserve aid and comfort if its enemies are Israel and the United States. The wars in the Middle East are the frontline of the offensive—a sixty-year aggression of Muslim Arabs against Israel, rationalized at each turn by epic lies that resonate with Western radicals: that the Arab aggressors are the victims; that the Jews stole Arab land; that there is a Palestinian entity desiring peace with the state of Israel. There is none. There is not even a single Palestinian leader who supports the existence of a Jewish state.

The Palestinians are the only people in history who in their majority support a national death cult, who worship the murderers of little children, including their own, and who proclaim the murderers saints and "martyrs." Their allies in the West are either stupendously ignorant or morally blind. Here is the self-revealing declaration of the associate director of Middle Eastern Studies at the University of Wisconsin: "The state terror unleashed from the skies and on the ground against the Gaza Strip as we speak has nothing to do with Hamas. It has nothing to do with 'Terror.' It has

---

[3]Said in different ways by Hamas leader Ismail Haniya to an interviewer in 2008: "The Jews love life more than any other people, and they prefer not to die;" Spengler, "Dolphinplasty as a Principle of Governance," *Asia Times*, May 19, 2009; http://www.atimes.com/atimes/Middle_East/KE19Ako1.html; and by Hezbollah leader Hassan Nasrallah to an interviewer in 2004: "We have discovered how to hit the Jews where they are most vulnerable. The Jews love life, so that is what we shall take from them. We will win because the Jews love life, and we love death;" Aryeh Tepper, "We Love Death," *Jewish Ideas Daily*, April 6, 2011

nothing to do with the long-term 'security' of the Jewish State.... Strip away the clichés and the vacuous newspeak blaring out across the servile media and its pathetic corps of voluntary state servants in the Western world, and what you will find is the naked desire for hegemony; for power over the weak and dominion over the world's wealth. Worse yet, you will find that the selfishness, the hatred and indifference, the racism and bigotry, the egotism and hedonism ... the callousness with which we indulge in them all are endemic to our very culture; thriving here like flies on a corpse."[4] In other words, what it has to do with is the evil Jews and their evil American allies.

The author of this repulsive treason, Wisconsin professor Jennifer Loewenstein, is herself a Jew, obviously of the self-hating kind. Hers is a sordid lineage, going back to the "capos" who shoveled fellow Jews into the Nazi ovens and collaborated with their executioners. Like many of her political comrades in the secular and religious left, she has joined the forces of Islamic barbarism that are ranged against the civilized peoples of America and Israel. And she is only one of many. In the midst of the global war that radical Islam has declared on the West, the conflict in Gaza has revealed again the presence of a fifth column in our midst, so detached from its own communities and civilized values that it now constitutes a clear and present danger.

---

[4]Jennifer Loewenstein, "If Hamas Did Not Exist," *CounterPunch*, January 1, 2009; http://www.counterpunch.org/2009/01/01/if-hamas-did-not-exist/

The Campus War Against the Jews

The Campus War Against the Jews

Opposing the Campus War Against Israel

The radical Islamic state of Iran is leading a global movement for a second Holocaust—the elimination of Israel from the face of the earth. The Islamic terrorist organizations Hezbollah and Hamas are calling on Muslims to destroy the Jewish state and kill the Jews, in those exact words. And on campuses across the United States, radical professors and student groups are lining up to support the genocide.

The day Israeli troops left Gaza—a territory that has been used as a launching pad for three aggressive wars against the Jewish state—Hamas terrorists began rocket attacks on Israel, which were only halted by an Israeli counterattack three years later, in December 2008. As Israel was defending itself from the Hamas attacks, University of California sociology professor William Robinson assembled pictures of Nazis persecuting Jews—pictures that university administrators described as "lurid"—and emailed them to all the students in his course on globalization. Included with them was a diatribe about how the Israeli soldiers fighting Hamas terrorists were no different from fascist troops in World War II, destroying the city of Warsaw.

Announcement of "Stop the War Against Israel Week," October 9, 2009; http://frontpagemag.com/2009/david-horowitz/stop-the-campus-war-against-israel-and-the-jews-by-david-horowitz/

Robinson's propaganda message had no educational context, was unrelated to the subject of the course, and allowed for no alternative viewpoints. It had nothing to do with education. It was purely an act of aggression, part of an intensifying war against the Jews that has broken out on many fronts across American higher education. Here are other examples:

- A University of Rochester sit-in during Israel's defensive war in Gaza intimidated school administrators into backing a demand for the university to divest from companies doing business with "the Israeli war machine."
- During Israel's war to defend itself from 7,000 unprovoked rocket attacks launched at civilian targets from the Hamas-run Gaza strip, "teach-ins" were held on campuses across the country, alleging that Israel is a Nazi apartheid state and that the Hamas terrorists are freedom-fighters.
- An event at UCLA's Center for Near Eastern Studies encouraged the audience in a "Zionism is Nazism" chant and portrayed the genocidal terrorists of Hamas as peace-seeking, unjustly provoked victims.
- At the University of California Irvine graduation ceremonies, members of the Muslim Student Union wore green stoles mimicking those of suicide bombers, with the Arabic word *shahada* ("martyr") printed on them.

This campus war against Israel and the Jews, with its ominous overtones of the 1930s, has the further agenda of stigmatizing America and the West for not joining the anti-Israel *jihad*. It is a campaign that has been building for several years. At one level, it is a war of symbols. Campuses are adorned with banners in which the Star of David is joined to the swastika by an equal sign; student governments and academic senates push measures for disinvestment from Israeli ventures, based on the libel that Israel—the only democratic and tolerant state in the Middle East—is morally equivalent to the racist apartheid regime of South Africa. In a cynical reversal of the Biblical story, the genocidal Islamic world is cast as David and tiny, outnumbered Israel becomes Goliath.

The campaign increasingly threatens real, as opposed to merely rhetorical, violence. Pro-*jihad* groups such as the Muslim Students Association, an organization that supports Hamas and is an arm of the Muslim Brotherhood, now has hundreds of campus chapters and regularly sponsors Islamic prophets of hate. These activists have dropped the pretense that it is only Israel, not Jews, that they have targeted. In demonstrations at UCLA, members of the Muslim Students Association showed that they make no such distinction as they chanted "Death to Israel!" in almost the same breath as "Death to the Jews!"[1] At a pro-Palestinian demonstration at UC Irvine, members of the Muslim Student Union threatened Jewish students with violence and chased them off campus.[2]

The campus alliance between Muslim supporters of the Islamic *jihad* and secular radicals has been winning these battles. In large part, this is because of the support they receive from faculty members who use their classrooms to reinforce the virulent anti-Israel and anti-American messages of the *jihad.* They are abetted by administrators who otherwise rigorously punish even the suspicion of hate speech; they are so cowed by the campus left that they refuse to apply similar standards to the Jew-haters on their faculties and among their campus organizations. But the real problem is that this campus war has been going on for so long now, and has been so one-sided, that it has created a culture of stigma for Israel and the Jewish students who support Israel, or who criticize the genocidal ambitions of Hamas and other Islamo-Fascist groups involved in the Palestinian cause.

During the week of October 12–16, 2009 the David Horowitz Freedom Center is organizing a nationwide protest whose theme

---

[1] "UCLA's Fight Against the War on Terror," Bruin Alumni Association, Chapter 2; http://www.bruinalumni.com/articles/waronterror2.html
[2] "Creating Hate at UC Irvine," *StandWithUs,* http://www.standwithus. com/app/iNews/view_n.asp?ID=1033

will be "Stop the Campus War Against Israel and the Jews." We intend to attack the culture of stigma that has placed a target on the back of every Jew attending a college—to support students who are standing up to the hate and fighting back. We will do this in several ways:

- In a series of pamphlets and flash videos, we will document the fact that the all-out, totalitarian attack on Israel is in fact motivated by Jew-hatred. These publications will show the full range of the left's anti-Semitic assault—in classrooms, in administrative decisions, and especially in the abusive arena of campus politics.

- We will report on the bigotry Jewish students experience as part of their every day academic and social lives. A series of first-person accounts that will dramatize the crushing way in which the virulence of the hatred against Israel affects individuals, especially when they speak up, in or out of class, with an opposing view.

- We will establish alliances with Jewish student groups under attack, and with Christian groups defending Israel. We will also reach out to Scholars for Peace in the Middle East, an embattled faculty organization that attempts to promote an even-handed discussion of Israel and Palestine on campus, and increase their visibility and influence. We will do the same with individuals such as Professor Alan Dershowitz, who has waged an often lonely struggle against the university "divestment" movement, one of the left's most potent weapons in its offensive against Israel.

The centerpiece of the Freedom Center's campaign to "Stop the Campus War Against Israel and the Jews" will be a week-long series of demonstrations. Based on the Center's successful "Islamo-Fascism Awareness Weeks," these teach-ins will feature films, lectures, and panel discussions with figures such as Nonie Darwish, Yossi Olmert, Robert Spencer, Daniel Pipes, and myself. By revealing the irrational hatred of the left's attack on Israel, by documenting its anti-Semitic overtones and its support for terrorist groups, this week of demonstrations will win space for an honest discussion of Israel and the Middle East conflict, and will expose the objectives of the campus left.

2

Genocidal Acts at UC San Diego

The last time I visited this campus was forty years ago. At that time, I came to have lunch with Professor Herbert Marcuse, a malicious Marxist who had made a reputation for himself and become a hero to the left by advancing the proposition that if you can claim to speak on behalf of the oppressed, you have the right and the obligation to silence people who disagree with you.[1] This, of course, is the creed of every run-of-the-mill dictator, and it is the creed of the progressive left today. It is appropriate, and not coincidental, that I arrive here during "Israeli Apartheid Week" or, as I prefer to refer to it, "Hitler Youth Week."

I use that reference because what is going on here is part of a globally organized movement centered in the Arab Muslim Middle East to finish the job that Hitler started. Unlike the Nazis, who hid their "final solution" from ordinary Germans and the world at large, Muslim radicals shout it from the rooftops, put it in their organizational charters and get applauded for doing so by millions of Muslims who want to see it happen. And the left contributes to the effort by conducting auxiliary campaigns to help the genocide along.

Israel's birthday is coming up this month, along with Israeli Apartheid Week, and these leftists will commemorate it as the

---

This speech was delivered at the University of California, San Diego on May 10, 2010 and has been edited for publication, May 28, 2010; http://frontpagemag.com/2010/david-horowitz/the-war-against-the-jews-at-uc-san-diego-2/
[1] This is my parsing of Marcuse's concept of "repressive tolerance."

"Nakba," which is Arabic for "catastrophe"—the name they have given to the creation of the world's only Jewish state. These Nakba celebrations represent genocidal intentions, since they seek the obliteration of a people's homeland. They are supported by this California public university, which otherwise prides itself on its diversity and respect for others. Jews are apparently excepted. The "Israeli Apartheid Wall," which is the centerpiece of the events this week at the University of California San Diego, was created with the help of $8,500 in student funds. Another $32,000 in student funds went to the sponsoring organization, the Muslim Student Association, for the anti-Israel speakers it brought in. The hate week is supported by several university departments, including Ethnic Studies, Visual Arts and Literature, and by a division of the university, Thurgood Marshall College, which happens to be named for a civil-rights activist.

It is fitting that one of the featured speakers should be Angela Davis, a protégée of Marcuse, an academic icon and a lifelong Communist who has devoted herself to furthering the agendas of the most oppressive, blood-soaked movement in recorded history. For her services, Davis received a Lenin Prize from the East German police state, the most wretched and ruthless of all the Soviet satellite regimes. Davis is also notable for having bought an arsenal of weapons for a young Black Panther who attempted to hold a judge and his courtroom hostage; the Panther blew off the judge's head and got himself killed in the process. Davis comes to this event as the leader of a twenty-year campaign to end what she calls the "Prison-Industrial Complex" and free America's "political prisoners," whom she defines as any incarcerated person with a darker skin tone. Her movement is actually doubly racist; first, because it singles out black and Hispanic criminals for "liberation;" and second, because 95 percent of their crimes are committed against black and Hispanic people. Angela Davis bears the title "University Professor" at this state-wide institution, which means that she makes a six-figure income, is provided with a personal staff and is honored in a way that only a handful of university faculty are. A revered figure among the academic left, she makes scores of appearances every academic year, receiving $10,000 honoraria to spread her hatred of white people, of Jews, and of America to college audiences.

Ecclesiastes famously said, "There is nothing new under the sun," and the older I get, the more impressed I am by this observation. My parents were card-carrying members of the American Communist Party, which meant that they were pawns, witting and unwitting, of the Soviet empire. They called themselves progressives and believed they had joined a movement to bring social justice to all mankind. In 1956, the leader of world Communism gave a secret speech about the crimes that Stalin had committed in the name of social justice, which included the murders of millions of people, including millions of Communists. Nikita Khrushchev decided to give the speech because the post-Stalin leaders of the Soviet Union were afraid a new Stalin would emerge and slaughter them, too. Like today's leftists, my parents hated the anti-Communists of the political right and called them liars when they confronted progressives with the crimes their hero had committed. The anti-Communists claimed that Stalin had killed ten million people. When the archives were opened and the truth was revealed, the correct figure was shown to be four times that number. That's an interesting fact in itself: the right understates the truth, while the left, in the name of "social justice," overstates the lie.

When Khrushchev's speech appeared on the front page of *The New York Times*, its impact was devastating to the progressive cause to which my parents had devoted themselves. Progressives were demoralized and unable to regroup. So their children—my generation—launched a new left. We fatuously believed that there could actually be a *new* left, untainted by the crimes of the old and unlikely to repeat them. But our understanding of the world and our agenda for the future—"social justice" (meaning equality enforced by government)—were fundamentally the same. The American founders did understand, and therefore asserted, that politically enforced equality would mean the end of liberty and individual freedom. This was a wisdom we ignored as our new left quickly revealed that it was no different from the old—embracing Communists in Vietnam and Central America and eventually Islamic totalitarians in Gaza and the Middle East.

About the time I was having lunch with Herbert Marcuse, I was also raising a considerable sum of money for the Black Panther Party in order to buy a church in East Oakland to house a Panther school. I was then the editor of *Ramparts*, the largest magazine of the left, and had recruited our bookkeeper, Betty Van Patter, to maintain the school's financial records, because I believed our own propaganda that a "racist" federal government would shut down the school if the Panthers failed to keep their books properly. In December 1974, Betty Van Patter disappeared, and by the time the police fished her body out of San Francisco Bay, I knew the Panthers had killed her. I further knew that every progressive friend I had was a potential threat to me and my four children, because if I said what I thought, members of that community would denounce me as a CIA agent and a racist, and I couldn't be sure of what consequences might ensue.

So, for me, Israeli Apartheid Week—where secular progressives join hands with theocratic fascists and disregard the realities in front of their eyes—is a case of *déjà vu* all over again. On this campus, we are witnessing a "protest" in support of a movement worse than the Nazis, which broadcasts from the rooftops its plan to obliterate the Jews, to obliterate Israel and to obliterate America. Have you noticed a single Muslim country distancing itself from this plan or denouncing its spokesmen—Iran's Ahmadinejad, Hezbollah and Hamas—for proclaiming this solution to the problem posed by the existence of infidel Jews and Americans? Even *one* Muslim state out of the 57? When people say Islam is a religion of peace, I'm sure that's true for some individual Muslims, and I've said so many times. But when you look at the organized Muslim community, where do you see people who are willing to stand up for peace, who will defend the right of the Jewish state or

Jews to exist, or are willing to pass a UN resolution condemning the genocidal terrorists of Hezbollah and Hamas? Those people are so invisible and so inconsequential, it's as if they didn't exist.

Now allow me to deal with some of the lies perpetrated by the Muslim Student Association and their "Israeli Apartheid Week" on this campus. On the "apartheid" wall of hate funded by this university, there is a map that pictures Israel, Gaza and the West Bank. It is labeled "occupied Palestine." That is a lie. There is no occupation of a country called "Palestine." There were no Palestinian lands to be stolen when Israel was created. Israel was created in the same way that Jordan, Syria, Lebanon, and Iraq were created—out of the ruins of the Ottoman Turkish empire. The Turks are not Arabs. They had ruled the entire region for 400 years, since the 16th century, until they joined the powers that were defeated in World War I. At the end of that war, the victors— Britain and France—divided up the spoils. The "Palestine Mandate," which was part of these Turkish spoils, did not refer to a people but to a geographical region. It is a term like "New England." There are New Englanders, but they do not constitute an ethnicity or a nationality. The people who lived in the region of Palestine for the previous thousand years called themselves Arabs, not "Palestinians." The word "Palestine" is not even an Arab word. It is Roman in origin. When the Romans drove the Jews out of their homeland, Judea, in the first century CE, they renamed it after the Jews' enemies, the Philistines, who were Europeans, not Arabs. Hence the name "Palestine." The claim that Israel is "occupied Palestine" is a lie of Hitlerian proportions. It has the same genocidal intention. And it is funded by the University of California on this campus.

A second version of this lie focuses on Jewish settlements in the West Bank, as though these were an extension of the so-called "occupation." The hate-week displays put up by the Muslim Student Association show the West Bank dotted with the settlements of Jewish interlopers. Let me put to you this question: If you are not a xenophobe or a racist, what is wrong with Jewish settlements—with Jews settling on the West Bank or in Gaza? Why is a Jewish settlement a problem? There are more than a million Arab Muslims settled permanently in Israel as Israeli citizens. They have more rights than the Muslims of Gaza, more rights than Muslims in the West Bank, more rights than the Muslims in Iran, more rights than the Muslims in *any* Muslim country. Jews welcome Muslims as settlers in their country. But Arab Muslims do not welcome Jews. They are racists and Judaeophobes, and that is the only reason why Jewish settlements are a problem for them.

Consider that the Jews of Israel have been attacked in three aggressive wars within a single generation—wars designed to push them into the sea. By every precept of international law, they had (and have) the right to annex those territories from which they were attacked, and even to expel the populations that joined the aggressions. That is precisely what happened to the Germans after World War II. East Prussia was the industrial heartland of Germany. Ethnic Germans had inhabited it for a thousand years. But after Germany invaded Poland twice in a generation, the allied powers said: enough. As part of the peace that followed the war, they expelled twelve million Germans from East Prussia and gave the land they had inhabited to Poland. There was no international outcry over that. The Israelis had every right to take the same measures to secure peace in the Middle East in 1948 and 1967. In 1948 they could have expelled all the Arabs who had not left Israel, the way the Arabs expelled the Jews living in their countries at the time. But the Israelis didn't. In 1967 they could have expelled all the Arabs living in Gaza and all the Arabs on the West Bank. But they didn't. They preferred to live in peace with their Arab neighbors. The Israelis extended their hands to them even as their peace offers were rejected. The Israelis then built universities in the West Bank and made it a booming economy, an economy the PLO has since destroyed. Now, as a reward for their generosity, the Israelis are being threatened with extinction by these same people.

A third lie featured in the Muslim-sponsored hate-fest this week is that there are five million Palestinian refugees who should be returned to their homes in Israel. The contemporary records show quite clearly that, when the Arab armies invaded Israel, the Arab governments called on those Arabs living in the area to flee and promised them they would be returned to their homes by the victorious Arab armies. In war, people flee because they are scared; and some were undoubtedly driven out. Eventually, there were an estimated five or six hundred thousand Arabs who fled. But there were also six hundred thousand Jews who were driven out of Iraq, Morocco, Tunisia and other Arab lands where they had lived for centuries. Jews were the largest ethnic community in Baghdad until the 1930s, when Iraq sided with the Axis powers.

The Arab propagandists and their University of California supporters now claim that there are more than five million Palestinian refugees, even though there were only a tenth that many originally and only 10 percent of that number are still alive. But why are there *any* Palestinian refugees? It is sixty years later. There are no longer any Jewish refugees, because Israel re-settled them. The Arabs did not re-settle the Arab refugees. The Arab refugees were not even re-settled in Jordan, whose territory includes 80 percent of the original Palestine Mandate and whose population is 70 percent made up of Arabs from the mandate. A Hashemite minority rules Jordan, but there are no calls for the self-determination of Palestinians in Jordan. Palestinian Arabs are not *allowed* to settle in the other Arab states. In short, the reason there are Palestinian refugees is that the PLO, Hamas and the Arab states *want* them to be refugees—want them to be confined in miserable camps, where they can use them for propaganda and as cannon fodder for the war to purge the Jews from the Muslim Middle East. The refugee camps are bases for the terrorist armies of the Islamic *jihad.* The United States and Israel, along with other countries, have poured billions of dollars into the refugee cause, most of which ended up in the Swiss bank accounts of the real oppressors of Palestinians—the leaders of the PLO and Hamas. Yasser Arafat died with a Swiss bank account reported to be worth $35 billion. That was money donated by Jews and Americans and taken out of the pockets of Palestinians, while the thief and terrorist Arafat remains an officially revered figure among them.

The centerpiece of the Muslim-sponsored hate week on this campus is the so-called Apartheid Wall, which is itself two lies. The wall being protested—the wall in Israel—is not a wall but a security fence, and it is not an "apartheid" fence because it is not designed to enforce a separation of races or ethnicities. There are, as I previously observed, a million Arabs living in Israel with more rights than the Arabs of any Arab country. The fence was not erected to keep Arabs out. It was erected to keep *terrorists* out. The West Bank and Gaza are terrorist camps whose governments honor, support, and orchestrate the terrorist war against Jews in Israel. What if the Jews took down the wall? We know from the past exactly what would happen. Israel's security fence did not appear out of the blue. The wall was a desperate last measure the Israelis devised after years of watching their children slaughtered by suicide bombers in discos and pizza parlors. In the wake of their crimes, the Palestinian Authority honored the murderers as heroes and martyrs to be emulated. If a whole people is supporting murderers, you have to separate that people from the intended victims. The erection of the fence has stopped virtually all of these terror attacks. What the hate week on this campus is really calling for, when it calls for removal of the fence, is a renewal of terrorist attacks against the children of Israel.

As I said at the outset, there are whole departments of this university that are sponsoring this hate week and, thus, the war against the Jews it encourages. The sponsors include the Visual Arts Department, the Literature Department and the Ethnic Studies Department, along with the Thurgood Marshall College. If you look at the codes this university claims to live by, you will see that chief among them is respect for diversity—for the ethnicities of students who attend this school. But there is no respect for Jewish students at this campus when a week of hate is thrust in the faces of Jewish students, courtesy of university faculties and administrators.

There are thirty campuses across the nation hosting Israeli Apartheid Weeks this spring, including the University of California Irvine, UC Berkeley, UC Santa Barbara, UC Santa Cruz, UCLA, Boston University, Brandeis, Brown, University of Wisconsin, University of Houston, Brooklyn College, University of Chicago, DePaul, Columbia, University of Illinois, University of Minnesota, University of Washington and others. Behind each and every one of these hate weeks is the Muslim Students Association. Many people on this and other campuses mistake the Muslim Students Association for a cultural organization that represents all Muslims. It is no such thing. The Muslim Students Association was created by the Muslim Brotherhood and is a sister organization of the terrorist organization Hamas. It is a recruiting organization for the Brotherhood. More than a dozen of its former presidents at American universities have gone on to high-level positions in Al-Qaeda and other terrorist groups, the most prominent being Anwar Awlaki, the leader of Al-Qaeda in Yemen. Awlaki was president of the Muslim Students Association at Colorado State.[2]

Hasan al-Banna, the founder of the Muslim Brotherhood and the architect of terrorist *jihad*, was an admirer of Nazism whose organization translated *Mein Kampf* into Arabic. The father of Palestinian nationalism, Haj Amin al-Husseini, was one of al-Banna's protégés and is revered to this day by the Palestinian Authority and Hamas as the father of Palestinian nationalism. Haj Amin al-Husseini was a Nazi. In the twenties and the thirties, he preached the extermination of the Jews and inspired two celebrated massacres of Jewish settlers. During the Second World War he went to Berlin to work with Hitler to recruit Arabs to the Nazi cause. He devised his own plan to create an Auschwitz in the Middle East, and was thwarted in setting up his death camps only because Rommel was defeated at El-Alamein. After the war, he

---

[2]"Anwar Al-Awlaki's American Journey," Clifford D. May, *National Review Online*, October 6, 2011; http://www.nationalreview.com/content/anwar-al-awlaki%E2%80%99s-american-journey

and al-Banna led the Arab crusade against the creation of the Jewish state.

Why is the Muslim Students Association allowed to sponsor hate weeks against Israel and the Jews, which violate the diversity principles and ethical codes of every one of these universities? Where is the outrage over the lies the Muslim Students Association spreads, along with its incitements against the Jewish state? Shame on the University of California for hosting this event. Shame on Thurgood Marshall College and the faculties that sponsored it. Shame on the campus leftists who are supporting a genocidal campaign, and shame on the Muslim students who use the shield of their religion to advance the Islamic war against the Jews.

You've been a very civil audience in the midst of a very uncivil week of events. Thank you for coming.

• • •

[NOTE: A Question and Answer Session followed, which included this exchange.]

> ***Jumanah Imad Albahri:*** Good evening. I just wanted to say thank you for coming to campus tonight and presenting your point of view. It's always valuable to have two sets of views going on at the same time. Very useful. My name is Jumanah Imad Albahri and I am a student here at UCSD. I was reading your literature. I found that much more interesting than the talk. And I found some interesting things about the MSA, which is an organization that is very active on campus and it is hosting our annual "Hitler Youth Week." You should come out to those events. If you could clarify the connection between the MSA and Jihad terrorist networks, because last I checked, we had to do our own fundraising and we never get help from anyone. So if you could clarify the connection between UCSD's MSA, or if you don't have such information, if you could connect other MSAs on UC, because the connection wasn't too clear in the pamphlet.
>
> ***David Horowitz:*** Will you condemn Hamas here and now?

Jumanah Imad Albahri: I'm sorry, what?

Horowitz: Will you condemn Hamas?

Albahri: Would I condemn Hamas?

Horowitz: As a terrorist—genocidal—organization?

Albahri: Are you asking me to put myself on a cross?

Horowitz: So you won't. I actually have had this experience many times. You didn't read the pamphlet ["The Muslim Students Association and the Jihad Network"], because the pamphlet gives chapter and verse on the connection.[3] The main connection is that the MSA is part of the Muslim Brotherhood network as revealed in the documents produced by the FBI in the Holy Land Foundation trial.

Albahri: I don't think you understood what I meant by that. I meant, if I say something, I'm sure that I will be arrested for reasons of Homeland Security. So if you could please just answer my question.

Horowitz: If you condemn Hamas, Homeland Security will arrest you?

Albahri: If I support Hamas—because your question forces me to condemn Hamas—if I support Hamas, I look really bad.

Horowitz: Well, if you don't condemn Hamas, obviously you support it. Case closed. I had this same experience at UC Santa Barbara where there were fifty members of the Muslim Students Association sitting right in the rows there.[4] And throughout my hour talk, I kept asking them, "Will you condemn Hezbollah and Hamas?" And none of them would. And then, when the question period came, the President of the Muslim Students Association was the first person to ask questions. And I said, "Before you start, will you condemn Hezbollah?" And he said, well, that question is too complicated for a yes/no answer. So I said, okay, I'll put it to you this way. I am a Jew. The head of Hezbollah has said that he

---

[3]"The Muslim Students Association and the Jihad Network," http://www.discoverthenetworks.org/Articles/MSA%20and%20Jihad%20Network%20v5b-1.pdf

[4]See "Fear and Loathing in Santa Barbara," above.

hopes that we will gather in Israel so he doesn't have to hunt us down globally. *For it or against it?*

Albahri: For it.

Horowitz: Thank you. Thank you for coming and showing everybody what's really going on here.[5]

---

[5]"David Horowitz at UCSD 5/10/2010," http://www.youtube.com/watch?v=8fSvyvourTE

3

It's Time for Jews to
Stand Up for Themselves

I was not looking forward to my speech at Brooklyn College last night during "Israeli Apartheid Week." The campus atmosphere was so hostile to Jews that no student organization was willing to host my appearance, not even the Jewish organizations—and with 3,500 Jewish students on campus, there were several. My visit was only made possible by the courage of one professor, Mitchell Langbert, who reserved a room in the school library; the bravery of one student, Yosef Sobol, a Jewish immigrant from Ukraine who organized the event; and the intervention of a single university trustee, Jeffrey Wiesenfeld, who arranged for a formidable campus police presence to guarantee security at the event.

At Brooklyn College, as at other schools, the student paper, *The Excelsior*, is an independent entity for which the university takes no responsibility. *The Excelsior* is edited by a 9/11 "truther" who declared on the Internet that a memorial should be erected to the leader of the 9/11 attacks, Mohammed Atta, and his terrorist accomplices. This editor has turned *The Excelsior* into an anti-Israel propaganda sheet. Despite the fact that the Jews who attend Brooklyn college are members of an ethnic minority—which the FBI reports is the victim of eight *times* the number of hate crimes

March 11, 2011, http://frontpagemag.com/2011/david-horowitz/its-time-for-the-jews-to-stand-up-for-themselves/

as are committed against Muslims—the faculty at Brooklyn College chose as a requirement for all incoming freshman that they read a single book: about discrimination against Arabs. The book is called, *How Does It Feel to Be a Problem? Being Young and Arab in America.* Despite the fact that a third of its student body is Jewish, Brooklyn College has hired an instructor who was an activist for Hamas, an organization that is officially committed to "obliterating" the Jews.

For two weeks prior to my arrival, an adjunct professor at the college had been calling on students and political radicals to protest my appearance, while denouncing me as a "racist" and "McCarthyite." This professor is a Muslim member of the International Socialist Organization, a communist party that seeks a "dictatorship of the proletariat" in America. During my speech, he urged students and outsiders to attack the event, both outside and inside the auditorium. As at all my campus speeches these days, I was accompanied by my bodyguard, Floyd Resnick, who also serves as a campus bodyguard for Ann Coulter and other conservative speakers. Two days before the event, he called campus security and was told the university's policy was that protesters who tried to obstruct my speech would not be removed from the room. On hearing this, I accepted that I might not be able to speak at all, or that, if I did speak, it would be a struggle to be heard.

At this point, something totally unexpected happened. Jeffrey Wiesenfeld, a trustee of the City University of New York, of which Brooklyn College is a part, entered the arena. Wiesenfeld demanded that the university protect the students who had invited me, and the event itself. In all my years of traveling to universities, more than four hundred of them, this had never happened. As a result of Wiesenfeld's intervention, seven armed and imposing guards stood at the entrance to the hall. They inspected the attendees with metal detectors and searched their bags before they entered. The campus chief of public safety was there too, along with an official from the university who warned would-be protesters that they would be removed if they obstructed my speech.

As a result of these precautions, I was able to speak for an hour in a civil atmosphere, and the students who attended were able to hear what I had to say. Let me pause for a moment to say that threats of campus violence and obstructions of speakers, which are the work exclusively of leftists and Muslim radicals, would disappear overnight if university administrators did their job, and if university trustees met their responsibility to ensure that an appropriate atmosphere prevails on their campuses.[1] Would that there were a hundred trustees like Jeffrey Wiesenfeld.

Brooklyn College is a commuter school. It was a rainy and blustery evening when I arrived but the library auditorium was filled with over a hundred people, mainly students, virtually all of them either Jewish or Palestinian. The Palestinians were all members of a recently created "Palestinian Club." The Jews represented about 80 percent of those present. I began by asking everyone how it felt to go through a "checkpoint" as they had that evening. The "injustice" of Israeli checkpoints was of course a focus of recent demonstrations by the Palestinian Club. I said, "Well, our checkpoint made *me* feel safe, and that is the point of checkpoints—to protect the innocent from attacks by people who want to silence or kill them." I then addressed the atmosphere of intimidation that prevailed at Brooklyn College as a result of the attacks by the anti-Israel left. The Brooklyn College administration had ignored and thereby encouraged these attacks, as had university administrations across the country. I recalled how Nazis and Communists in the 1930s had conducted a joint campaign to break up the public meetings of their opponents, and how that had spelled the end of democracy in Germany and the rise of the totalitarian state.[2]

---

[1] For further discussion, see Volume VII in this series, *The Left in the University.*

[2] David Horowitz, "Opposing the Palestinian War Against the Jews," March 25, 2011; http://frontpagemag.com/2011/david-horowitz/opposing-the-palestinian-war-against-the-jews/ For a video of the speech, cf. http://www.youtube.com/watch?v=xnFlv9vDmSQ

The frontline battle in our present war with totalitarianism, I told them, was the First Amendment right to disagree. When protests were designed to shut down speakers, when speakers were defamed in advance of their appearances, one side of the argument was effectively silenced. If this were allowed to continue, we would soon lose our democracy. The attacks on freedom of speech had already gone so far in this country that one couldn't mention terror and Islam in the same breath without being labeled a bigot or an Islamophobe, and accused of calling *all* Muslims terrorists. Even President Bush, who had defended us against the attacks of Islamic terrorists, could not identify our enemies by name for fear of offending other terrorists or their sympathizers, or Muslims in general. He could not identify them as Islamic *jihadists*, which is in fact what they call themselves.

My speech happened to coincide with the opening of congressional hearings on the radicalization of Muslims in America. On my hotel television screen, I had watched the attacks on those hearings from the Democrats and the left. We had reached a moment in our history when we could not even make inquiries about the threat of domestic terrorism posed by Islamists—who are responsible for seventeen thousand terrorist attacks since 9/11—without being attacked as "McCarthyites" and "bigots." This was the prime political strategy of all Islamic terrorists and their enablers: to identify anyone who speaks about Islamic terrorism as someone who is attacking "all Muslims." The terrorists naturally seek to identify themselves with Islam, to hide themselves and their sinister agendas in the Muslim community and use it as a protective shield.

If criticism of religiously inspired terror is seen as an attack on the religion itself, the terrorists gain the protections of religious freedom. But the charge that an attack on Muslim terrorists is an attack on all Muslims is an insult to the Muslim community, a form of religious and ethnic abuse. All Muslims are not terrorists; but there are also not enough Muslims coming forward to separate themselves and Islam from the radical *jihad*, or to condemn terrorist organizations like Hamas. I mentioned Dr. Zuhdi Jasser, a Muslim who had testified at the hearings. He said, "This is our problem, and it is our responsibility to solve it."

That was my introduction. I then read a series of statements by Palestinian leaders and by the spiritual head of the Muslim Brotherhood, each of whom essentially promised to finish the job that Hitler had started. Here are two:

Mahmoud Al-Zahar, a founder of Hamas, said in 2007: "There is no place for you Jews among us, and you have no future among the nations of the world. You are headed to annihilation."

In that same year, Ahmad Bahar, acting chairman of the Gaza parliament, said:

> "Be certain that America is on its way to disappear.... Allah, take hold of the Jews and their allies, Allah, take hold of the Americans and their allies ... Allah, count them and kill them to the last one and don't leave even one."[3]

It doesn't take a rocket scientist, I said, to know who these people are. "They are Nazis, and they want to kill the Jews and destroy the Jewish state. Their goal is not peace but to push the Jews of Israel into the sea. On campuses all across America, the Muslim and socialist left are chanting 'From the river to the sea.'" At this point, I was interrupted by a voice from the audience who turned out to be the Muslim Marxist organizer of the protest, who completed the chant: "Palestine will be free." I pointed out that the eastern boundary of Israel is the Jordan River and the western boundary is the Mediterranean Sea, so "this is just another way of saying we want to obliterate your Jewish state and push you into the sea. These are Nazis." The embargo on free speech is already so far advanced in America, I continued, that we speak of a "peace

---

[3]"Jews & Americans—'Allah ... don't leave even one'," *Palestinian Media Watch*, from Palestinian TV (Fatah), Apr. 20, 2007; http://palwatch.org/main.aspx?fi=427 Also, see "Faces of Palestine," April 6, 2012, http://frontpagemag.com/2012/frontpagemag-com/faces-of-palestine/

process" as though there were one. There is not a single Palestinian leader willing to recognize the Jewish state. Both Hamas and the Palestinian Authority want to "liberate" Palestine "from the river to the sea." How can you make peace with people who don't want you to exist? How can you negotiate a peace with Nazis who want to kill you? You can't. You have to demand that they stop being Nazis, or that the people who support them elect other leaders. We have to stop capitulating to the censors of our language, I said, and call things by their right names. That is the only way to have clarity and to begin to be able to defend ourselves.

I then asked why the left is willing to embrace Hamas Nazis who want to kill the Jews. I suggested that leftists would answer this question by claiming that Palestinians are oppressed, and that it is the Jews who are responsible for their suffering. The Jews stole their land and put them under military occupation and have since subjected them to all manner of indignities, like checkpoints. I then said, "Let's put off the question as to whether there is any truth in these claims, and just look at the claim that suffering explains their resort to suicide bombings and their desire to kill the Jews and push them into the sea. For thousands of years, nations, ethnic groups, races and religions have suffered. They have been enslaved, they have been occupied, they have been oppressed. But never in the history of mankind, until now, has there been a people like the Palestinians who strap bombs on their own children and tell them to blow themselves up and kill other children, and that if they do they will go to heaven and become saints. No other religion besides Islam makes murderers into saints. In the entire history of mankind, no people has sunk to such moral lows as the Palestinians in their war against the Jews."[4] This is a "sick culture," I said.

---

[4]These are not precise quotes. For the text of my remarks, cf. http://frontpagemag.com/2011/david-horowitz/opposing-the-palestinian-war-against-the-jews/

I then went over the claims that the Jews are actually oppressing Palestinians—beginning with the claim that the Jews stole Palestinian land. I went over the history of the Middle East, the fact that prior to the creation of Israel, the land belonged to the Turks—who were not Arabs, let alone Palestinians—for four hundred years. The Arabs' claim to Israel, I said, was about as credible as a Dutch claim to the city of New York. I pointed out that the state of Jordan, which was also created out of the Palestine Mandate, was 70 percent Arab, and was ruled by a Hashemite minority. Yet no one was calling for *their* liberation. That was because the true goal of the Palestinian liberation movement is not a Palestinian state but to push the Jews into the sea.

I discussed the other indefensible lies that make up the case against Israel and the justification for Arab and Palestinian aggression, beginning with the claim that Jewish settlements on the West Bank are a problem. "There are a million Muslim Arabs settled in the state of Israel who enjoy more rights as Israeli citizens than the Muslims or Arabs in any Muslim or Arab state. If Muslim communities in Israel are not a problem, why are Jewish communities in the Arab world or on the West Bank or in Gaza? Because the Arabs and Muslims of the Middle East are racists and refuse to live side by side with any non-Arab or non-Muslim people. That is the straightforward, factually accurate, politically incorrect answer. There were two democracies in the Middle East after the Second World War: Israel and Lebanon. Lebanon was actually a Christian democracy. Democratic Lebanon has been destroyed by the Islamic *jihad,* and the Christians of the entire Middle East are under the gun or in flight."[5]

I had encouraged the Brooklyn students to erect a "Palestinian Wall of Lies" that my Freedom Center and I had created to combat the malignant "Israeli Apartheid Wall" that the campus left, along with the Muslim Brotherhood groups, were going to erect during

---

[5]Ibid.

"Israeli Apartheid Week."[6] When the Brooklyn College administration learned of these plans, they banned both walls—one with
the hate-filled lies and praises of Hamas assassins, and one with
the facts. This is what a victory looks like in collegiate America
today.

If the anti-Israel campaign had been directed against African-
Americans or any other campus ethnic group—including and
especially Muslims—no university community would tolerate it.
But because it is directed against Jews, Israeli Apartheid Week is
protected and funded by student governments and protected by
university administrators. Moreover, and most disturbingly, the
Jewish organizations on campus have been unwilling to stand up
for themselves and claim the same rights and respect as the groups
who are attacking them. The Hillel organization on the Brooklyn
College campus is a thousand Jews strong but it would not sponsor
our event. The Palestinian Club is a hundred Muslims strong, but
they came to attack it. Only one of the many Jewish organizations
on campus—Students United for Israel—was willing to co-spon-
sor the event.

By now, readers of this report are probably wondering about the
reaction of the members of the Palestinian Club who came to
protest my speech. They are wondering how the members of the
Palestinian Club responded to the detailed arguments I made
against their claims and self-justifications, or to my statement
that, while Palestinians were indeed suffering, the cause of their
suffering was the policies of their own leaders and the Arab states
which, for sixty years, rejected peace because they want to push
the Jews into the sea. The answer is that they didn't. It was as
though they had not heard a word. I have had the same experience
on scores of campuses, where I have confronted audiences that
include sizeable contingents from the Muslim Students Association and their leftwing allies. The reactions at the end of my talks
are always the same.

---

[6]http://www.walloflies.org

When members of the Palestinian Club went to the microphones to ask questions after the speech, they all had one talking point—the strategic talking point of the *jihadists:* "Mr. Joe McCarthy"—this is how the leader of the protest actually addressed me—"you said that all Muslims are terrorists...." I pointed out that I had said just the opposite, which didn't stop the others from standing up to make the identical charge. Despite the fact that they were college students, not one even made a pass at questioning the history I had reviewed or the facts I had presented. I was told afterwards that almost every member of the Palestinian Club was from Ramallah in the West Bank. But not one of them spoke as a Palestinian. I had said that Palestinians elected two terrorist governments to rule over them; that Palestinians were willing to kill their own children in order to kill other children; that their schools taught their children to hate and kill Jews; that as a people they had sunk to the lowest moral level in history. I had said that they were indistinguishable from Nazis. But not one Palestinian in that room stood up to defend themselves *as Palestinians.* One woman shrieked, "Do you want to go lynch all Muslims in America?" To a man and woman, they said, "You are accusing all *Muslims* of being terrorists."[7]

One questioner actually did offer an intellectual challenge to an argument I had made, and did attempt to defend Palestinians as

---

[7]From the transcript:
Interruption by a member of the Palestinian Club: "Do you want to go lynch all the Muslims in America?"
Audience member: "Sit down."
Member of the Palestinian Club: "Lynch me! Lynch me!"
Audience Member: "Shut up!"
Member of the Palestinian Club: "Yeah, you're racist. Is that what you want to do? You want America to go around killing all the Muslims in America?"
Member of the Palestinian Club: "Do you want to go lynch all Muslims in America? You're racist, racist. Yeah, you're racist." Exits the room— "Killing the Messenger: The Left Strikes Back," March 13, 2011, http://frontpagemag.com/2011/david-horowitz/killing-the-messenger-the-left-strikes-back/

an ethnic group, as opposed to a religious sect of Islam. This person was a Jew from Hillel who suggested that Japanese kamikaze pilots were akin to suicide bombers, and so Palestinians were not the only people in history who had sunk so low. But of course, kamikaze pilots were soldiers, not civilians; they targeted battleships and aircraft carriers, not women and children in pizza parlors.

When it was over, I was glad I had come. I was proud of the small vanguard of Jewish students who had invited me and braved the attacks. I was proud of Jeffrey Wiesenfeld, the Jewish trustee who had gone out of his way to protect me and the students who came to hear me. And I was gratified that they understood my message and would take it to the rest of the Jewish community at Brooklyn College. It is the same message I take to other campuses where my audiences are mainly non-Jewish. Israel is the canary in the coal mine. If we in America cannot stand up for Israel, we cannot defend ourselves.[8]

---

[8]This idea is the theme of George Gilder's *The Israel Test*, Richard Vigilante Books, 2009.

4

Suicidal Jews

This spring, we are attempting to place in student papers an advertisement featuring a "Palestinian Wall of Lies" to counter the "Israeli Apartheid" walls that the Muslim Students Associations have erected on college campuses with the support of student funds and the encouragement of the student press.[1] Unlike the Muslim efforts, our ads have met with resistance from campus editors, whom it would be overly generous to call ignorant. In those few cases where student papers published the ad, its appearance was met with outraged letters, particularly from Jews. Our ad was specifically devised to answer the propaganda that portrays Israel as an apartheid Nazi state occupying Arab land, while the Palestinians are presented as innocent victims of Israeli theft and oppression. The statements in our ad were strictly factual, which may account for the absence of reasoned challenges to any of its statements or the offer of any evidence that would contradict its claims.

In fact, all the rejections of the ad by campus editors have been on grounds that it was offensive to ethnic or religious groups— clearly Arabs, Palestinians and Muslims. To my knowledge, there has never been a single editorial in any campus paper, let alone in the 15 that have rejected our ad so far, decrying the "Israeli Apartheid Weeks" staged on their campuses and promoting

March 24, 2011, http://frontpagemag.com/2011/david-horowitz/suicidal-jews-and-the-anti-semites-they-ignore-and-sometimes-embrace/
[1]http://www.walloflies.org

monstrous slanders against Israel and its Jews. What is really taking place on American campuses is a hate campaign against Israel and the Jews—along with a parallel campaign to censor any response to these hateful attacks by Muslim and Palestinian campus groups.

Even more disturbing is the response of campus Jewish groups to our attempts to confront these lies directly and refute them. The largest and most important of the Jewish groups, Hillel, has actually joined in a coalition with anti-Semites to support their attacks on us. At Florida State University, Hillel is working to protest our efforts in coalition with the Muslim Students Association—the Hamas-supporting sponsor of the hate weeks. They have called their protest "The Coalition Against Hate." At Brown, the student Hillel, which has written no letters protesting Israeli Apartheid Week, sent this one to *The Brown Daily Herald*:

> To the Editor:
> The student leadership at Brown-RISD Hillel would like to express its disapproval of an advertisement that ran on page 8 of yesterday's Herald. The advertisement propagated several Islamophobic, racist and hurtful untruths by linking all modern Arab leadership to Nazi ideology and equating Islam with violence.

There was no attempt by the Brown-RISD Hillel students to demonstrate that our claims were untrue. Instead they simply asserted that we were bigots and not associated with them (since I was a Jew):

> Though neither Hillel nor any affiliated students had anything to do with the advertisement, we feel compelled to declare that there should be no place for these spiteful, bigoted words in the Brown—or any—community, even under the guise of political free speech. We stand staunchly beside any members of our community who feel alienated and attacked by the advertisement.
> We trust that the Brown University community will be wise enough to view the 'Wall of Lies' advertisement as an unfortu-

nate example of hatred and as unrepresentative of Hillel or the Jewish community.

The Brown-RISD Hillel Student Executive Board[2]

The student leadership at Brown-RISD Hillel was upset not with the Muslim Students Association, sponsor of the Israeli Apartheid Weeks across the country, but with those of us who have had the temerity to correct the hateful lies spread by enemies of the only Jewish state. According to Brown Hillel, there are "Islamophobic, racist and hurtful untruths" in our ad which consist in "linking all modern Arab leadership to Nazi ideology and equating Islam with violence." What our ad said was: "Today Arab leaders call for the destruction of the Jewish state and routinely deny that the Holocaust with which their forebears collaborated actually took place."

Is this actually the case? Mahmoud Abbas, the head of the Palestinian Authority, has actually written an entire book of Holocaust denial. Hamas, which is the government of Gaza, promises in its charter that "Israel will exist and will continue to exist until Islam will obliterate it." Perhaps the Hillel Student Executive Board would like to name a Palestinian leader who does not call for the destruction of the Jewish state. Following this futile effort, they should attempt to explain how the truth can be described as "bigoted." And then they should explain how they expect normal people to regard their embrace of Palestinians—whose leaders without exception call for the destruction of the Jewish state—as anything but lending support to their genocidal cause.

---

[2] "Reactions to Yesterday's Full-page Advertisement," *The Brown Daily Herald*, March 15, 2011; http://www.browndailyherald.com/2011/03/15/reactions-to-yesterdays-fullpage-advertisement/

5

Palestinian Wall of Lies
[Text of Ad Placed in Campus Newspapers]

Myth 1: Israel Occupies Arab Palestine

This is a genocidal claim made by the Muslim Students Association and other pro-Arab groups. It is genocidal because it obliterates the Jewish state. If Israel is actually "Occupied Palestine" then there is no legitimate Jewish state in the Middle East.

Since Roman times when the Philistines inhabited the region around the Jordan (hence the name "Palestine") there has never been a political entity—neither a province nor a state—called "Palestine" and no one claimed there was until well after the United Nations created Israel in 1948. The land on which Israel was created by the U.N. was also used by the colonial powers to create Syria, Iraq, Lebanon, and Jordan. It was land that had belonged to Turkey for 400 years. The Turks are not "Palestinians" and are not even Arabs.

There never was an Arab country called "Palestine" or inhabited by "Palestinians." Before the creation of the Palestine Liberation Organization in 1964, which was sixteen years after the birth of Israel, no Arab political entity was called by that name.

Myth 2: Israel Is An Apartheid State

The term Apartheid refers to the segregation of groups on the basis of ethnicity or race, and the denial of basic civil rights to the

---

http://frontpagemag.com/2011/frontpagemag-com/palestinian-wall-of-lies-a-genocidal-campaign-on-americas-campuses/

segregated group. There is no such segregation in Israel. Arabs are granted full civil rights under Israeli law, which forbids discrimination on the basis of race, creed, or sex. Arabs take part fully in Israeli society and government. Arab citizens of Israel vote in national elections, have representatives in the Israeli Parliament, sit on the Israeli courts and on the Israeli Supreme Court benches, and serve as tenured professors teaching in Israeli colleges and universities. The Arab citizens of Israel have more rights, and enjoy more freedom, education, and economic opportunity than the Arabs of any Arab state.

Myth 3: The Arabs Want Peace and a State on the West Bank

The Arab nations rejected peace and a state on the West Bank first in 1948 when it was offered to them by the U.N. and then in 2000 when it was offered by Presidents Clinton and Barak. In 1949, the West Bank and Gaza Strip, which the U.N. had designated as a homeland for the Arabs, were annexed respectively by Jordan and Egypt. When the Palestinian Liberation Organization (PLO) was formed in 1964 its covenant made no mention of liberating the West Bank or Gaza from Jordan and Egypt. The PLO leadership stated that its goal was to "push the Jews into the sea." Today the "liberation" of Palestine "from the river to the sea" is still the goal of Hamas and the Palestinian Authority (PA). The war in the Middle East is about the desire of the Arab nations and Muslims to destroy Israel; it is not about the desire for a Palestinian state.

There are 1.4 million Arabs living in Israel with civil rights that are the envy of the Arab world. Israeli Arabs vote in Israel's elections, have representatives in the Israeli Parliament, sit on Israeli courts and on the Israeli Supreme Court, and serve as tenured professors teaching in Israeli colleges and universities. The Arab citizens of Israel have more rights, and enjoy more freedom, education, and economic opportunity than the inhabitants of any Arab or Muslim state.

Myth 4: The Holocaust Is Europe's Problem; Palestinians Had No Role In It

The father of Palestinian nationalism, Haj Amin Al-Husseini, planned death camps for the Jews in the Middle East. Haj Amin Al-Husseini, was a devoted follower of Hitler who spent the war in Berlin, recruited an Arab legion to the Nazi cause and planned a "Final Solution" for the Jews of the Arab world. The Muslim Brotherhood, which created Hamas, the government of Gaza, translated Mein Kampf into Arabic in the 1930s and called for the destruction of the Jewish state at its birth.

Myth 5: Israel's Security Fence Is an "Apartheid" Wall

This is two myths in one. The West Bank fence is a fence, not a wall. About 97 percent of the fence is made of chain-link material. The remaining 3 percent is concrete, designed to repel sniper fire in particular areas. The fence was built in 2003 in response to thousands of suicide bombings and rocket attacks on Israeli citizens by Palestinian terrorists, sponsored and armed by the Palestinian Authority and Hamas. The fence was built to keep out terrorists, not Arabs.

In the years since the construction of the fence, terrorist attacks have declined by more than 90 percent. The fence is Israel's legitimate defense against a ruthless and amoral terrorist aggressor.

Myth 6: Israel Is the Cause of the Refugee Problem

The Palestinians claim there are 5 million Palestinian refugees who fled Israel during the 1948 war. This is false. There were only 500,000 Arab refugees from the 1948 war—an unprovoked war that Egypt and four other Arab states had launched against the newly created state of Israel. In the aftermath of the war, 500,000 Jewish refugees were driven out of the Arab states in the Middle East. There are no Jewish refugees today, sixty years later, because Israel resettled them. Why are there still Arab refugees? The Arab regimes have been given billions of dollars by Israel and the United States to relocate their refugees. But the Arabs are still in refugee camps. While Israel resettled Jewish refugees, no Arab country would take in the "Palestinians" who were forced into camps and were kept there by the Arab regimes to stir up hatred against the Jews. The refugee "issue" has been created by the Arab regimes as a weapon in their war against the Jews. It should be resolved by resettling the inhabitants of the refugee camps in the West Bank and Gaza where almost all of them have lived all their lives.

Myth 7: Israel Commits War Crimes By Killing Civilians

This is the Big Lie, coming as it does from some Palestinians who have made terrorist attacks on civilians a weapon of choice, and who make martyrs and national heroes out of suicide bombers.

The Gaza strip was a base for 7,000 rocket attacks against schoolyards and townships in Israel before the Israelis responded in 2007. During Israel's airstrikes on Gaza rocket sites there was one civilian death for every 30 terrorists. By contrast, a 2001 study by the International Committee of the Red Cross[1] found that the civilian-to-military death ratio in wars fought since the middle of the 20th Century has been 10:1—ten civilian deaths for every soldier death. In other words, the Israelis protect civilians at a rate 300 times greater than any other national army. As Harvard Law School Professor Alan Dershowitz observes, "No army in history has ever had a better ratio of combatants to civilians killed in a comparable setting."

Myth 8: Jews Have Little Historical Connection To Israel

Jews have lived continuously in the land of Israel for over 3000 years; the Arabs arrived through multiple invasions, beginning in

---

[1]http://en.wikipedia.org/wiki/International_Committee_of_the_Red_Cross

the 7th Century AD. In the year 70 AD, when the Jewish civilization was already over 1000 years old, the Romans forced most of the Jews of Judea and Samaria (now the West Bank) into exile. By the end of the 19th Century, the majority population of Jerusalem was Jewish.

Myth 9: The Koran Describes Jerusalem As Holy To Islam

The Koran does not mention Jerusalem because Mohammed never set foot in the city. Jerusalem was conquered by Muslim armies in 636 after the death of Mohammed. Muslim jihadists claim that the Koran mentions "The Farthest Mosque"—Al-Aqsa in Arabic— and that this is a Koranic reference to Jerusalem. This is a lie. The Al-Aqsa Mosque in Jerusalem had not been built when the Koran was written, so the reference is to some other (or any other) "farthest mosque." In contrast, Jerusalem is and has always been a holy city to Jews. The daily prayers of the Jews are focused on Jerusalem. The Hebrew Bible mentions Zion and Jerusalem a total of 809 times.

Myth 10: The Temple of Solomon Is Not Jewish

This myth is one of many designed to steal the history of the Jews in order to justify erasing them from the Middle East. When the Palestinian Authority was established in 1994, it immediately began a campaign to delegitimize Israel by rewriting history with the intention of denying Israel's right to exist. Among its false claims is that the remains of the Temple of Solomon—the Western Wall—are in fact the remnants of the Al-Aqsa Mosque. The Al-Aqsa Mosque was deliberately built on top of the Temple after the Muslim conquest to humiliate the conquered.

6

Hillel's Coalition with Israel's Enemies

On Monday, March 28, *The Daily Pennsylvanian* printed our "Palestinian Wall of Lies" ad, which responded point by point to the damaging falsehoods spread by the Muslim Students Association during their Israeli Apartheid Weeks.[1] When the *Pennsylvanian* editors objected, we removed the word "Palestinian" from the title. This was our concession to the campus political orthodoxy, which forbids juxtaposing the words "Palestinian" or "Muslim" to the words "lies" or "terrorism" in the same factual sentence but has no problem with putting "Israeli" and "Apartheid" or "Israeli" and "terrorism" in similar juxtapositions, thus spreading actual lies about a militarily threatened democratic state. When our ad appeared, it was attacked not only by Muslim groups seeking to destroy the Jewish state but, in concert with them, by leaders of Hillel, the largest Jewish organization on campus. Here is their joint "response" to our ad, followed by my response.[2]

March 31, 2011, http://frontpagemag.com/2011/david-horowitz/hillel%E2%80%99s-coalition-with-the-enemies-of-israel-becomes-increasingly-unseemly-2/

[1] http://www.walloflies.org

[2] Besan Abu-Joudah, Logan Bayroff, Ariel Fisher, Elisheva Goldberg, Sarah Shihadah, "A Statement of Principles," March 30, 2011; http://www.thedp.com/article/2011/03/guest_column_a_statement_of_principles

On Monday, the David Horowitz Freedom Center took out a full-page advertisement in *The Daily Pennsylvanian* and college newspapers around the country. It was an ad full of dehumanizing hate speech about the Palestinian people particularly and the Muslim, Arab and pro-Palestinian communities generally. We, as leaders of the Jewish and Muslim communities and as leaders of the pro-Israel and pro-Palestinian groups on campus, are joining together to collectively condemn such hateful and inflammatory rhetoric and those who espouse it.

We propose that we, as Israeli and Palestinian advocates, bring the same level of open-mindedness and intellectual rigor to our advocacy as we do to our studies. When discussing this issue, we resolve not to check our inquisitiveness or our tolerance at the door. We should be able to view each other's efforts not as incitements that require either response or dismissal but as invitations to expand our understanding of the issues and each other.

Today and going forward, we stand united in our suffering and against our suffering. We are united in the conviction that this moment of hate will serve as the catalyst for us to come together and learn from each other. These conversations will not be easy, but they are essential in the process of reconciliation between our communities and the development of a shared vision for the future.

We all dream of peace, but we also recognize that in our dreaming we must not fall into complacent slumber. We must remain alert to the hatred and intolerance that surround us and guard ourselves—and each other—against them. Our generation has not inherited an easy task, but we resolve that those who see enmity as inevitable, or hatred as natural, will never go unchallenged. By our unity, commitment, action and friendship we vow to build and defend a new framework of respect, humility and constructive creativity.

We believe that the publication of this horrifying and divisive document is an opportunity to come together as one community and address the status quo that has gone unchallenged for too long. We are exasperated by the oversimplification of an issue that deeply affects millions of human lives. We reject the idea

that there is no alternative to this fruitless, polarizing antago-
nism. We are deeply disappointed by the fact that both sides have
convinced themselves that they have nothing to learn from the
other and nothing to say that the other will respect. We reject the
extension of this attitude to our campus.

We are no longer satisfied with a world in which Muslims,
Jews and Christians, as well as those who identify as pro-Israel
and pro-Palestinian, are compelled to suffer silently every time
extremists perpetrate hate in the name of the convictions we
hold most dear. We recognize that these attacks and libels de-
humanize not only those they target but also those in whose
name they claim to speak—the individuals whose peaceful
voices and opinions are drowned out in a sea of discrimination
and hatred. We refuse to be complicit in destructive ignorance.
*This guest column was written by: Besan Abu-Joudah, College
and Wharton junior, former Penn Arab Student Society vice president Logan Bayroff, College sophomore, Forum for New Israel
Dialogue president Ariel Fisher, College senior, former Hillel
Education chairman Elisheva Goldberg, College senior, Kedma
editor-in-chief Sarah Shihadah, College freshman, Penn for
Palestine, Penn Arab Student Society. The following people are
signatories: Maryam Alireza, Penn Arab Student Society presi-
dent Humna Bhojani, Penn for Palestine president Sarah Ijaz,
Muslim Students Association president Tamar Karpuj, Hillel
Israel Sector chairwoman*

To the editor:

On Wednesday, *The Daily Pennsylvanian* printed a response to
our Wall of Lies ad signed by a coalition of Jewish and Muslim
campus leaders. In several rhetoric-heavy paragraphs, they called
our ad "dehumanizing hate speech" and "hateful and inflammatory." It would have been nice to see one citation from the ad
that was alleged to be hate speech; or one argument that the
claims made in our ad were not true. There was no such citation
and no such argument, only hate speech against us for writing the
ad. It seems reasonable to conclude that this resort to emotion is
because there is no argument to be made for the slanders that

Israel is an "apartheid state" or that Israel "occupies" Arab land. Or perhaps these students were not up to the task. Shame on those who signed the article, and shame on their teachers for not providing them with the ability and good manners to answer arguments they disagree with instead of demonizing those who make them.

Sincerely,

David Horowitz

Following is an additional letter I wrote to one of the signers of the attack, a former Hillel education chairman:

Dear Elisheva Goldberg,

I don't pretend to understand what would motivate you to attack a statement of facts defending Israel with such hate-filled vitriol as you do in the article you have jointly signed with Palestinian groups. I would like to see any statement by you personally, or Hillel generally, condemning the Israeli Apartheid Weeks and Walls organized by the Muslim Students Association, undoubtedly with support from the Palestinian groups you have embraced. If you do not respond to this email I will conclude that you made no such statements, and that you prefer to attack Jews defending themselves against slanders whose intent is clearly genocidal.

The purpose of this email is formally to offer to debate you, or anyone you may propose, as to the veracity of the claims our ad makes in defense of Israel or, alternatively, of the claims made by the Palestinian groups you have aligned yourself with against Israel.

Sincerely,

David Horowitz

I did not receive a reply from Elisheva Goldberg, who subsequently graduated and went to work for Peter Beinart and a J Street-affiliated group.

7

How Not to Defend Yourself
as a Jew at Yale

A t Yale the other week, Students for Justice in Palestine, one of the most aggressive and vicious supporters of Palestinian terrorism, played a stunt to dramatize their anti-Israel agenda. Members of the SJP put "Eviction Notices" under the dorm-room doors of Yale students, warning them that their rooms were going to be "demolished in three days" for no reason. According to a report of the action in the *Yale Daily News*, the eviction notices were designed "to raise awareness about the plight of Palestinians whose homes are being demolished by the Israeli government."[1] In a sane world, such a claim would have zero credibility. Why would any government, let alone one as humane and democratic as the government of Israel, go around randomly demolishing people's homes? What agenda would be served by that?

In fact, the homes that Israel has demolished belong to terrorists who blow up pizza parlors and buses and Passover services, hoping to kill as many innocent Jews as possible. It is all part of a sixty-year unrelenting war that Arabs and Muslims have waged against the existence of a non-Arab, non-Muslim state in the

April 29, 2011, http://frontpagemag.com/2011/david-horowitz/how-not-to-defend-yourself-as-a-jew-at-yale/
[1]Tapley Stephenson, "Flyers Threaten Eviction, Raise Awareness," *Yale Daily News*, April 22, 2011; http://yaledailynews.com/blog/2011/04/22/flyers-threaten-eviction-raise-awareness/

Middle East. This is a fact overlooked not only by terrorist support groups like Students for Justice in Palestine but by the editors of the *Yale Daily News*. Naturally, some Yale students ignorant of this history, and bombarded by Palestinian lies spread by left-wing faculty and student organizations, are unable to distinguish reality from fiction: "I was really confused at first," a Yale sophomore named Helen McCreary told the *Yale Daily News*, "but I think I understand why [Students for Justice in Palestine] did it. None of us have had our house randomly destroyed by the government."

The eviction notices explained to the credulous that they "were not meant to be an attack on Israel or Israelis, but rather on the actions of the Israeli state." But, as everyone knows, Israel is a democracy and its government reflects the sentiments and will of its people—including a million Muslim Arabs who are Israeli citizens with more rights than the citizens of Gaza or the West Bank under Palestinian rule. In short, this is a distinction without a difference; the attack on Israel is an attack on Israelis and Jews—and Israeli Arabs. By the same token, 100 percent of the Palestinians living in the West Bank and Gaza vote for terrorist organizations—either Fatah or Hamas. But if one were to draw the conclusion that Palestinians as a people supported terrorism, that opinion would be banned from the pages of the *Yale Daily News* and every other college newspaper as offensive to an ethnic group—although there is no ethnic group "Palestinian."

How did Yale's Jewish organizations respond to this malicious attack from a Hamas-supporting, Israel-hating campus group? According to the *Daily News* reporter, "a member of the Yale Hillel board and the co-president of Yale Friends of Israel criticized the flyers for being 'counterproductive' and 'disrespectful,' and also 'hyperbolic.'" But responding in such generalities did not come close to addressing the outrage that had been committed. Hillel did not want to think of upsetting Students for Justice in Palestine, which is a group that would like to see Israel destroyed and the Jews pushed into the sea. Too harsh? That is precisely what the SJP slogan, chanted on campuses across the country, promises: "From the river to the sea, Palestine will be free." One glance at a map of the Middle East will show that the eastern border of Israel is the Jordan River and the western border is the Mediterranean Sea. In other words, "Free Palestine from the river to the sea" means the obliteration of Israel. As it happens, this is the explicit goal of SJP's favorite Palestinian party, Hamas, enshrined in its charter: "Israel will exist and will continue to exist until Islam obliterates it."

On a brighter note, the *Yale Daily News* did publish an intelligent response to the eviction protest by two Jewish undergraduates, who pointed out, in an op-ed piece aptly titled "Evicting the Truth," that the demolition of homes by Israel was not a policy of random sadism but an attempt to discourage terrorists from killing Jews—at random.[2] Even these two defenders of Israel, however, could not muster the courage to confront the sinister reality of the SJP attack, which they described merely as "silly." They concluded their argument on this note: "Yale has a long tradition of serious conversation and intelligent dialogue. The time has come for organizations like SJP to contribute meaningfully. Let's have a real conversation; we'll even bring the *matzah*."[3] Yes, by all means bring the *matzah* to dine with people who want to obliterate you.

For Yale Hillel's self-abasing Jews, however, even sugarcoating your enemy's venom ("counterproductive," "hyperbolic," "silly") is an insufficient gesture of submission. You must also distance yourself from Jews who stand up to their enemies: "'We try to act constructively and respectfully on these issues, not divisively and hyperbolically,' said Josh Kalla '13, Israel Chair on the Hillel Board. Kalla noted that when the David Horowitz Center, a pro-settlement organization, published an incendiary full-page advertisement in the *News*, the [Joseph] Slifka Center [for Jewish Life at

---

[2]Leah Sarna and Yishai Schwartz, "Evicting the Truth," *Yale Daily News*, April 22, 2011; http://www.yaledailynews.com/news/2011/apr/22/schwartz-and-sarna-evicting-truth/
[3]Ibid.

Yale] also published a full-page advertisement, criticizing the Horowitz Center's approach to the debate."[4]

The ad we placed in the *Yale Daily News* was headlined: "The Palestinian Case Against Israel Is Based on a Genocidal Lie" (namely, that Israel occupies Palestinian land).[5] We didn't see the Slifka Center attack until later because it was available only in the print version of the paper. When my office called the Slifka Center and requested a copy of the ad from Steven Sitrin, its executive director, Sitrin barked into the phone, "We don't have it"—then, in as hostile a manner as he could muster, hung up the receiver. After failing to get the cooperation of Mr. Sitrin, I received a copy of the Slifka Center ad from the *Yale Daily News*. The ad was the response of Yale's Jews to Palestinian anti-Semites at Yale. Its gravamen was as follows: Horowitz is an Islamophobe; facts are hateful if they offend your enemies; and you are welcome to attend our forthcoming dialogue with the Ground Zero Mosque Imam Feisal Abdul Rauf, who will be appearing with our rabbi at the Slifka Center.[6]

As it happens, the director of Hillel for the Philadelphia region, Howard Alpert, has characterized as "incendiary" the contents of our advertisement, which we called "a factual reply to common anti-Israel propaganda." For the Slifka Center and Yale Hillel, a factual defense of the Jews in the Middle East is "incendiary" because it upsets the Israel-haters. But a campaign to portray the only existing Jewish state as an evil force that systematically

---

[4]Tapley Stephenson, "Flyers Threaten Eviction, Raise Awareness," *Yale Daily News*, April 22, 2011; http://yaledailynews.com/blog/2011/04/22/flyers-threaten-eviction-raise-awareness/

[5]This ad was also placed in *The New York Times*, May 2, 2011.

[6]Nathaniel Zelinsky, "A Jewish Student at Yale Stands Up," *Front Page Magazine*, March 26, 2011; http://frontpagemag.com/2011/front-pagemag-com/a-jewish-student-at-yale-stands-up/; Tapley Stephenson, "Imam Discusses Park51, Muslim Identity," *Yale Daily News*, March 24, 2011; http://yaledailynews.com/blog/2011/03/24/imam-discusses-park51-muslim-identity/

demolishes the homes of innocents is not incendiary. It's just "hyperbolic."

In closing, it should be observed that the *matzah* overture, with which the two undergraduates concluded their op-ed, was not incidental. To conduct their malevolent attack on the Jews, Students for Justice in Palestine had chosen the precise week Jews all over the world celebrate Passover, a religious commemoration of their flight to freedom from slavery in Egypt.

8

Andrew Sullivan's Defense of Tony Kushner

Andrew Sullivan has posted an attack on CUNY trustee Jeffrey Wiesenfeld for blocking a politically motivated honorary degree that was to be given to the over-rated, Israel-demonizing playwright Tony Kushner.[1] Andrew's intelligence is on display in the opening paragraph of his piece, where he reiterates his clear-headed views of Kushner's inflated literary reputation. Kushner's Pulitzer Prize-winning agitprop, *Angels in America*, is a puerile embarrassment. In recognizing this, Andrew shows that he is capable of breaking out of the bubble of liberal derangement when it suits him. All the more reason that Andrew's attack on Wiesenfeld is an illustration of the unhinged attitudes of current "critics" of Israel, who are in practice apologists for Hamas and their willing Gaza subjects.[2]

The Palestinian case against Israel, as we noted in a half-page ad we placed in *The New York Times*, is built on a genocidal lie that Andrew seems to have swallowed whole.[3] Andrew wonders how apologists for Jew-hating Arab aggressors in the Middle East can be regarded as anything but reasonable critics. After all, Israel

May 7, 2011, http://frontpagemag.com/2011/david-horowitz/andrew-sul-livans-misguided-defense-of-the-regrettable-mr-kushner/
[1] Andrew Sullivan, "The Mindset of Jeffrey S. Wiesenfeld," *The Dish*, May 6 2011; http://dish.andrewsullivan.com/2011/05/06/the-mind-of-jeffrey-s-wiesenfeld/
[2] http://www.discoverthenetworks.org/printgroupProfile.asp?grpid=6204
[3] "The Palestinians' Case Against Israel Is Based on a Genocidal Lie," *Front Page Magazine*, May 3, 2011; http://frontpagemag.com/2011/front-pagemag-com/freedom-centers-ad-in-todays-new-york-times-1/

refuses "to give up land conquered in war." Come again? Israel conquered nothing. Israel is the target of would-be conquerors whom it has managed to thwart through five or six (depending on how you count them) aggressive wars waged against the tiny Jewish state since 1948.

In 1948, the Arabs declared an unprovoked war on the Jews for having been given an internationally recognized mini-state on land previously possessed by the non-Arab Turks, who had held it for 400 years. That 1948 war—a racist war to expel a non-Arab people from the Middle East—has continued unabated for sixty years. Determined to "push the Jews into the sea," the Arab aggressors refused to sign peace agreements in 1949, in 1967, in 1973 and in 2000. When Israel unilaterally withdrew its troops from Gaza in 2006, absent a peace signed by the Arabs, Gaza instantly became a terrorist state, firing 7,000 rocket attacks into Israeli schoolyards and towns for more than a year before Israel struck back. Shame on Andrew for implying that this was not self-defense, and for calling Gaza "conquered land," as if Israel had been the aggressor. This is not reasonable criticism of Israel, Andrew; it is apologetics for war criminals.

Andrew then accuses Israel of insisting on "populating that land with its own people." Excuse me. We are still talking about the ruins of the Turkish (not Arab) empire. Since the Palestinian Arabs have never come to terms with the postwar status-quo, they are aggressors who have by all recognized laws of war forfeited their right to the land they were offered by the UN in 1948 and rejected. Pay attention to the character of the people whom the Jews are forced to deal with here. Five years ago, Israel forcibly extricated 7,500 law-abiding, productive Jews from Gaza because, without the presence of Israeli troops, they would have been slaughtered by the Palestinians. Not because of anything they had done, but because they were Jews. These are Nazis, Andrew; and that is why Kushner's support for them is regarded with such distaste by people like Jeffrey Wiesenfeld and myself.

You refer to the "brutal bombardment" of Gaza. Excuse me but, again, no. What country would allow itself to be assaulted by 7,000 rockets randomly shot into populated civilian areas without retaliation? And where was your outrage over these terrorist attacks, or over the fact that 100 percent of Palestinians support terrorist governments that have sworn to destroy the only Jewish state on earth?

Despite your raised eyebrows over Wiesenfeld's mild statement, the Palestinians have indeed earned themselves a special place in the annals of human depravity. In thousands of years of human suffering, there has never been a people that has strapped bombs onto its own children, instructed them to blow up other children, and treated them as martyrs and national heroes when they did. This is a sick, evil culture. The suffering of the Palestinians is self-inflicted, and no one can release them from their suffering but themselves.

9

Defaming Nonie Darwish

Tablet magazine has published a bizarre attack by Jeremy Seth Davis on an incredibly brave Arab defender of Israel and the Jews.[1] Nonie Darwish is the daughter of an Egyptian general who was chief of intelligence for Gamel Abdel Nasser when Gaza was part of Egypt, the West Bank had been annexed by Jordan, and nobody referred to Arabs as "Palestinians." Darwish's family lived in Gaza, where her father created the Fedayeen, the first terrorist organization dedicated to the murder of Jews and the destruction of the Jewish state. Her father was responsible for the murder of numerous Israeli civilians before he was killed by the Israeli Defense Forces in a targeted assassination.[2] At the time, Nonie was eight years old.

In her memoir *Now They Call Me Infidel*, Darwish describes how she was brought up in a Muslim Arab culture of hate, and how she gradually freed herself from this culture—coming to understand that it was the very hatred she had been taught, unjustly directed against the Jews, that had killed her father. A particularly compelling incident she relates concerns her brother's decision to check himself into an Israeli hospital to be treated for a

July 7, 2011, http://www.tabletmag.com/jewish-news-and-politics/71736/anti-defamation/[1]Jeremy Seth Davis, "Heretic," *Tablet,* June 30, 2011; http://www.tabletmag.com/jewish-news-and-politics/71348/heretic

[2]Yossi Melman, "Targeted Killings—A Retro Fashion Very Much in Vogue," *Haaretz,* March 24, 2004; http://www.haaretz.com/print-edition/features/targeted-killings-a-retro-fashion-very-much-in-vogue-1.117714

burst appendix, rather than go to an Arab hospital in Gaza. Even though he was the son of a terrorist whom the Israelis had killed, her brother trusted his life with Jews rather than with his fellow Arabs. This decision taught his younger sister that the demonic image of the Jews that had been instilled in her as a small child was false, a travesty of the truth. This is what led her to turn against the Muslim-Arab culture of hate and to found an organization called Arabs for Israel, dedicated to defending the Jews from the genocidal campaign that her own people were waging.[3]

For this sin, Jeremy Seth Davis has described her as a renegade and an "apostate," comparable to those Jews in the Middle Ages who converted to Christianity to join in the attack on their fellow Jews. Merely to state Davis's thesis is to refute it. The Jews of the Middle Ages were tiny minorities, forced to live in hostile Christian societies that regarded them as God-killers. They were burned at the stake for refusing to convert to Christianity, and entire communities were expelled from countries they had resided in for centuries, on grounds they were a poisonous presence that could no longer be tolerated. By contrast, there are a million and a half Arabs who are Israeli citizens with more rights as Israelis than Arabs enjoy in 22 Arab states. There are 300 million Arabs living in those states. Jews are a tiny minority occupying .02 percent of the land mass of the Middle East. They are among the most isolated and persecuted peoples on the face of the earth. Even in America, the number of official hate crimes against Jews is nearly *ten times* greater than that of hate crimes against Muslims or Arabs.[4]

In the Middle East, the head of the Islamic Republic of Iran has called for the extermination of the Jews, a sentiment met with no noticeable dissent by the leaders of other Muslim states. In Gaza, the leader of Hamas has warned Jews, "you are headed for

---

[3] http://www.arabsforisrael.com/
[4] Hate Crimes Statistics, Federal Bureau of Investigation, http://www2.fbi.gov/ucr/hc2009/data/table_07.html

annihilation"—while, in Lebanon, the leader of Hezbollah has expressed his hope that Jews will all gather in Israel so he won't have to hunt them down globally. On its official TV programs and in its public schools, the Palestinian Authority lionizes terrorists who have murdered innocent women and children merely because they are Jews. Leaders of the Palestinian Authority and Hamas publicly call for the "liberation" of Palestine "from the river to the sea," which is today's code for the original Arab war cry: "Push the Jews into the sea."

In the context of this genocidal campaign to solve the Jewish problem by getting rid of the Jews, Nonie Darwish travels to college campuses to defend them and to warn others about the dangers of Muslim and Arab Jew-hatred. When she arrives, she is verbally attacked and physically threatened by members of the campus left and most venomously by members of the Muslim Students Association—an arm of the Muslim Brotherhood, and sponsor of campus outrages that libel Israel as an "apartheid state," alleging that Israel has stolen the land of a (fictional) Palestinian state. Davis finds admirable these assaults on a middle-aged Arab woman for having the temerity to defend Jews. In his rendering, they are an understandable response to her "apostasy," as though she were a religious heretic—when in fact she is merely someone who has the decency and the courage to be outraged by the fanatical Jew-hatred publicly expressed by her Muslim and Arab compatriots.

If Davis wants a parallel to the defenders of Jew-hating Christians in the Middle Ages, it is those Jews who have joined the genocidal coalition of Arabs and Muslims intent on destroying the Jewish state. These are the Jews who joined the flotilla to Gaza, organized by the Muslim Brotherhood to break the blockade against arms shipments to the Hamas terrorists who had sworn to obliterate Israel. These are the Jews who join Muslim Brotherhood organizations on college campuses in obstructing the speeches and threatening the safety of speakers like Darwish, who defend the Jewish state. They are also, as it happens, upholding the oppression of women and gays and other minorities in Islamic states. Jeremy Seth Davis writes of Nonie, as though it were a negative commentary, that she is supported by conservatives; or that her defense of free speech, women's rights, gay rights, and Jewish rights in the face of Muslim attacks mirrors comments made by conservatives. A better question to ask is: why aren't liberals and progressives supporting Nonie Darwish, and defending these victims of Muslim attacks?

A Malignant Cause

I want to thank Brandon Hartness, the Committee for a Better Carolina, and Christians United for Israel for inviting me to speak tonight. I wish I had also been invited by Jewish groups on this campus, but they are in a state of denial when it comes to the threat facing Israel and the Jews.

The subject of my talk is Israel, but it is really about America as well. Israel is the canary in the coal mine. When you watch Hassan Nasrallah, the head of Hezbollah, lead tens of thousands of Muslims in Lebanon in chants of "Death to America! Death to Israel!" you understand the fates of the two are linked. When you hear Iran's dictator, Mahmoud Ahmadinejad, lead similar crowds in chants of "Death to Israel! Death to America!" you see that they are linked. The coiner of the slogan linking them as enemies of Islam (and also the secular left) was the Ayatollah Khomeini, father of the modern *jihad* against the West, who called America "The Great Satan" and Israel "The Little Satan."

When gauging human conflicts, it is important to look at people's intentions. Probably none of you ever wondered why we don't have missiles pointing towards our northern neighbor, or an army stationed on the Canadian border. That's because we understand that, whatever resentments Canadians may have against us, and such national resentments are normal to human communities,

---

Edited transcript of a speech given at the University of North Carolina Chapel Hill on March 12, 2012; http://frontpagemag.com/2012/david-horowitz/the-war-against-the-jews-of-the-middle-east/

their main intentions towards us are friendly and benign. But if people had understood or correctly read Hitler's intentions in the 1930s, 70 million lives might have been saved. Hitler systematically violated the international peace agreements that were meant to keep Germany from re-emerging as a major aggressive power. Then he took Austria and a major piece of Czechoslovakia, foreshadowing his designs to take on the world. But there were always people in the West, leaders in the West, who said, "We can do business with Hitler, we can negotiate with him, we can appease his appetites short of war." And they were wrong.

The Jews, too, misread Hitler's intentions. There would be a lot more Jews in the world today if the Jews had understood the intentions of the Nazis. There were five hundred thousand Jews imprisoned in the Warsaw Ghetto. But they didn't think the Germans were going to kill them. Even when the Germans put them in these ghettos which they were not allowed to leave, the Jews didn't wake up. They formed governing councils and organized themselves, identifying all their inhabitants as though they were citizens of a normal state. And this simply made it easier for the Germans to ship them out to the concentration camps and the gas chambers. They thought they were going to work- camps. All in all, they made it easier for the Germans to kill them because they thought the Germans were too civilized to commit such heinous crimes. The Jewish communities of Europe misread the intentions of the Germans, and now they no longer exist.

So I want to begin this talk tonight by reading some statements made by Palestinian leaders, which express their intentions towards the Jews. Mahmoud al-Zahar is a founder of Hamas and one of its current leaders. This is what he has said: "There is no place for you Jews among us, and you have no future among the nations of the world. You are headed for annihilation." Ahmad Bahar, who is acting chairman of the Gaza parliament and a member of Hamas, has said: "Be certain that America is on its way to disappear. Allah take hold of the Jews and their allies. Allah take hold of the Americans and their allies. Allah count them and kill them to the last one, don't leave even one." On the official Hamas website, there is a video of a Hamas suicide bomber who can be seen saying this: "My message to the Jews is that there is no god but Allah. We are a nation that drinks blood and we know that there is no blood better than the blood of Jews. We will not leave you alone until we have quenched our thirst with your blood and our children's thirst with your blood."

Yusuf al-Qaradawi, the spiritual leader of the Muslim Brotherhood, spoke not long ago to millions of reverent Muslims on Al Jazeera TV and said this: "Throughout history Allah has imposed upon the Jews people who would punish them for their corruption. The last punishment was carried out by Hitler by means of all the things he did to them—even though they exaggerated this issue— he managed to put them in their place. This was divine punishment for them. Allah willing, the next time will be at the hands of the believers."[1] In other words, Islam intends to finish the job that Hitler started—or Muhammad, for that matter. The prophet Muhammad has said, as recorded in a holy *hadith:* "The Day of Judgment will not come about until Muslims fight the Jews, when the Jew will hide behind stones and trees. The stones and trees will say, 'O Muslims, O Abdullah, there is a Jew behind me, come and kill him.'"[2] This genocidal saying of the prophet is quoted in the Hamas Charter, which also says: "Israel will exist and will continue to exist until Islam will obliterate it, just as it obliterated others before it."[3]

On American campuses across this country, members of Students for Justice in Palestine and the Muslim Students Association

---

[1]Sheik Yusuf Al-Qaradawi, "Allah Imposed Hitler Upon the Jews to Punish Them," *Middle East Media Research Institute* (aired on Al Jazeera TV, January 30, 2009); http://www.memritv.org/clip_transcript/en/2005.htm

[2]"Islam and Anti-Semitism," *Wikipedia,* http://en.wikipedia.org/wiki/Islam_and_antisemitism

[3]Hamas Charter, (Hamas Covenant 1988), http://avalon.law.yale.edu/20th_century/hamas.asp

chant: "From the river to the sea, Palestine will be free." The river is the Jordan, which is Israel's border to the east; the sea is the Mediterranean, which is Israel's border to the west. "From the river to the sea" is Israel. What Students for Justice in Palestine are chanting, what members of the Muslim Students Association and their leftist allies are chanting, is a statement of intention to obliterate the state of Israel.

What is "Palestine"? The name is not Arabic. It is a name that was given to Judea and Samaria, which is now called the West Bank, and which is the historic homeland of the Jews. In 66 AD the Jews had the bad judgment to rebel against the Roman Empire; they were defeated, and a million Jews were killed. To humiliate the Jews of Judea still further, the Romans renamed their homeland after their enemies, the Philistines. There were no Arabs in the region at that time. The Philistines were red-headed Aegean sailors, not Arabs. For 2000 years after that, there was no people calling itself Palestinian. In fact, there was no people calling itself Palestinian until 1964, fifteen years after the state of Israel had been created, which is one of the reasons that Newt Gingrich recently observed that the Palestinians are "an invented people." Palestine is the name of a region, like "New England." If you were talking about Palestinians in 1948, you would have been talking about Jews. We inhabit a kind of surreal universe now, particularly in universities, which are the most conformist institutions in our country, which is why these facts might seem strange. The university has become a one-party state where people on the left talk to each other and nobody challenges them, which is why everything I'm going to say tonight will probably seem strange. But if you can overcome your emotions and look at the facts, you'll see that everything I'm saying is accurate.

The, Big Lie repeated by Hamas and the PLO, by everyone on the political Left and by all supporters of the Palestinian cause, is the claim that Israel occupies Palestinian land, or that it occupies Arab land. In fact, the land that Israel was created on, which is the same land that Syria, Lebanon, Iraq and Jordan were created on, belonged to the Ottoman Turks for 400 years prior to that. Turks are not Arabs. The Turks joined the losing side in the First World War, and when the war was over the Ottoman Empire was dismantled. This accorded with international law and international tradition. After the war, the European victors were given mandates over the conquered empire, and they carved out these five nations. The "Palestine Mandate" was a piece of the defeated empire, a region and not a people. Along with the Jews, there were Arabs living in the Mandate, but there was no "Palestinian people." In 1922, Churchill assigned 80 percent of the Palestine Mandate to a state he named "Trans-Jordan," which is now the state of Jordan. Seventy percent of the people living in this area were Arabs who inhabited the region called "Palestine." In other words, 70 percent of Jordan is "Palestinian." But you never hear anybody complain that Jordan is "occupied" Palestine. Jordan is 80 percent of the landmass of the original Palestine Mandate. Where is the movement for self-determination of Jordan's Palestinians? There is none. There is none because the agenda of the Palestinians and their leftwing supporters is not to create a Palestinian state but to push the Jews into the sea.

> [At this point about 40 members of the audience, most of them members of the Muslim Students Association and Students for Justice in Palestine, and supporters of Hamas—some wearing *keffiyehs*, the terrorist symbol created by Yasser Arafat— marched out of the room on a pre-arranged cue.[4]]

Goodbye, everybody. These are supposed to be college students, supposed to be at this school to learn.

To continue, the British and the United Nations divided the remaining 20 percent of the original Palestine Mandate between the Jews and the Arabs. They divided the remaining 20 percent equally, except that they gave the Jews three slivers of land, not

---

[4]http://www.youtube.com/watch?feature=player_embedded&v=AZjpSC_USpU

exactly contiguous, and 60 percent of that land was an arid desert. The Arabs were awarded the west bank of the Jordan River, which is the historic homeland of the Jews. But the Arabs rejected their share of the land, and on the day Israel was created in 1948, eight Arab dictatorships attacked the Jews with the stated intention of pushing them into the sea. That war has never ended. It is the Arabs' aggression against the state of Israel, their desire to push the Jews into the sea, that is the cause—the sole cause—of the conflict in the Middle East.

Following their victory in the 1948 war, the Israelis offered to sign a peace with the Arabs and live side by side with an Arab state. But the Arabs did not want a Palestinian state, then or for the next sixty years. They rejected a state every time it was offered to them because that has never been their goal. Their goal is to expel a non-Muslim people from the region, and make it Muslim. Islam is—and has always been—an imperial religion that expands by force. No one can leave Islam. For apostates, the sentence is death. Similarly, once an area is Muslim, it has to remain Muslim. That is the creed.

When the war ended in 1949, Egypt annexed Gaza and Jordan annexed the West Bank. There was not a peep out of the entire Arab world about the annexation of Gaza or the annexation of Jordan, or the fact that the so-called Palestinians not only lacked a home, they didn't have the land they had been promised to build on. Why was there no protest? Because the war was not about self-determination for the Palestinians or the Arabs. It was, and still is, about getting rid of the Jews.

The founder of the Muslim Brotherhood, Hassan al-Banna, was an admirer of Hitler. In 1948, al-Banna said, "If the Jews get a state in Israel, Islam will push the Jews into the sea." That is the agenda, and it has never changed. In 1964, when the West Bank was still part of Jordan and Gaza still part of Egypt, the Egyptian dictator Nasser sponsored the creation of the Palestine Liberation Organization as a weapon against the Jews. You can read the original PLO charter on the Internet. You will not find a word about liberating the Palestinians of the West Bank, or about self-determination for the Palestinians of Gaza. The PLO mission, as stated in its charter, is all about obliterating the Zionists—Israel—the Jews.

As a result of Israel's victory in the 1967 war, the West Bank and Gaza were liberated from Egypt and Jordan. That war was the second Arab aggression in 20 years whose stated purpose was to destroy the Jewish state. When Israel won the war, it offered to return Gaza and the West Bank to Arab rule in exchange for a peace treaty that would recognize Israel's right to exist. The Arabs rejected the offer. The aggressors all met in Khartoum in 1967 and issued a joint statement which is generally referred to as "The Three No's"—"No recognition of Israel; No negotiation; No peace." That is the reason Israeli troops continued to occupy Gaza and the West Bank. Their purpose was to prevent further aggressions by the Arab states through these corridors, and also to prevent their use as terrorist launching pads by the PLO and Hamas.

Israel cannot just unilaterally withdraw from these territories and allow those who seek its destruction to attack again. They need to have a peace treaty that recognizes their right to exist, and they need to redraw their borders to make their territory more defensible. It is the internationally recognized procedure for dealing with aggressors, when they lose, to redraw the map so that the victims have a greater ability to defend themselves the next time. Germany attacked Poland twice in the 20th century, so in 1945 the Allies took the entire region of East Prussia, which was the industrial heartland of Germany, and gave it to Poland. How many Germans do you think had to be resettled? *Twelve million.* Twelve million Germans were uprooted from places they had inhabited since the Middle Ages. And nobody complained. If the Jews had acted the way other nations act, they would have annexed the West Bank in 1967 and they would have moved all the Arabs into Jordan, which is a majority Palestinian state. But they didn't do that. The Jews tried to be nice. They thought: if we're nice to them, they'll be nice to us. No, they won't. They hate you, and want to push you into the sea.

In the years preceding the 1993 Oslo accords, when Israel was the ruling authority in the West Bank and Gaza, the Israelis poured hundreds of millions of dollars into these territories and created universities; the economy of the West Bank grew at a rate that was the fifth-fastest in the world. Then came the so-called "Oslo peace process," which established the Palestinian Authority, brought the terrorist Arafat back from Tunisia and gave him control of the West Bank and Gaza. Within six months of Palestinian rule, the standard of living in Gaza had declined by 25 percent and the unemployment rate went from 10 to 40 percent. These are the real oppressors of Palestinians: the PLO and Hamas.

The malicious intentions towards the Jews are not extraneous to this struggle. They *are* the struggle. The father of Palestinian nationalism is Haj Amin al-Husseini, the Grand Mufti of Jerusalem, who led massacres of the Jews in the 1920s and 1930s *because* they were Jews—well before the creation of the state of Israel. Al-Husseini was a Nazi—literally—who went to Berlin to serve Hitler. Al-Husseini was a protégé of Hassan al-Banna, the founder of the Muslim Brotherhood. He recruited an Arab legion to fight for Hitler, and also drew up his own plans to create a death camp for Jews in the Middle East. The only reason his plan wasn't implemented was that Montgomery defeated Rommel in the battle of El Alamein. Today, al-Husseini is honored on the West Bank with a holiday as the founder of the Palestinian cause.

This is a Nazi movement. The statements I read at the outset of this talk are Nazi statements. The difference is this: Hitler concealed his plans for the Final Solution because he thought the German people were too civilized to accept them. The Palestinians and their Iranian allies shout their plans from the rooftops. Where in the Muslim world is the great dissent from this evil summons? It is too bad that all our Muslim friends have left the room and did not stay to hear this; but notwithstanding the evil intentions of Muslim leaders in the Middle East, there are good Muslims and there are bad Muslims, and most are probably good Muslims— decent, law-abiding, desirous of peace. But there were good

Germans, too, and in the end they didn't make a damn's worth of difference. I will know a moderate Muslim when he or she stands up and condemns these kinds of statements and the actions they inspire. It's not really that hard to know who your friends are. But a lot of people have difficulty in knowing who their enemies are, and that is the problem we are facing today.

Israel is in a very hard place. A significant portion of its plight is its own doing—not reading the intentions of its enemies. The Oslo peace accords were a disastrous mistake. When Oslo began, the terrorist Yasser Arafat was in exile in Tunisia. For the sake of peace with people who wanted to push them into the sea, the Jews brought Arafat back to Ramallah and armed his terrorist "police force" with 40-thousand weapons. Instead of sowing the seeds of peace, this offering was taken as an opportunity by Israel's enemies to begin a new phase in their war of extermination, one in which the Hamas Nazis are dictating the tactics—suicide bombing in particular, and now rocket attacks from the territory of Gaza, which Israel had evacuated in order to give peace a chance.

Why do people fall for these illusions? Why would they think that other people, having stated quite clearly their goal to obliterate them, might be persuaded by appeasement and withdrawal to give up that goal? It's the "hopey-changey" thing in all of us. The wish is father to the thought. We want things to be better; we don't want to face the fact that there is evil in the world, and that it has to be contained by superior force. People don't want to hear that. On our college campuses today, you can't even inform people about the threats we are facing. Our Freedom Center has produced a pamphlet, written by Dan Greenfield, about Muslim hate-groups on campuses; it describes in great detail the malevolent activities of the Muslim Students Association and Students for Justice in Palestine.[5] I tried to place an ad for that pamphlet in thirty college

---

[5]Daniel Greenfield, "Muslim Hate Groups on Campus," January 20, 2012; http://frontpagemag.com/2012/frontpagemag-com/muslim-hate-groups-on-campus-2/

papers. Only one, Ohio State, agreed to print it—a paid advertisement, mind you. Of course, there was a big eruption when it appeared in the Ohio State paper.

On a college campus, you can't talk about Palestinians having evil intentions. That's offensive. According to the editor of one of the papers to whom we submitted our ad, it's a "generalization" and that's unacceptable. You can't say all Palestinians support terrorism or the war to obliterate the Jewish state. That would be racist. All right, where is the Palestinian "Peace Now" organization? Tell me that. Where is the Palestinian standing up in the West Bank or Gaza, or in the United States, for the rights of Jews? There are hundreds of thousands, if not millions, of Jews who are standing up for what they perceive to be the rights of Palestinians. But there are no Palestinians or members of the Muslim Students Association refuting the lie that Israel is an "apartheid state." It's all about intentions. It's all about culture. And the Palestinian culture is a culture of hate.

Don't tell me that Palestinians in their majorities, and through their elected governments, support suicide bombers because they are desperate; that "the Israelis have tanks, we have suicide bombers." People have been oppressed in many places for thousands of years, horribly oppressed; but never in the entire history of mankind has an oppressed people strapped bombs on its own children and sent them to blow themselves up and kill other children, telling them that if they do, and they are lucky enough to be male, they will go to heaven and receive 72 virgins as a reward for their good deed. That is sick. Gaza is a death-cult created by Hamas. A similar cult exists in the West Bank, run by Hamas's ally the Palestine Liberation Organization, which lionizes the murderers of children, makes national heroes of terrorists who set out to target children. Who does this but psychopaths? The Palestinian regimes have institutionalized psychopathic behavior. You can see it on the Web—the preachers preaching "death to Jews," the little kids dressed up as suicide bombers, the children's television cartoons encouraging them to murder Jews.

There was a documentary on HBO called *A Death in Gaza*, made by liberals, which was about this death cult. The filmmakers followed two twelve-year-old boys who were hanging around Hamas, aspiring to be suicide bombers. They recited poems in their school classes about becoming suicide bombers. It was a very sad picture. During the film, one of the kids was shot. Suddenly he was transformed back into a little kid no longer boasting about becoming a suicide bomber but crying for his mother, screaming in pain. In another sequence, one of the boys was playing "rock, paper, scissors" with a Hamas terrorist. When the kid went back home, the filmmaker said to the terrorist: "I see that you use this kid as a runner and lookout. Isn't that a little dangerous for a twelve-year-old? He could get killed." The terrorist answered: "Oh, we have thousands of kids like that we can replace him with."

At the end of the film, the director himself is killed. Nobody knows who killed him. He is out in the field and is shot. The film ends with a sequence with the kids. After they come through the terrible experience of one of them being wounded and in pain, the filmmakers ask them what they'd like to be now, and they say, "filmmakers." That's how sick that situation is. These kids begin their lives, like most kids, with hope and decent aspirations, and the adults turn them into aspiring terrorists. This is a whole society geared to bringing up its children to kill Jews.

I've talked to campus leftists who are supporting the Palestinian cause, and they're not stupid. So why are they sucked into this sickness, into being apologists for evil? I have some insight into this because I grew up in the left. My own parents were Communists and I was one of the founders of the New Left, so I have a fairly educated view as to what might go on in the minds of those who are seduced by causes. Everywhere one looks in this world, one can see misery and suffering. If the world could be changed to eliminate the suffering, who would not want to see that happen? Progressives and leftists are social redeemers. They want to repair the world and alleviate the suffering. What they refuse to see is the awful legacy of the movements that have actually set out to change the world. Nazism was one. If we just rid the world of the Jews and the mongrel races, we can create heaven on earth. Communism was another. If we just get rid of the capitalists—the 1 percent—we can create paradise on earth. What Communist progressives created, in fact, was the most oppressive state in the history of the world. In the name of "social justice" they murdered 120 million people, in peacetime, created unimaginable poverty and man-made famines. That's what progressives produce when they get the power to pursue their ends.

The lesson of this history is that you can only change the world a little piece at a time. There's a reason we are where we are and not somewhere else. The obstacle to the realization of all progressive utopias is human nature. You can read all the Marxist and leftist texts ever written and never encounter a serious consideration of what people are actually made of—what they are capable of—and consequently why it is so difficult to produce a society of human beings that is fundamentally different from the way human beings have lived since the beginning of recorded time. In the absence of such sobering reflection, the fantasy persists: we're going to change the world. It is the fantasy that inspires Osama bin Laden and the *jihadists:* We will make everybody Muslim and force them to live under *sharia* law, and then the world will be a holy place. And if you don't agree to be holy, we'll kill you— exactly the same mentality as the Nazis and the Communists.

There's a natural affinity between all movements for an earthly redemption. That's why the Islamists have been able to make common cause with progressives and have learned to talk in the language of the left—the totalitarian language of social justice. It's a noble idea, but it is also an impossible—and therefore horribly destructive—dream.

Jews Who Stand with Their Enemies

L ast week I travelled to Chapel Hill, North Carolina to speak about the Middle East and the campus campaign to demonize Israel as an apartheid state. I was invited by Christians United for Israel and the Committee for a Better Carolina, a conservative student group whose leaders also are not Jewish. I mention this otherwise irrelevant fact because they asked me specifically to speak about the war against Israel in the Middle East; and when I asked their leader Brandon Hartness why, he said to me, "because there is no one making a strong argument for Israel on this campus."

As on most campuses, there is a large and active campus Jewish group at Chapel Hill, namely Hillel. But UNC Hillel was not about to invite me or to sponsor this speech. In fact, UNC Hillel had attacked me the previous spring when these same students, again led by Brandon Hartness, put up a banner created by the Freedom Center to refute the genocidal lies that make up the Palestinian case against Israel.[1] We called the banner the "Wall of Lies" to counter the "Israeli Apartheid Walls" of the Muslim Students Association and the lies inscribed on them.[2] The most fundamental of these lies is that Israel "occupies" Arab land, and that this occupation is the source of the conflict. The lie effectively

---

March 19, 2012, http://frontpagemag.com/2012/david-horowitz/jewish-students-who-stand-with-israel%E2%80%99s-enemies-and-call-them-brothers/
[1]http://www.wall-of-truth.org/
[2]See Part II, Chapter 5, "Palestinian Wall of Lies," above.

delegitimizes the Jewish state and underpins the claim that Palestine extends "from the river to the sea"—which would obliterate Israel completely.

When the "Wall of Lies" banner was erected on the UNC campus last spring, two directors of Hillel—Ari Gauss and Sheila Katz—wrote a letter to the *Daily Tar Heel* dissociating themselves from our Wall and defending the Muslim Students Association, which the Wall identified as the group making the false claim. This was not the first or only attack on the Wall of Lies by liberal Jews active in the university community, and was mild compared to others, which had denounced me as an "Islamophobe" and "racist." At the University of Pennsylvania, Hillel students had voiced these slanders in a joint letter signed by members of the Hamas-supporting group "Penn for Palestine" and the Muslim Students Association.[3]

In an attempt to understand these reactions, I contacted Hillel officials at Penn and attempted to explore ways to work with them. At a bare minimum, I hoped to avoid being attacked by Jews for my efforts to defend the Jewish state. I met with Hillel's regional director in Philadelphia, Rabbi Howard Alpert, and more than a dozen Jewish student leaders. Hillel had issued policy guidelines forbidding its local chapters from entering working partnerships with organizations that did not defend the existence of the Jewish state—which should have included the Muslim Students Association and Students for Justice in Palestine. Unfortunately, this was a policy not always observed by the local chapters, which were independently funded and run. But my contacts with Hillel directors who shared my views of the conflict, including Rabbi Alpert, made me want to work with them to change that.

From my discussions in Philadelphia, I drew two conclusions. First, I had made a mistake in not discussing the ads with members of Hillel before placing them. The appearance of the ads

---

[3] https://secure.donationreport.com/productlist.html?key=5DGIXYHTR-FJI

inevitably created a local firestorm, thanks to the aggressive behavior of the Muslim student organizations and the political left, which attacked them as "Islamophobic" and "racist" at every turn. This was a standard operating procedure of the left generally, whose goal is never to engage an opinion that challenges its core beliefs but instead to demonize and marginalize it. In pursuit of this goal, leftists have shown no qualms about implicating others in their smears, making any group on campus that is Jewish or "pro-Israel" a party to the crime.

The second observation was that my approach to the defense of Israel was fundamentally different from that of most Hillel chapters. I believed that the way to combat genocidal claims and intentions was by identifying them for what they were and confronting them. By contrast, members of Hillel—even those who understood these malevolent agendas—felt that the defense of Israel should be positive; that it should stress the tolerance, creativity and generosity of the Jewish state, while refraining from identifying its enemies and their supporters with the genocidal intentions they held. In my view, the refusal to identify Israel's enemies with their malignant goals weakened the case for Israel's defense. The left understands that demonizing one's adversary as a "colonial occupier" is the most effective argument, even though it requires disregarding the facts. But pro-Israel groups like Hillel, from fear of offending the Muslim organizations and the left, give their most important asset away at the outset. This forces them to play defense, which is always the weaker position. The left understands that intimidation through name-calling is an effective technique—which is why so many Jewish students are reluctant to "provoke" them by speaking blunt truths.

After my discussions in Philadelphia, I decided to submit the ad I planned to run in the UNC student paper—the *Daily Tar Heel*—to the UNC Hillel director, Ari Gauss. The ad was designed to expose the connections of the leading sponsor of the "Israeli Apartheid" weeks to the Islamic *jihad* against Israel and the West, and thus to put the other side on the defensive. It was headlined,

"Where Are They Now?" and featured nine former presidents of the Muslim Students Association who had gone on to leadership positions in Al-Qaeda and other terrorist organizations. The most famous among them was Anwar Awlaki, mentor of the Christmas bomber and the Fort Hood assassin, who had previously been president of the Muslim Students Association at Colorado State University. Since the Muslim Students Association is basically a recruitment front for the Muslim Brotherhood, this should come as no surprise, yet these facts were invisible on university campuses. Also featured in the ad was the pamphlet we had produced, written by Daniel Greenfield and titled "Muslim Hate Groups on Campus."[4] The pamphlet documented the anti-Jewish hate-weeks and other outrages committed by the Muslim Students Association and Students for Justice in Palestine. Greenfield also traced the groups' lineage back to the Muslim Brotherhood and Hamas.

After receiving my email with the proposed ad, Ari Gauss sent this reply:

> While it's unspeakably upsetting and problematic that our campuses are supporting individuals that become leaders in terrorist organizations, my chief concern about the ad is that it's not clear to me 1) how connected one campus MSA may be to another and 2) specifically, how connected UNC's MSA chapter is to the national entity or other campus MSA chapters. To run this ad in UNC's paper suggests that UNC's MSA is connected to the others in some meaningful way and part of the problem. I'm not convinced that this is the case.

I have heard this argument from more than one Hillel director, and it always puzzles me. Why would an organization take on the same name as an already-existing national organization like MSA, which has chapters on virtually every campus, if it were not related to it? Wouldn't the national MSA sue any unrelated

---

[4]Daniel Greenfield, "Muslim Hate Groups on Campus," January 20, 2012; http://frontpagemag.com/2012/frontpagemag-com/muslim-hate-groups-on-campus-2/

organization that appropriates its name and recruits members using its name? Of course it would. In any case, a quick search of the national MSA website shows that the UNC chapter is indeed one of the national MSA affiliates. Apparently Gauss didn't bother to look.

Because I wanted to work with Gauss and forestall an attack on my appearance by the campus Hillel, I let this go and agreed not to run the ad. In a phone conversation, Gauss explained to me that, in his view, the Muslim Students Association at UNC was "not political." Hillel worked closely, in fact, with the UNC-MSA chapter and had established a joint "Israeli-Palestinian Dialogue Committee" with its members. Gauss was very proud of the dialogue. I asked him if this "dialogue" was based on a public commitment by the MSA that the Jewish state had a right to exist on the land now called Israel. I got no satisfactory response but again chose to continue our own dialogue. Since I had withdrawn the ad, I asked Gauss if he would distribute our pamphlet, *Muslim Hate Groups on Campus*, to his Hillel students, because they (and obviously he as well) needed to be informed about what was actually taking place on campuses across the country. He said he would do this, so I sent him 50 copies.

When the speaking date was set, my office called Gauss to arrange an in-person meeting with him and some Hillel students. Jeffrey Wienir, who runs our campus programs, informed me that he was having trouble setting up such a meeting, because the Hillel students were "to the left" and didn't want to be in the same room with me. It would require Gauss's intervention to get any of them to agree. When I arrived at his office a few hours before my speech, we had a brief chat in which he reiterated that he had good working relationships with the Muslim Students Association. Then he introduced me to two students who were willing to meet with me, whose names were Jacob and Josh.

Josh Orol was the co-president of the campus Hillel. His partner, Jacob, was visibly agitated when I entered the room. "Why did you run that ad last year?" he asked, referring to the ad containing the Wall of Lies I had placed in the *Tar Heel*. I asked him what he objected to. He said its references to the Koran were wrong and it was an attack on a religion. Neither of us could remember what the ad actually said; in fact the only reference to the Koran was that Jerusalem, which the Palestinians now claim is a Muslim holy city, was never mentioned in it. But I jumped right in. "The ad doesn't attack Muslims," I said. Then I asked whether he didn't agree that Islam was problematic in a way that Christianity and Judaism were not. I pointed out that Christians worshipped a carpenter who preached non-violence and never committed a violent act in his life. By contrast, Muslims worshipped a warrior who spread his religion by force, killed those he considered infidels, and had committed genocide against an entire community of Jews— the Qurayza tribe—*because* they were Jews. To which Jacob responded: "Well, in the Torah, Joshua conducted a war of extermination against the Amalekites."

"That's true," I said, "except for this difference: there are no Amalekites around anymore and there haven't been for more than a thousand years. But there *are* Jews, and there are Imams and dictators all over the world screaming for our destruction." At this point, Josh Orol spoke up to support Jacob: "In the Torah it says that rabbis should decapitate a Jew who does not observe the Sabbath." "That's news to me," I replied. "But when was the last time you heard of a rabbi decapitating anyone, let alone a Jew, for not observing the Sabbath?"

Anxious to break free of this surreal discussion—all too typical of the left—I returned to Jacob's original question and said: "The reason I wrote the ad was to identify the Palestinian case against Israel as a genocidal lie; namely, that Israel occupies Palestinian land. In fact, Israel was created out of the Turkish Empire. The Turks are not Arabs, let alone Palestinians." This comment poured oil on the already crackling flames; the conversation became testy and passionate as the two of them claimed that this history didn't matter. What mattered was "international law" under which Israel's occupation of the West Bank, according to them, was "illegal" and therefore indefensible. It was the standard PLO/Hamas line. I deliberately didn't accuse them of spouting the Palestinian line; but whatever I did say provoked an outburst from Josh Orol, who proclaimed with ardor that he considered the head of the Muslim Students Association not only his friend "but my brother."

I said, "If you consider him your brother, you might ask him whether he believes the Jews have a right to a Jewish state in the land that is Israel and, if he does, would he state that publicly."

"I could not do that," Josh replied. "It would be insulting." This spoke volumes about the suppliant attitude of the co-president of campus Hillel towards Israel's enemies.

Ari Gauss, who had not spoken until then, said it was time to conclude the conversation. I reached into my pocket and pulled out our pamphlet *Muslim Hate Groups on Campus,* thinking that Josh Orol should become acquainted with its contents. "Have you seen this?" I said. He hadn't. I realized then that Gauss hadn't distributed the pamphlets to his Hillel students as he said he would. "You've been remiss," I said to him. "Yes," he replied, "I've been remiss."

When I reached the hall where I was to speak, there were about 160 people assembled to hear me, about 60 of them students. I was a little concerned to see that the front rows were filled with students who were obviously Muslim, some with headscarves and at least one with a *keffiyeh,* the badge of Palestinian *jihadists.* Security is always an issue for me at such events, since I have been physically attacked on several campuses, and the words used by the left to defame me are easily translatable into incitements to violence. Nonetheless, this was a southern campus, and in my experience such campuses are generally better behaved than those in other regions.

My speech focused on two points: first, that the intentions of Israel's adversaries in the Middle East are genocidal, their goal being the obliteration of the Jewish state. Second, that this has been the goal of the Arab states and the Palestinians since Israel's creation in 1948. The rest of my speech was devoted to a historical narrative in which I documented the disinterest of the Palestinians in self-determination or in establishing a state. The 40 members of the MSA and Students for Justice in Palestine who had positioned themselves in the front rows didn't bother to wait around for the historical review. About fifteen minutes into my talk, they stood up on cue and marched out in unison. They had come only to protest, and were uninterested in hearing the facts or disputing them.

I learned from the report in the *Daily Tar Heel* the next day that the leader of the walkout was Mariem Massmoudi, a member of the Muslim Students Association and "co-founder" of the "Israeli-Palestinian Dialogue Committee" that Gauss had praised. I also learned, from an article in the Internet magazine *The Blaze*, that Massmoudi was not merely interested in Muslim culture and religion; she was a political activist and self-styled "revolutionary" whose father was an important figure in the network of Muslim Brotherhood fronts, of which the Muslim Students Association was one.[5] The headline in the *Daily Tar Heel*—"Student-Led Walkout of Horowitz Lecture Protests 'Destructive' Remarks"— gave Massmoudi the public relations victory she wanted.[6] The characterization of what I said as "destructive remarks" was the comment she had given to the reporter about the speech she hadn't stayed to hear.

This kind of "reporting" is not unusual for campus papers, which are normally run by leftists and whose editors are often as concerned, as are the activists, that the campus community not be

---

[5]Mytheos Holt, "UNC Students Walk Out of Pro-Israel Talk—Led by Student Whose Father Is Tied to Muslim Brotherhood," *The Blaze*, March 13, 2012; http://www.theblaze.com/stories/unc-students-walk-out-of-pro-israel-talk-led-by-student-whose-father-is-tied-to-muslim-brotherhood/

[6]Caroline Leland, "Student-led Walk-out of Horowitz Lecture Protests 'Destructive' Remarks," *Daily Tar Heel*, March 14, 2012; http://www.dailytarheel.com/index.php/article/2012/03/studentled_wal kout_of_horowitz_lecture_protests_destructive_remarks

exposed to politically incorrect opinions. The article beneath the headline ignored the substance of my speech, quoting only one remark I had made, which turned out to be a useful one. Accompanying the headline report were three column-length attacks on the editorial page, accusing me of being an anti-Muslim bigot. The attacks came from the president of the Muslim Students Association, the president of Students for Justice in Palestine, and the president of the campus Hillel, Josh Orol. It was obviously a coordinated assault.

The piece by Josh Orol was the most damaging, as it came from a fellow Jew who claimed to be pro-Israel. His attack was headlined: "UNC Hillel Won't Stand for Vilification of Muslim Students." It began: "As co-president of UNC Hillel, I was surprised to receive an invitation from the Committee for a Better Carolina to publicize David Horowitz's upcoming speech. I would have hoped that our opinions were already publicly known: UNC Hillel does not support Horowitz's repeated vilification of Muslims." The only attempt Orol made to justify the specific claim that I vilified Muslims—rather than Muslim *jihadists*—was this: "To make the broad claim that Arabs want to kill Jews—and that Islam is a militant religion bent on the destruction of Israel and the United States—is to destroy the principle of pluralism that the freedom of speech is meant to uphold." Naturally, Orol didn't quote anything I had said or written—and I have written thousands upon thousands of words on Islam and on the Middle East war. The reason he provided no quote is that there is none. I made no such claims. In my speech, I said the Arab states that attacked Israel in 1948, 1967 and 1973 did so with the intention of destroying the Jewish state and pushing the Jews into the sea. I also said Hamas is a terrorist organization dedicated to the destruction of the Jews. Conflating Hamas terrorists with all Muslims is the propaganda goal of Hamas, of its parent organization the Muslim Brotherhood, of the Muslim Students Association, of Students for Justice in Palestine, and of the campus left. This is how the terrorists and Jew-haters protect themselves, and how students like Josh

Orol who claim to speak in the name of the Jews become their enablers.

In an attempt to alert the campus community to the slanders it was being fed, and to set the record straight, I wrote a letter to the *Daily Tar Heel*. The *Tar Heel*'s editor, Steven Norton, refused to publish my letter, despite his paper's officially stated commitment to journalistic fairness and "involving . . . seldom heard opinions in our community." The letter summed up my feelings on this whole disturbing episode:

> Apparently, it is easier for the presidents of campus Hillel and the Muslim Students Association to condemn a defender of Israel than to condemn those who call for the destruction of Israel and America, and the murder of their inhabitants. Hassan Nasrallah, the head of Hezbollah, has called for "Death to America" and "Death to Israel," as has Mahmoud Ahmadinejad, the president of Iran. The spiritual head of the Muslim Brotherhood, Yusuf al-Qaradawi, has said that the Holocaust was a just punishment for the Jews and [he wishes] that the followers of Allah would finish the job that Hitler started.
>
> In their *Tar Heel* columns, the presidents of MSA, Hillel and Students for Justice in Palestine accuse me of being an anti-Muslim bigot. This is a lie exposed by the *Tar Heel*'s own reporter, whose one direct quote from my speech had me accurately saying, "There are good Muslims and there are bad Muslims." I also said that "the majority of Muslims [are] decent, law abiding citizens . . . who want peace." I then pointed out that there were also good Germans, but that in the end they didn't make "a damn's worth of difference." This is a true statement, and no one would accuse me of being anti-German for making it.
>
> Unfortunately, conflating Muslim terrorists with all Muslims is a typical tactic of campus apologists for *jihadists* who are at war with Israel and the United States. Opponents of the Islamic *jihad* against the West, like myself, are routinely accused of being "anti-Muslim," which is a term designed to shut down debate and make opponents of genocidal movements seem the indecent ones—instead of those who make excuses for them.

Mahmoud Al-Zahar, the co-founder of Hamas and one of its current leaders, has said: "There is no place for you Jews among us, and you have no future among the nations of the world. You are headed for annihilation." If the Muslim Students Association on this campus does not support Hamas or this statement, its leaders should say so.

This goes for all the Muslim Students Associations on American campuses. If they do not support the destruction of the Jewish state, and if they condemn the Hitlerian sermons of Muslim Brotherhood leaders like Yusuf al-Qaradawi, they should say so. And if they do not, Hillel should have no partnerships or "dialogues" with them, and Hillel students should not think of them as "brothers."

This was the less-than-satisfactory conclusion of my visit to the University of North Carolina. It pretty well summed up my experience on scores of other campuses I visited to try to counter the campaign to demonize Israel—a campaign spearheaded by campus fronts for the Muslim Brotherhood as part of the holy war the Muslim world is waging against the Jews of the Middle East.

Index